God strengthens

God strengthens

Ezekiel simply explained

Derek Thomas

 EVANGELICAL PRESS

EVANGELICAL PRESS
12 Wooler Street, Darlington, Co. Durham, DL1 1RQ.

© Evangelical Press 1993
First published 1993

British Library Cataloguing in Publication Data available

ISBN 085234 310 8

Printed in Great Britain by the Bath Press, Avon.

To my children,
Ellen and Owen,
in anticipation that, one day,
they will grow to love Ezekiel, too.

Contents

Preface

As I remarked in the preface to my volume on Isaiah, *God Delivers,* this series is meant to be read by 'the average reader'. In order to meet that requirement (which is difficult, for no two readers are quite the same), as well as produce a book of moderate length (Ezekiel has 48 chapters!), I am forced into making sacrifices. Readers who use this volume in order to explain a particular verse may well be disappointed because the comment is either brief or, possibly, non-existent. I can only beg their sympathy for the difficulty of my task.

What I have done, however, as opposed to a standard commentary, is to attempt to produce something that can be read in large doses. (I am not suggesting that commentaries are unreadable — though I could suggest one or two that are! — rather, that they are designed, I think, for consultation.) I have come across a number of folk who have used other books in this series as devotional helps to their daily reading of the Bible. That is, I suggest, the best way to use this volume. If you are going to read this book *instead* of the actual text of Ezekiel, then the profit will be minimal. Only as these musings of mine help you to understand God's Word itself will you gain as God intends you to.

I am once more grateful to many for help in the publication of this volume. I am indebted to Evangelical Press and its staff for many helpful comments incorporated in this book. Three others come immediately to mind. First, I must thank Adam Loughridge, former professor of the Reformed Presbyterian College, Belfast, who kindly sent me his sermon notes on Ezekiel, preached in the 1960s at the prayer meetings of Cregagh Road Reformed Presbyterian

Church. Handling these notes was, as Gollum in Tolkien's *Lord of the Rings* was wont to say, 'precious'! Here and there, alliterative headings appear in the text which are probably his and not mine. Second, I mention my own, untiring congregation, who have listened patiently as I have attempted to bring these chapters of Ezekiel to life at prayer meetings. Third, I thank my family for their willingness to see me locked in my study for many hours, particularly of late when the deadline set for its completion had long since passed. Children ought to know they have a father, and mine have recently begun to wonder. It is to them in particular I dedicate this book.

Derek Thomas
Belfast
November 1993

Introduction

To this day, at a place called Al-Kifl, near the ancient ruins of Babylon in Iraq, there lies what is claimed to be the burial tomb of Ezekiel. The book of Ezekiel may as well lie buried with him, for few Christians read it, and fewer still find it profitable reading.

It is said that during a first-century controversy as to whether Ezekiel should be included within the canon of Scripture, Rabbi Hanina-ben Hezekiah used upwards of 300 jars of oil in his night lamp studying the book. Most Christians could not claim to have used the equivalent of one jar of oil! If we may cite Augustine's remark that just as there are shallows in Scripture where a lamb may wade, so there are depths where an elephant may swim — Ezekiel, we may concede, is for elephants![1]

Allow me to expand on this a little by citing two characters, well known to children everywhere. The first is Alice, of Lewis Carroll's *Alice in Wonderland*. One day, she muses to herself: 'What is the use of a book without pictures or conversations?'[2] I know how she feels, and at the end of a day, with insomnia beckoning, a book with 'pictures and conversations' is just the ticket to send me to sleep!

My second character is J. M. Barrie's creation, Peter Pan. I guess most of us have grown to love him over the years. From my earliest days I have identified with this underdog and his swashbuckling escapades with the fearsome Captain Hook. Pan has a line which I sometimes repeat to myself, and it goes like this: 'I just want always to be a little boy and have fun.'[3] Living this fantasy is as popular today as it ever was. Even King David entertained himself with fantasies, expressing a desire to fly away from life's problems, like the doves he noticed doing so when a sudden noise disturbed their tranquillity (Ps. 55:6). This was not wise (for it is often not God's plan that we run away from trouble), and Pan's memorable line, while it makes for good fantasy, is decidedly unwise as a healthy philosophy of life.

Some Christians approach their reading of the Bible a bit like Alice (looking for the pictures), or else like Pan (avoiding the difficult bits in favour of the well-known and familiar). Fans of Alice will be drawn to Ezekiel (initially at least) because it opens with a fantastic picture, as vivid and colourful as any to be found in the book of Revelation. Fans of Pan, however, will find the book tough — far too tough for little boys to bother with. Too bad! For God does not want us to be 'little boys' for ever. He wants us to grow up! 'Let us leave the elementary teachings about Christ', writes one New Testament author, 'and go on to maturity' (Heb. 6:1). Clearly, there were fans of Pan in his day, too.

You, on the other hand, show greater promise — I venture so to so guess — for by the very act of reading these words you have shown some interest in getting to know Ezekiel better. You have, perhaps, been touched by the remark of Paul's that *every part of Scripture* is profitable in some way or another (2 Tim. 3:16-17); or, perhaps like me, you have been humbled at the thought of meeting Ezekiel some day in heaven and having to confess, shamefacedly, that you never got around to reading his book! Or perhaps you have a far more profound notion: that since the Holy Spirit saw fit to inspire the book of Ezekiel in precisely this way (a little difficult in parts) you and I had better knuckle down to some serious study and get on with trying to understand what it is that God is saying to us (for in the last analysis, what the Bible says, God says).

How are we to do this? 'Think in every line you read', wrote the Puritan Thomas Watson, 'that God is speaking to you.'⁴ It is, of course, the wise way to read Scripture as a whole, and Ezekiel in particular. And reading it this way will yield rich rewards. One fascinating statistic emerges in Ezekiel: that of the 359 occurrences of the phrase, 'This is what the Sovereign Lord says' in the Old Testament, one third of them (122) are in Ezekiel! The book claims (in a sense at least) more than any other to be from God. The widespread neglect of it is therefore all the more puzzling.

The man

I have called the book *God Strengthens*, partly because it dovetails nicely with a similar volume I have written on Isaiah,⁵ and more importantly, because the word 'Ezekiel' means precisely that: 'God strengthens' (or hardens; see comments on chapter 3). Why should Ezekiel be called by this name? Two answers seem to be forthcoming from the book itself: firstly, because Ezekiel faced fierce and sustained opposition to his message (3:8), and anyone who has ever tried to preach in such circumstances will know the need for divine help; and secondly, not only Ezekiel, but all God's people need to be reassured of his help in times of weakness. 'I will bind up the injured and *strengthen* the weak,' God promises his flock in exile in Babylon (Ezek. 34:16), using the same word as Ezekiel's name to convey this reassurance. Both Ezekiel himself and the church of his day were to be reminded of God's power every time they heard the prophet's name mentioned in conversation. This must have been wonderfully reassuring to the faithful who perceived the significance of his name.

Ezekiel's ministry came at a time when Judah was collapsing to the Babylonians. As a young lad, Ezekiel saw the decline of Assyria, the growing power of Babylon, the foreign control of Jerusalem (Egypt in 609 B.C.) and the defeat of Egypt and Assyria by Nebuchadnezzar at Carchemish (605 B.C.). In 603 B.C. Nebuchadnezzar deported many of Judah's leading men, including Daniel, and Ezekiel must have guessed that his turn would come. The next few years were unstable: Jehoiakim succeeded in ruling Judah as Babylon's puppet king for three years, until an attempt at rebellion got the better of him. The result was another of Babylon's deportations (597 B.C.) — this time to include Ezekiel himself. It was the start of his exile and years of ministry for the Lord.

Having been trained as a priest (1:3), and been deported into exile at the very age he was to begin his priestly service (i.e. twenty-five years of age), Ezekiel was further charged with the office of a prophet (3:1). This was a ministry he faithfully carried out for the next twenty-seven years (29:17). One of the most touching moments in his entire ministry comes at the death of his wife (24:15-27). He is given the extraordinary charge forbidding his mourning of her in any way. This he carries out without complaint of any kind, even though he loved his wife dearly (24:16). This incident, more than any other, makes me admire this man more than I can adequately express. Ezekiel often comes across as a bland, unsympathetic figure without any of the character traits of, say, his contemporary (and mentor?) Jeremiah. But this is too superficial a view. Ezekiel's greatness emerges in his total, unquestioning willingness to do God's will — no matter what the cost! He is an example of total consecration to the work of God. Christian workers everywhere will have cause to bow in admiration of this man's saintliness.

His message

A mere glance at the outline of the book will reveal that the task Ezekiel was told to perform was a difficult one. The first twenty-four chapters are full of unremitting judgements. These will prove difficult to read — but read them we must! God was angry with his people for their enormous crimes against the love he had shown them. We, too, need to know how utterly holy God is, and how he cannot tolerate sin, if we are to make progress in our relationship with him.

Strawberries and cream are one of God's great gifts to us, and I for one am grateful for having tasted them; but they are only good occasionally, and a constant diet of such delicacies would ruin our health and vitality. If all we read are God promises of blessing, without the counter threat of punishment for disobedience, our understanding of the ways of God is going to be seriously out of shape. Every now and then, we need to sit down and let these chapters hit us with all the power of a force 10 gale. Only then will the dross of misconceived notions about God be blown away.

Ezekiel does have another message to deliver. Like other prophets, there was a ministry of tearing down to perform, but there was also a ministry of building up (Jer. 1:10). At the heart of Ezekiel's message is God's faithfulness to his covenant of grace. The promise of the coming Messiah was remembered by the prophets who lived *before* the exile (Isa. 9:5-6; Amos 9:11; Micah 5:1-5) and *on the eve* of the exile (Jer. 23:5-6; 30:9), as well as *after* the exile (Zech. 12:8). It was also to be the theme of prophets who lived *during* the exile, and in particular Ezekiel (34:23-24; 37:21-25). It should be a thrilling thought to know even before we start our journey, that, as one writer puts it (commenting upon 11:14-25), 'The prophecy is essentially Messianic.'⁶ We are going to find the footsteps of Jesus in these chapters!

The other half of Ezekiel's message (judgement being the first) is that of restoration and blessing. It is a fascinating study to catch the references to the restoration of a remnant of his people to the land again (6:8-10; 7:16; 9:4-8; 11:13,14-20; 12:16; 14:22; 16:62-63 etc.). Bible readers through the ages have come to all sorts of fanciful notions as to what these passages mean. During the course of our study, I have had occasion to point out where I disagree with some of them. In doing so, of course, I criticize only the view, not the person who holds it. There are times when I have admitted to being unclear about certain passages. These are failures on my part, but I take refuge in the knowledge that both Daniel (Dan. 12:8) and Peter (2 Peter 3:16) said something similar — Peter about some of Paul's writings, and Daniel about his own!

But that is enough by way of an introduction. It is time to start our study!

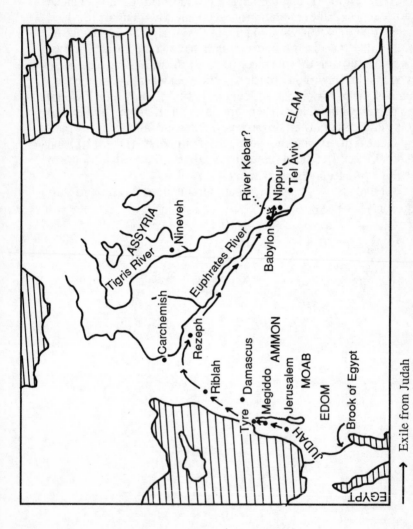

→ Exile from Judah

Map 1. The ancient Near East in the time of Ezekiel showing Judah's nearest neighbours

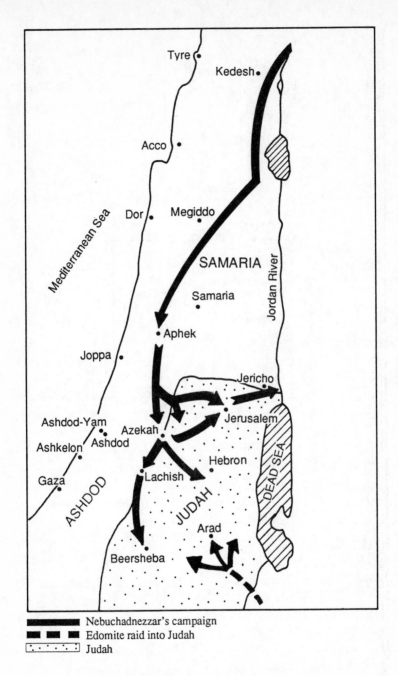

Map 2. The Babylonian invasion of Judah

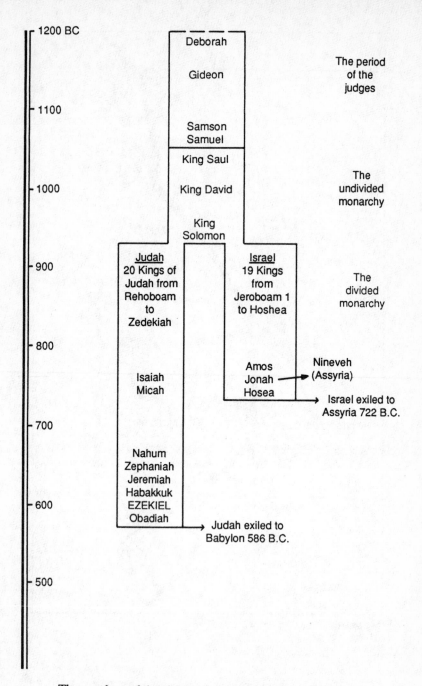

The prophets of the eighth, seventh and sixth centuries B.C.

Part I
Ezekiel's vision, commission and message
Ezek. 1 - 5

1.
Meeting God

Please read Ezekiel 1:1-28

Christianity is a religion of the word. God has set down all that he requires of us to know concerning himself, his plans and purposes, in the Bible. Over two million Bible words, written over a period of 1,500 years by some forty different authors, underline the fact that words are essential for Christianity. But a stubborn truth persists in making itself known: most people remember pictures better than they remember words. That is why Bible writers (and behind them, the guiding hand of the Holy Spirit) pepper their words with vivid word-pictures to throw light on what these words mean. Ezekiel is full of word-pictures!

Only C. H. Spurgeon could use the text, 'A window shalt thou make to the ark' (Gen. 6:16, AV; cf. 8:6) to establish the need that sermons should contain illustrations, adding the thought that: 'Ezekiel, in his vision of the temple, saw that even to the little chambers there were windows suitable to their size'![1] It is the same thought that led G. K. Chesterton to write in a child's picture book:

Stand up, and keep your childishness,
Read all the pedant's creeds and strictures
But don't believe in anything
That can't be told in coloured pictures![2]

The opening verse relates how, along with the book of Revelation, this prophecy is packed with intricate sketches: **'I saw visions of God'** (1:1). Coloured pictures abound throughout Ezekiel's prophecy, but as we shall see, the pictures are not Ezekiel's but God's. And, more importantly, these God-given pictures need interpreting. It is a message and not a picture that Ezekiel will be called to deliver to God's people. Pictures, without interpretation, are dangerous vehicles for truth: folk are prone to make of them what they will. That is why we shall have to root everything Ezekiel *saw* in what he *knew* of God in the Scriptures then available to him.

History: God's unfolding plan (1:1-3)

Before we look at these visions, we are given a historical reference point that helps us focus on the exact features which made these visions relevant: **'It was the fifth year of the exile of King Jehoiachin'** (1:2). Jane Austen caught the spirit of many when, in her book *Northanger Abbey*, she has the character Catherine Morland say, 'I can read poetry and plays, and things of that sort, and do not dislike travels. But history, real solemn history, I cannot be interested in. Can you?'[3] No Christian who seriously desires to know what the Bible teaches can adopt this attitude. When Paul says, 'In your thinking be adults' (1 Cor. 14:20), he implies that we are bound to take history seriously when we read the Bible.

The exile to which Ezekiel refers is that of Babylon in 597 B.C. The end of the seventh century and beginning of the sixth century B.C. had seen the ascendancy of Babylon in the ancient Near East. Jerusalem was attacked on three specific occasions as part of a Babylonian expansionist policy during the years 605, 597 and 587 B.C.[4] The city was first attacked by Nebuchadnezzar in 605 B.C. during the reign of Jehoiakim — the setting of the opening chapter of the book of Daniel (Dan. 1:1).

Ezekiel, along with many others, was taken into captivity during the second of these deportations, which took place in the reign of Jehoiakim's son, Jehoiachin (2 Kings 24:8-15). The opening verse informs us that Ezekiel was in his **'thirtieth year'**.[5] Assuming that this refers to Ezekiel's age, then the prophet would have been twenty-five years old at the time of his deportation. He, along with many other Jews, had refused to acknowledge the legitimacy of Zedekiah's reign (the puppet king who had replaced Jehoiachin, 2 Kings 24:17-18) and five years later Ezekiel is still using Jehoiachin as the legitimate reference point of history. (Readers should refer to the chart on page 18: 'The prophets of the eighth, seventh and sixth centuries B.C.').

Ezekiel's youth

Assuming Ezekiel was thirty when he received his call to be a prophet, his youth fell during the declining years of the mighty kingdom of Assyria and the reign of the reformer King Josiah in Judah (640-609 B.C.).

Ezekiel, **'the son of Buzi'** (1:3), was born at one of the most significant times in Old Testament history, for in 621 B.C. the 'book of the law' (Deuteronomy?) was found during a time of temple repairs (2 Kings 22:8-10; 2 Chron. 34:8-18). The result was a reformation along the lines of the sixteenth-century reformation in Europe led by Martin Luther. It was also the period of the prophet Jeremiah's ministry. To have grown up during a time of revival and reformation, and to have had the privilege of the ministries of Josiah and Jeremiah, must surely have made an impression on the young Ezekiel. He had seen what God could do. If Judah now resembles a valley of dry, dead bones, God can bring them to life! (37:1-15). We, too, must learn to formulate our theological convictions in the light of what God has done in the past — and what he promises to do in the present and future.

Ezekiel's call to service

Ezekiel was both a **'priest'** (1:3) and a 'prophet' (2:5). If the argument is correct that Ezekiel was carried into exile in his twenty-fifth year, this would be especially significant since the Levites entered into the priesthood at this age (Num. 8:24) and may have served a period of five years as an apprentice (cf. Num. 4:3).[6]

Summing up, two features now emerge about the times in which Ezekiel preached.

1. A time of great change

To those whose lives have been shattered by sudden, catastrophic providences, Ezekiel's ministry should strike an immediate, sympathetic chord. Ezekiel knows all about suffering: in chapter 24, just five years later when Ezekiel would have been only thirty-five, we read of the death of his wife (24:18).

2. *A time of near despair*

We can imagine Ezekiel sitting **'by the Kebar River in the land of the Babylonians'** (1:3) recalling days spent in the temple at Jerusalem when a boy. Some of his companions had wept, unable even to raise a familiar song (Ps. 137). Ezekiel, instead of learning at the feet of experienced Levites in the temple at Jerusalem, was forced into exile, his entire life changed and seemingly destroyed.

But such frustrations reckon without God's supervision. Writing of events in 1939, at the outset of the Second World War, Dr Martyn Lloyd-Jones remarked, 'I feel that there is a tremendous opportunity for preaching. At the moment what is wanted is the comforting note to help people over the shock. But, following that, the need will be for the prophetic note to awaken the people.'[7] Ezekiel's opening chapter does both of these things. Later on, the prophetic note will sound with tremendous force, but for now, the fact that God had called a prophet from among the exiles on the Kebar River, and given him great visions of God's glory, must have helped them over the shock of it all. No matter what may be happening, God is still in control. He neither abandons, nor forsakes; Ezekiel was assured that **'the hand of the Lord was upon him'** (1:3). When this seventy-year exile eventually came to an end, this expression would prove to be the very same source of strengthening for Ezra (Ezra 7:6,28) and Nehemiah (Neh. 2:8,18). Ezekiel, who knew his Bible, would have read the words of Moses: 'Be strong and courageous. Do not be afraid or terrified because of them, for the Lord your God goes with you; he will never leave you nor forsake you' (Deut. 31:6). But the content of these visions, as we shall see, serves another, more sobering purpose: God was coming in judgement upon disobedient Jerusalem.

'I saw visions of God' (1:4-28)

God made Ezekiel wait for five years before speaking to him. That is something we have to face up to in our own experience. There are times when silence speaks louder than any words. The people of Judah in exile had to be made aware that God was angry with them for their sin. But, God's anger, though necessary, is tempered with mercy. Ezekiel's call to be a prophet (2:5) was God's way of reassuring his people that his covenant with them was sure. Accompanied as it was by a vision of God's glory, in almost the same way as Isaiah's call had been 150 years earlier (Isa. 6), it was a remarkable demonstration that not even their sin can destroy his sovereign rule.

It is quite possible that Ezekiel had heard of Jeremiah's words describing the nature of a true prophet as opposed to a false one. The hallmark of a true prophet was that he had stood before the Lord of glory in the midst of his council of angels (Jer. 23:18). What Ezekiel is about to see is a cherubim-driven chariot bearing a great crystal-like expanse upon which sits enthroned a figure of awesome glory. It is to this vision that we must now turn.

The vision is, in fact threefold: the second and third evolving out of the first.[8] If we are unused to reading Ezekiel (or books similar to it, like the book of Revelation) then we shall be at sea in this chapter. Ezekiel is painting 'coloured pictures' and we must be careful not to let our imaginations run away. The details of the vision serve only to heighten the overall picture. The secret of interpretation here, as with similar passages in the rest of the Bible, is to get the overall picture first and let the details sort themselves out.

Ezekiel's first vision began with a **'windstorm coming out of the north'** (1:4). Adding more detail, Ezekiel describes **'an immense cloud with flashing lightning and surrounded by brilliant light'**, and concludes by saying, **'The centre of the fire looked like glowing metal.'** A storm is brewing of immense proportions! No one who knows the Old Testament prophets need wonder what this vision is about. The **'north'** is always the region from which Judah's enemies came. The land of Israel in the north had already capitulated in Isaiah's time to the Assyrians. Now it was the Babylonian ascendancy in the Middle East that threatened to destroy Judah also. Jerusalem had already been attacked twice (in 605 and 597 B.C.). It is now 592 B.C. and in five years' time Jerusalem would be destroyed entirely. Judah had not learnt the lesson that disobedience to God would lead to judgement.

Following the collapse of the Assyrian empire there followed a brief ascendancy of Egyptian power to the south-west. The reformer king Josiah was to lose his life at the hands of Pharaoh Necho in a famous battle at Megiddo in 609 B.C. (2 Kings 23:29). Egyptian power over Judah lasted for only four years, during which time Jehoahaz was deposed (after only three months) and replaced by a

puppet king, his older brother Jehoiakim. The rise to power of
Nebuchadnezzar in Babylon was to spell the end of the Egyptian
menace. In 605 B.C. the Babylonians attacked and defeated Egypt
at Carchemish, inflicting heavy casualties (Jer. 46:2). The Egyptians fled homewards and the Babylonians annexed both Philistia
and Judah. It was of this that Jeremiah had warned, and perhaps
Ezekiel had heard: 'Flee for safety without delay! For I am bringing
disaster from the north, even terrible destruction' (Jer. 4:6). It is not
without significance that Jeremiah, too, had begun his prophecy
with a vision of 'a boiling pot, tilting away from the north' (Jer.
1:13).

It is not, however, sufficient to see in the reference to the 'north'
merely the Babylonians, for the vision is essentially a vision of God.
Nor are these in conflict, for the vision is of God coming to judge
Jerusalem, using the Babylonians as his instrument of wrath.[9]

The vision seems to be constantly evolving and Ezekiel's focus
changes. The dark cloud is actually alive with winged creatures —
four **'living creatures'** which tell of the rule of God. One is
immediately reminded of the comfort Elisha drew from a similar
vision when harassed by predatory invasions by Arameans (2 Kings
6:17).

In Ezekiel 10:1-22 these creatures are called cherubim.[10] Several
important details are now brought into focus. They were like a man
in appearance (1:5). They each had four faces and four wings
(making sixteen faces and sixteen wings in all, 1:6; so that from
whatever angle Ezekiel looked, he could see all four faces at once),
two of their wings being extended so as to touch each other and the
other two wings used to cover themselves (1:11).[11] Their legs were
straight, and their feet were like those of a calf (1:7, the calf probably
denoting agility; cf. Ps. 29:6; Mal. 4:2). As they moved (supporting
the chariot-like structure described later in the chapter) they seemingly had no need to turn around — they were able to move in any
direction without having to change positions (1:12). The point being
made is that this complex vision could see in any direction at any
time and could quickly move there without any delay.[12]

In addition, Ezekiel points out that their four faces were that of
a man — the chief of all; a lion — the chief of the animals; an ox —
the chief of domesticated animals; and an eagle — the chief of the
birds, possibly representing intelligence, ferocity, strength and
freedom.

Wheels within wheels

As the prophet continues to describe what he sees, his eyes now focus on wheels **'on the ground beside each creature'** (1:15) Each wheel was intersected by another, probably at right angles, thus enabling the wheels to move quite easily in all four directions, as the cherubim themselves did (1:12, 19-21). This supernatural, fantastic chariot could move fast, in any direction, **'wherever the Spirit would go'** (1:20).

But all this has merely been a preparation for the real focus of the vision: the firmament (NIV **'expanse'**, 1:22) and the throne of glory. Carried aloft by the four living creatures together with their wheels, was a vast, **'awesome'** platform (1:22). As the creatures flew about carrying this **'sparkling'** expanse (1:22), the sound they made was like **'the roar of rushing waters, like the voice of the Almighty, like the tumult of an army'** (1:24). Then the climax of the vision appears: a **'throne of sapphire'** (1:26) and on the throne was **'a figure like that of a man'**. The 'man' is also of fantastic appearance: he seems to be on fire! (1:27). And all around him there is the glow of a multi-coloured rainbow (1:28).[13]

Who is this 'man'? 'I willingly embrace the opinion of those fathers,' says John Calvin, 'who say that this is the prelude to that mystery which was afterwards displayed to the world, and which Paul magnificently extols when he exclaims, "Great is the mystery —God is manifest in the flesh." (1 Tim. 3:16).'[14] The God of the Old Testament is none other than Jesus Christ! It is Jesus who comes in this chapter in the form of a divine warrior. Nor is this in any way in contradiction to the New Testament picture of Jesus. The counterpart to this vision which is about to unfold is what Paul refers to when he speaks of the day 'when the Lord Jesus is revealed from heaven in blazing fire with his powerful angels. He will punish those who do not know God and do not obey the gospel of our Lord Jesus' (2 Thess. 1:7,8). Ezekiel's prophecy is all about the coming of Jesus Christ. Several truths about God (Christ) emerge in this opening chapter.

1. God is the Judge

It is important to note that Ezekiel was impressed not just by what he saw, but also by what he heard![15] Several times in this chapter,

Ezekiel tries to describe the sound that accompanied the vision, for it was the 'voice of the Almighty' (1:24). Later in the prophecy, Ezekiel will draw attention to the impressive sounds that accompanied the visions (3:13; 10:5,13; 43:2). It is the same feature that is celebrated in Psalm 104:

> He makes the clouds his chariot
>   and rides on the wings of the wind...
> But at your rebuke the waters fled,
>   at the sound of your thunder they took to flight
>
> (Ps. 104:3,7; cf. Ps. 29).

When the psalmist describes God as 'riding' on a wind-driven chariot (Ps. 104:3), accompanied by a terrible sound, it is the same verb that is used in Genesis 3:8 to describe God 'walking' in the garden 'in the cool of the day', following Adam and Eve's transgression. The point of Genesis 3 is not to tell us that God was out on some leisurely walk, but that he was coming in judgement, accompanied by all the terror that later 'comings' in the Bible evoke.

Sound also accompanied the visions of Isaiah and John (Isa. 6:4-8; Rev. 1:15).[16] Of greater significance is the fact that such a 'noise' is said to accompany the Lord's return at the end of the age (1 Thess. 4:16; 1 Cor. 15:52; 2 Peter 3:10; Rev. 1:10,15; 4:5; 10:3; 11:19).[17] Clearly, Ezekiel is telling us that God is coming in judgement! But it is important to stress that God's 'coming' evoked a twofold response: 'The terror which the manifestation was fitted to inspire was terror only to the guilty; while, for the penitent and believing, there was to be the brightest display of covenant love and faithfulness.'[18]

2. God is holy

'Fire' (1:4) is a frequent symbol of God's holiness, purity and awesomeness in Scripture (Exod 3:2,3; 13:21; 19:18; 1 Kings 18:24,38; 2 Thess. 1:7; Heb. 10:27; 12:29; Rev. 1:14; 2:18). And storm clouds are frequently used in Scripture to depict the Lord's coming in wrath (Ps. 29:3-9; 104:3; Isa. 29:6). The Second Coming of Christ is depicted using the same imagery of storm and fire (Matt. 24:30; 26:64; 1 Thess. 4:17; 2 Thess. 1:7). Ezekiel saw only **'the appearance of the likeness of the glory of the Lord'** (1:28) in burning fire and brilliant light, but it was enough for him to fall down prostrate on the ground. Moses hid his face, because he was afraid to look upon God (Exod. 3:6). Isaiah was overwhelmed by his own sinfulness when he saw the glory of God in the temple (Isa. 6:1-5). Daniel, too, had collapsed and fainted at a similar sight (Dan. 10:9). Peter and John had similar experiences (Luke 5:8; Rev. 1:17). We, too, ought to 'tremble' as we read God's Word in Ezekiel (Isa. 66:5).

3. God is all-powerful

Everything about this vision speaks of power and strength. But of particular interest is the fact that Ezekiel uses the term 'Shaddai' (meaning 'Almighty') to refer to God in verse 24. This name, first used by God when speaking to Abraham in Genesis 17:1, reminds us of Jesus saying in Mark 14:62: 'And you will see the Son of Man sitting at the right hand of the Mighty One and coming on the clouds of heaven' (Mark 14:62). God is almighty. His power extends over the entire universe. He can do with it whatever he wills. As Creator he stands above all other powers. The ultimate rule belongs to Jesus Christ. Providence, though dark and unfathomable, is not capricious. In the context of Ezekiel and the impending threat of Babylonian domination, this must surely have proved to be a comfort to the exiles along the Kebar River as well as those in Jerusalem who might have heard Ezekiel's prophecy. When we remember that God is in control, there is no need for panic or fear.

4. God rules

In the opening chapter of Ezekiel we are reminded that God rules over all. Ezekiel is only a servant in the unfolding of God's kingdom. As the nations gather for war, God is overruling every event in order to accomplish his grand design. Prophet after prophet saw visions of God's throne: Micaiah (1 Kings 22:19), Isaiah (Isa. 6:1) and Daniel (Dan.7:9); and the psalmist celebrated God's reign (Ps. 93:1; 96:10; 97:1; 99:1). The kingdoms of the world rise and fall, but Ezekiel sees a God who is above them all. His plans and power stretch into eternity. What is Nebuchadnezzar in comparison? Nothing!

God's way with those of his people who find themselves in trouble is to cause them to look to Christ — a sovereign Christ. Ezekiel's response to this awesome sight was to fall down (1:28; he

is told to get up in 2:1). As Calvin was to remark in the opening of
his *Institutes of the Christian Religion*, 'For if in broad daylight we
either look down upon the ground or survey whatever meets our
view round about, we seem to ourselves endowed with the strongest
and keenest sight; yet when we look up to the sun and gaze straight
at it, that power of sight which was particularly strong on earth is at
once blunted and confused by a great brilliance, and thus we are
compelled to admit that our keenness in looking upon things earthly
is sheer dullness when it comes to the sun.'[19] God's way of letting
us know how sinful and unworthy we really are is to let us glimpse
the glory and splendour of Christ. God is concerned to show himself
as the God of **'glory'** (1:28), a 'glory' that will, one day, fill the earth
(Num. 14:21; Ps. 57:5; 72:19; Isa. 11:9; Hab. 2:14). And God's aim
is not to constrain man's submission by force, but to ravish our
affections with irresistible displays of the treasure of his glory.
When God is our treasure, submission is our pleasure!

The beatific vision

The vision cannot be left there. When Ezekiel saw 'the likeness of
the glory of the Lord' (1:28), he was following that which others had
seen (Isa. 6:1) and promised (Ps. 24:3-6; 73:24-28). When Jesus
gave the beatitude, 'Blessed are the pure in heart, for they will see
God' (Matt. 5:8), he meant his disciples to understand that even
now, they beheld God! Speaking to Philip in the upper room, Jesus
said, 'Anyone who has seen me has seen the Father' (John 14:9).
When Jesus came into the world, the long hoped for day of the vision
of God had arrived in part. In Jesus, God makes himself visible.
Even now, Christians have the Spirit of glory and of God resting
upon them (1 Peter 4:14). But what we experience now does not
compare to what we shall 'see' in heaven (1 John 3:2). Then we shall
see God's glory as we have never seen it thus far (Heb. 11:27).

It is that glory which John glimpsed when he tells us that 'The
Word became flesh and made his dwelling among us. *We have seen
his glory*, the glory of the One and Only, who came from the Father,
full of grace and truth' (John 1:14). 'There's glory for you,' Humpty
Dumpty said to Alice; to which she replied: 'I don't know what you
mean by "glory"!'[20] What John means by 'glory' is what he saw at
the transfiguration of Christ, when 'He was transfigured before

them,' and 'His face shone like the sun, and his clothes became as
white as the light' (Matt. 17:2). Throughout his earthly ministry
there was nothing to indicate who Christ really was. He was, to use
Luther's designation, incognito. What people saw was a suffering
servant. Now and then his glory was glimpsed in the miracles he
performed (John 2:11). But on the Mount of Transfiguration, by
way of confirmation to Jesus himself as to the nature of his true
identity, the ordinary was replaced by the glory that had always been
his. What the incarnation had veiled was momentarily revealed and
his whole person was irradiated with the most intense whiteness. It
was a reminder of what lay the other side of the cross.

But equally significant was the reminder to John of the glory that
all of God's people will share. As Christians we already share in the
glory of God (John 17:22), and there is glory to come (John 17:24).
Our bodies will be as glorious as his (Phil. 3:21). Knowing that we
are to stand in that glory of God's presence, we are even now to
know a joy which is 'inexpressible and glorious' (1 Peter 1:8). It is
a 'joy that results from being in the presence of God himself ... that
even now partakes of the character of heaven.'[21] And Ezekiel
anticipates this in his opening chapter as he stands in the glory of
God's presence. It is what Christians are said to do all the time if they
but knew it (2 Cor. 4:6).

Summary

God has shown his people that they are not forgotten; he has called
from among them a prophet to speak his Word. The visions of
Ezekiel have reminded us of some of God's great attributes: his
holiness and power in particular. But these 'coloured pictures' have
also depicted God's coming. If along the banks of the River Kebar
nothing seemed to be happening; if, as some imagined, God seemed
far away; if the prayers of his faithful people seemed unheard — the
truth was otherwise: God was on the move. The councils of heaven
were fully active. The rims of the wheels, which **'were full of eyes
all around'** (1:18), were meant to convey that God sees everything
that goes on. Nothing is hidden from him.[22] God has a plan which
every day unfolds before us. It involves the coming of his Son, Jesus
Christ, to rescue his people and destroy his enemies. Here is our
Deliverer: Jesus on a fiery chariot.

2.
Five commissions

Please read Ezekiel 2:1 - 3:27

'Men cannot be brought to order unless they are laid prostrate,' observes Calvin.[1] The vision of God's glory in chapter 1 had caused the prophet to fall on his face (1:28; 2:1). But God had work for this prophet to perform and the opening vision of his glory was meant to propel Ezekiel into service.

God makes demands on each one of us; that is his right. We are called to serve our Master. Ezekiel is about to set out on his life's task. Ahead lie the greatest of trials; but already Ezekiel is assured that the one whose figure was 'like that of a man' (1:26) is with him.

Sometimes we need to be told several times to do something — particularly if the task is difficult. It emerges that Ezekiel is given a fivefold commission (2:3; 3:4,11,17,22).

The messenger (2:1 - 3:15)

Several features come to the surface by way of a description of Ezekiel as God's messenger.

1. His title

He is called **'Son of man'** (2:1,3,6, and about ninety times elsewhere in Ezekiel). Commentators differ widely as to what this phrase means. Some point out that its usage elsewhere refers to the weakness of man: that he is *only* a son of man (cf. Num. 23:19; Job 25:6).[2] But its use in Psalm 8:4 and Daniel 8:17, as well as its being a title of Christ, have given rise to a different interpretation of the phrase. In Psalm 8 the 'son of man' is given a royal mandate:

'What is man that you are mindful of him,
   the son of man that you care for him?
You made him a little lower than the heavenly beings
   and crowned him with glory and honour.
You made him ruler over the works of your hands;
   you put everything under his feet:
   all flocks and herds,
   and the beasts of the field,
the birds of the air,
   and the fish of the sea,
   all that swim the paths of the seas'

(Ps. 8:4-8).

Though man is fallen and depraved, God has given him a power
to rule over the creation. He is a king. Ezekiel, already referred to as
a priest (1:3) and here in this chapter as a prophet (see below), is
being reminded by this expression, 'son of man', that he is also a
king. 'In this respect,' says van Groningen, 'it can be understood
why Ezekiel is, indeed, a type of Christ and why Jesus Christ himself
was prepared to take the phrase *Son of Man* as a suitable ascription
for himself.'[3]

2. *His authority*

The section 2:1 - 3:11 provides us with an account of Ezekiel's call
to be a prophet. It is similar to that of Isaiah (Isa. 6:5-13) and
Jeremiah (Jer. 1:7-10). Since we have already been told in the
opening chapter that 'The hand of the Lord was upon him' (1:3; and
this will be repeated again at 3:14,22; 8:1; 33:22; 37:1) it is not
surprising that we find Ezekiel speaking as God's mouthpiece,
driven by **'the Spirit'** (2:2) and using the characteristic, **'This is
what the Sovereign Lord says'** (2:4). This is the first of 122
instances of this phrase in Ezekiel![4] The biblical prophets, when
they preached, were, like John the Baptist, God's voices (Matt. 3:3);
and the biblical writers, when they wrote down these sermons, were
God's pens. 'This is why,' J. I. Packer observes, 'the biblical
writings are "holy" (2 Tim. 3:15): not because they deal with holy
things, but because the Holy God is their true Author.'[5] What
Ezekiel, and others like him, preached and wrote down was not
man's guesswork, or speculation, or wishful thinking. It was God's
utterance, and therefore inerrant truth.

3. His dependence upon God

It appears that without the Spirit's help, Ezekiel was powerless to obey God's command to rise to his feet (2:2). 'If any of us,' comments Calvin, 'is fit for rendering obedience to God, the prophet certainly excelled in this disposition, and yet the word of God had no efficacy in his case, until the Spirit gave him strength to rise upon his feet.'[6]

The same point is underlined in the third chapter when we are told that the people to whom Ezekiel ministered were **'hardened'** (3:7) — using the same word that is used of Pharaoh (Exod. 7:3). Perhaps Ezekiel wondered whether he could display the same courage that Moses had shown. He need not have been concerned, for God equips his servants for the tasks he calls upon them to perform. The repetition of the words **'hardened'**, **'hardest'**, and **'harder'** (3:8,9) seems to be a deliberate play on Ezekiel's name, which is made up of the Hebrew words for 'God' and 'hard', literally meaning 'God hardens' or 'God strengthens'.[7] God toughened him for the task.

We are never to approach any work for God from the perspective of our own natural abilities. 'Whoever, therefore, shall acknowledge that God is sufficient for overcoming all obstacles', Calvin concludes, 'will gird himself bravely for his work; but he who delays for calculating his own strength is not only weakened but is almost overcome.' He continues: 'Many are so full, yea so puffed out with confidence, that they bring forth nothing but wind. Hence let us learn to seek from God alone that fortitude which we need: for we are not stronger than Ezekiel, and if he needed to be strengthened by the Spirit of God, much more do we at this time need it.'[8]

These words, from his unfinished commentary on Ezekiel, were delivered at the Cathedral of Saint Pierre in Geneva. The condition of Calvin's health at this time is worth noting, if only to emphasize how greatly he himself needed to be strengthened by God. Having just recovered from a fever it is said that he overstrained his voice preaching in Saint Pierre, which brought on a violent fit of coughing, so violent that he broke a blood-vessel in his lungs and haemorrhaged. Added to this was the constant pain he suffered from piles, and he was weakened further by pulmonary tuberculosis. He was often carried to his duties in a chair or on horseback. Writing to Bullinger a little later, after preaching on Ezekiel had become impossible, he said, 'Although the pain in my side is abated, my lungs are so full of phlegm that my breathing is difficult and short. A stone in my bladder has been very troublesome for the last twelve days. Add to that our anxiety. For all remedies have so far proved ineffectual. Horse riding would have been best, but an ulcer in the haemorrhoid veins tortures me... Within the last three days the gout has also been very troublesome.'⁹ A month or so later he was dead.

Theodore Beza, writing the dedication to Calvin's unfinished commentary on Ezekiel, says of him: 'We have lost the very best and bravest.'¹⁰ It is of men like Ezekiel and John Calvin that the 'cloud of witnesses' is made up (Heb. 12:1). They are an exhortation to us to persevere in our faith, fixing 'our eyes on Jesus, the author and perfecter of our faith, who for the joy set before him endured the cross, scorning its shame, and sat down at the right hand of the throne of God' (Heb. 12:2).

4. His faithfulness

There are a number of ways in which faithfulness was called for. First, Ezekiel was asked to deliver this message *to his own people* — those who spoke his own language (3:5). The difficulty was recognized by Jesus when he spoke of prophets receiving honour everywhere apart from their own home town (Matt. 13:57). It is one thing to be faithful before complete strangers; it is another before those who know you intimately.

Second, God called for faithfulness *to the message itself.* We shall see in a moment the content of the message, but the fact that it is described as **'full of lament and mourning and woe'** (2:10) is sufficient to underline how difficult it was going to be to deliver it.

To deliver such a message required courage. Three times in a single verse Ezekiel is urged not to be afraid (2:6, and again at 3:9). Some might even be tempted to dilute it, or even tamper with it. That seems to be why Ezekiel is told that, unusually, the scroll was written **'on both sides'** (2:10). God demands that his prophets be *faithful*, declaring the *whole* counsel of God. Ezekiel is to be faithful to **'all the words'** God speaks to him (3:10). It is the same thought that is brought out later: 'Son of man, prophesy against the prophets of Israel who are now prophesying. Say to those who prophesy out of their own imagination: "Hear the word of the Lord! This is what the Sovereign Lord says: Woe to the foolish prophets who follow their own spirit and have seen nothing!'" (13:2-3).[11] False prophets, as Jeremiah had taught, speak 'from their own minds, not from the mouth of the Lord' (Jer. 23:16).

Ezekiel is in a long line of faithful preachers. They include Elijah, who opposed the entire national establishment, challenging the prophets of Baal and condemning the king and queen for murdering Naboth and seizing his vineyard (2 Kings 18:16-45; 21:17-24). Then there was Nathan, who dared to confront King David for his adultery with Bathsheba and his murder of her husband (2 Sam. 12:1-14). Amos stood up to the evil even in the king's sanctuary at Bethel, and predicted a terrible end for Amaziah, the royal chaplain, for trying to silence him (Amos 7:1-17). It is possible that Ezekiel knew Jeremiah and recalled how, when called upon to bring a message of national doom, God promised to make him 'a fortified city, an iron pillar and a bronze wall to stand against the whole land — against the kings of Judah, its officials, its priests and the people of the land' (Jer. 1:18). It is in this long line of courageous prophets that John the Baptist stands as a 'voice crying in the wilderness'. In Jesus' own testimony, he was the greatest of the prophets (Matt. 11:1-11).

It is in this same tradition that Paul urged the elders at Ephesus to be as courageous as he had been when he declared to them 'the whole counsel of God' (Acts 20:27, NKJV). God wants of us what was said of John Knox by the Earl of Morton at his grave: 'Here lies one who never feared flesh.'[12]

Third, Ezekiel's faithfulness reveals itself *in the face of opposition*. Hamlet told one of his players, 'Suit the action to the word, the word to the action.'[13] Words repeated several times bring out emphasis, as do the words **'rebel'** or **'rebellious'** which occur seven times in chapter 2 (2:3,5,6,7,8), and twenty-five times in the entire book. Clearly, Ezekiel is intent on getting us to grasp the point that rebellion is afoot! The people of Israel had been **'in revolt'** against God (2:3).[14] They were **'obstinate and stubborn'** (2:4). They refused to **'hear'** (2:5,7; cf. 3:6,7,10,11,27). This was something Isaiah had confronted a century earlier. He, too, had found it necessary to begin and end his book using the word 'rebel' as a description of God's people (Isa. 1:2; 66:24). Behind it lies a history of unfaithfulness to God's covenant. It is a theme to which Ezekiel will return later, accusing God's bride of becoming a 'prostitute' thus violating the marriage covenant with God (16:1-22, especially v.8).

Fourth, Ezekiel's faithfulness is apparent in the light of *the people's suffering*. As the glory-chariot of the first chapter rises into the sky, accompanied as it was by a great noise (3:12), Ezekiel once more finds himself at Tel Abib,[15] near the River Kebar, sitting among his suffering fellow-Israelites. The vision of glory is now over. And Ezekiel is suddenly filled with **'bitterness'** and **'anger of ... spirit'** (3:14). 'The strong hand of the Lord' had brought him into difficult areas and he resented it[16] — so much so that it took him seven days to get over it! (3:16).

If we are honest we shall have to confess that we, too, have felt this anger that Ezekiel experienced. It wasn't just that Ezekiel had been returned to the humdrum existence of his life in Tel Abib; that was, to be sure, a part of it. But the task of delivering what was in effect a funeral dirge to his own people who were already suffering seemed perhaps unfair and beyond his ability. God's ways did not seem to be right. How often we have felt such emotions! The fact that Ezekiel's response is portrayed for us with such frankness is meant both to comfort and warn: to comfort us in the knowledge that such a great man of God as Ezekiel had feet of clay, and to warn us that we need to watch out for similar responses in our own lives.

5. His obedience

Ezekiel, like the apostle John, was asked to eat the scroll on which had been written God's words (3:1-2; Rev. 10:8-10). The scroll itself was a leather parchment of some length rolled and tied in some fashion. God enabled Ezekiel to eat it! To his surprise, **'It tasted as sweet as honey'** (3:3). This illustrates the truth that God's Word is to be received with delight by his servants (Ps. 119:103). Jeremiah had said something similar: 'When your words came, I ate them; they were my joy and my heart's delight...' (Jer. 15:16). Obeying the Lord, in what appeared to be a difficult command, proved to be a pleasurable experience. It invariably does. 'Our wisdom', Calvin comments on 2:3, 'consists in nothing else but in attending to his instructions.'[17]

Ezekiel might well have recalled an incident some eleven years earlier, in 603 B.C. when Jeremiah's prophecies had been written down on a scroll and read aloud in the temple. King Jehoiakim was so incensed by its contents that he had the scroll burned and the order put out for Jeremiah's arrest (Jer. 36). Ezekiel's obedience and loyalty to God's Word were to be an initiation into a lifetime's service for God. The Lord was teaching him that to be really effective for God in our Christian lives, his Word has to become a part of us (Job 23:12).

The watchman (3:16-27)

For seven days Ezekiel nursed his anger, until God came and spoke to him again in what was to be the fourth commission (3:16-21).[18] Once again Ezekiel is merely the channel through which God's Word comes: the expression, **'The word of the Lord came to me'** (3:16; cf. 1:3) is the second of fifty occurrences in the book. There comes a time when we have to stop thinking about how we feel and get on with doing what God wants us to do. God wanted Ezekiel to become a **'watchman'** (3:17; cf. Isa. 56:10; Jer. 6:17; Hab. 2:1).

The duties of a watchman are to be spelled out later (18:1-32; 33:1-33). For now, God wants Ezekiel to become, not only his mouthpiece through whom he speaks, but his eyes and ears also.

The watchman stood on the ramparts of the city and watched for the coming of invaders, quickly blowing a trumpet to warn the entire city of the onset of danger. If a battle was taking place within sight of the city, it was the watchman who would give progress reports of it to the city's inhabitants (2 Sam. 18:24-27). The commission contained in itself a sign of God's continued favour to his covenant people: no matter how great their sin, he would not abandon them entirely. Even in Babylon he gave them a 'town crier' to warn them of dangers and summon them to action.

As a watchman, Ezekiel's task lay in two directions: to the **'wicked'** (3:18-19) and to the **'righteous'** (3:20-21). Under the ministry of the prophets the people were called to a true repentance and to return to God. The call to repentance focused on the covenant which God had made with them, as Ezekiel reminds them later (16:8). Israel were currently in breach of God's favour towards them, as their current status in exile showed so clearly. They must return, not only to the covenant, but to the God of the covenant.

Genuine repentance, as the *Shorter Catechism* teaches us, involves a change of direction. It is when a sinner 'out of a true sense of his sin, and apprehension of the mercy of God in Christ, doth, with grief and hatred of his sin, turn from it unto God, with full purpose of, and endeavour after, new obedience'.[19] Some of those elements are clearly in focus in Ezekiel's commission: **'Dissuade him from his evil ways in order to save his life ... turn [him] from his wickedness or from his evil ways'** (3:18,19). The basis of this appeal, as Ezekiel will make clear later, is 'Get a new heart and a new spirit. Why will you die, O house of Israel?' (18:31).

God's message to the wicked who refuse to repent is quite clear: **'You will surely die'** (3:18). It is the message he has made clear from the start (Gen. 2:17). But what of the righteous person who has now transgressed against God? What is in view in these verses is a criterion by which true disciples might be distinguished. They are such as continue in God's Word and ways. The backslidden have no hope in Scripture set before them *apart from repentance*. Such as have confessed the name of Christ and have fallen into a lifestyle of sin need to repent — quickly! Ezekiel's companions, even if they once professed to be believers, if now their lives are characterized by ungodliness and rebellion, cannot rest in the profession they once made. Jesus taught, in the parable of the soils, that it is possible to give all the outward signs of faith and obedience, and to witness for a time a good confession, showing zeal for the kingdom of God, and then to lose all interest and become indifferent, even hostile (Mark 4:1-20).

'We have come to share in Christ,' insists the author of Hebrews, 'if we hold firmly till the end the confidence we had at first' (Heb. 3:14). This is a message that Ezekiel will return to more than once. 'Even the most established believer is not safe,' suggests Fairbairn, 'unless he keep constantly in mind the dangers of his condition, and, with a godly jealousy over himself, perpetually watch and pray lest he fall into evil.'[20]

Human responsibility

God makes it plain that he holds Ezekiel accountable, insisting (twice) that any failure to warn the wicked of the consequences of their ways will result in the prophet having **'blood'** on his hands (3:18,20; 33:8). The language is similar in intent to that of the words of Paul when he said, 'Yet when I preach the gospel, I cannot boast, for I am compelled to preach. Woe to me if I do not preach the gospel!' (1 Cor. 9:16). The same Bible which teaches that, as King, God is sovereign (Gen. 45:8; 50:20; Prov. 16:9; 21:1; Matt. 10:29;

Acts 4:27-28; Eph. 1:11) also teaches that, as Judge, he holds each one responsible for the choices they make and the directions they take (Rom. 2:1-16; Rev. 20:11-13). The reaction of our finite and sinful minds may be to suggest that this is unfair, but this is misguided. 'One of you will say to me: "Then why does God still blame us? For who resists his will?" But who are you, O man, to talk back to God? "Shall what is formed say to him who formed it, 'Why did you make me like this?'"' (Rom. 9:19-20).

An acted parable

Once more Ezekiel returns to the plain and sees the glory of the Lord that had filled his soul a week earlier (3:22-23). Once again his reaction is to fall down on his face (3:23) and God's Spirit sets him on his feet (3:24). And once more God has something for Ezekiel to do: this time, not so much a listening, but a doing. Ezekiel is called upon to perform a kind of acted parable. This was to prove the first of many such gestures.

Three things were required of the prophet. First, he must stay at home (3:24), thereby indicating that whenever he appeared in future it was as God's messenger. When people saw Ezekiel coming it was the voice of God that would speak. Second, he was to be tied up (3:25), thereby indicating that he was God's prisoner, or slave. And third, whenever he was not speaking God's Word he was to be silent (3:26). He is not allowed to reprove the rebels of the exile unless God says so (3:26-27). This muteness was to last for almost seven and a half years, until the fall of Jerusalem (33:21-22).

God's calling for Ezekiel is one of total obedience. It is no less so for any Christian. We are 'slaves of Christ' (Eph. 6:6). Just as Ezekiel was totally at his Master's command, so must we be. 'Faithfulness to God must be the supreme rule, and his glory the chief aim.'[21]

In a final word that closes this section on Ezekiel's commissioning, the prophet hears something that would become all too familiar in Palestine centuries later: **'Whoever will listen let him listen, and whoever will refuse let him refuse'** (3:27). This was to be Jesus' theme too. Just as Ezekiel was to be held responsible for his actions, so everyone who hears the gospel will likewise be held responsible.

Summary

God has called Ezekiel five times to a life of service as a prophet of God. As prophet and watchman he is to be God's eyes, ears and mouth. The task is difficult and exacting. There are temptations to compromise and give up. But Ezekiel is to stand firm. He is to show by his lifestyle that he is dedicated to serving God, no matter what the cost may be. Above all, he is to be faithful and courageous. Like the other great prophets of the Old Testament, he is not to fear the face of any man. And he finds that in complying with God's demands, there comes a sense of delight and well-being. Ezekiel's wisdom consisted in attending to God's instructions.

3.
The siege of Jerusalem

Please read Ezekiel 4:1 - 5:17

The first three chapters have dealt largely with Ezekiel's calling and commission to serve as a prophet. What that commission entailed is now highlighted in chapters 4 and 5. Ezekiel is called upon to act out a prophecy of the coming destruction of Jerusalem in four different ways. Any who think that they can trust in Jerusalem to save them had better rethink their position; salvation is of the Lord and not of man.

In order to understand these acted prophecies we will have to brace ourselves for a bit of history.

From Jehoiakim to Zedekiah

Assuming that no interval of time has elapsed, chapter 4 opens in the year 593 B.C. Five years have elapsed since Nebuchadnezzar's forces first attacked Jerusalem in December of 598 B.C. That siege lasted for three months and coincided with the reign of Jehoiakim's son, Jehoiachin (2 Kings 24:8-12).

Jehoiachin was completely at the mercy of his circumstances; Scripture records of him that 'he did evil in the eyes of the Lord' (2 Kings 24:9). The three-month siege lasted until March of 597 B.C. when Jehoiachin decided that submission was the prudent course of action. Submission undoubtedly saved many lives and enabled Judah to retain its status as a kingdom.

Since Jehoiachin had proved disloyal, Nebuchadnezzar exacted retribution: he appointed a king of his own choice (Zedekiah), received tribute and exiled many of Jerusalem's subjects (3,023

according to Jeremiah 52:28, a figure which included both
Jehoiachin and Ezekiel).

Life in Jerusalem during this period was difficult. Zedekiah
consistently adopted pro-Babylonian policies despite a sizeable
number who sought opportunity to rebel. Ezekiel's contemporary
Jeremiah called such rebels 'bad figs', asserting that all the 'good
figs' had been deported (Jer. 24). Jeremiah thus put his finger on the
difficulty of the Babylonian deportation policy: namely, that the
best people were taken away and those that remained in Jerusalem
were 'second rate' and ineffective leaders.

One interesting event took place in 594 B.C. — about a year prior
to the events recorded in Ezekiel 1-5. At the probable instigation of
Egypt, representatives of a number of states gathered in Jerusalem
to discuss the possibility of a revolt against Babylon (Jer. 27:3). The
background to this meeting was a revolt against Nebuchadnezzar in
Babylon itself (December 595 - January 594); but order was
restored and the plotters in Jerusalem decided against revolution.

Five years later, Zedekiah could wait no longer and instigated a
rebellion, probably at the invitation of the ambitious Hophra, who
had acceded to the throne of Egypt in 589 B.C. (2 Kings 25:20; 2
Chron. 36:13).[1] At the back of it lay inordinate pride on the part of
Zedekiah and others that Jerusalem could not fall.

God teaches the proud lessons. In a swift and decisive response
Nebuchadnezzar sent his armies into Judah and proceeded to
destroy all the fortified towns and cities. At the close of 589 B.C.
Jerusalem was besieged (2 Kings 25:1). Before the close of the
following year, only three cities were still holding out: Jerusalem,
Lachish and Azekah (Jer. 34:7). Jerusalem was to know a brief
respite when Pharaoh Hophra's armies came to Zedekiah's rescue
(Jer. 37:5). Thinking that all was over, Jerusalem's citizens were
overjoyed — apart, that is, from Jeremiah.

But the hearts of the people of Jerusalem remained unchanged.
Having freed the slaves during the time of siege, they quickly re-
enslaved them as soon as Nebuchadnezzar's armies moved away
(Jer. 34:8-11). As well as condemning their unbelief and hardness
of heart, Jeremiah was to prophesy of Jerusalem's destruction.
When he attempted to leave the city on private business he was
arrested, flogged and thrown into a filthy dungeon where, apart
from the intervention of a palace official, he would have died of
thirst and starvation (Jer. 37:9 - 38:13). He was to remain in custody

until the city fell in August of 587 B.C. A month later the city was systematically destroyed — houses, royal palace, city walls and temple. The holy objects of the temple probably went up in flames; at least they were never to be seen again. It is this horrible future that Ezekiel is to reveal to the people of Judah along the banks of the River Kebar.

When things are bad there is always the possibility that they may get worse. What the exiles in Babylon had already suffered was only the beginning of their sorrows. God was about to teach them a lesson that they would find hard to bear.

Building a model of Jerusalem (4:1-3)

Taking **'a clay tablet'** (4:1), something probably about a foot square, Ezekiel was to depict on it the layout of Jerusalem under siege. There were to be ramps erected at the outer walls of the city, camps of soldiers nearby and battering rams to pound the city walls. In addition, Ezekiel was told to take **'an iron pan'** (4:3) — probably a cooking utensil — and use it as a barrier between himself and the city. The **'sign'** (4:3) that this constituted was not difficult to interpret: God was 'hiding his face' from his people, as the curse of the covenant had predicted (Deut. 31:17,18; 32:20). This is, no doubt, what Ezekiel told passers-by who enquired as to the meaning of the model.

The covenant people of Ezekiel's day had broken the covenant. They had served other gods. Though circumcised in the flesh, their hearts remained uncircumcised (Jer. 9:26; Ezek. 28:10; 31:18; 32:21-32). They had not made good the covenant. Whenever people turn to other gods, God turns from his people. This is the message Paul would have us consider: 'Consider therefore the kindness and sternness of God: sternness to those who fell, but kindness to you, provided that you continue in his kindness. Otherwise, you also will be cut off' (Rom. 11:22). There is safety in Christ, but only in Christ. 'The one who sows to please his sinful nature, from that nature will reap destruction; the one who sows to please the Spirit, from the Spirit will reap eternal life' (Gal. 6:8). Jerusalem's inhabitants, in the main, had sown sinful seed; they were about to receive their reward — God's wrath and displeasure.

A bed of woe (4:4-8)

The second of Ezekiel's enactments was to last for a total of 430 days and was heavy with symbolism. The prophet, having first preached God's message of punishment against Jerusalem (as represented in the clay model), was then to lie on his **'left side'** (4:4) for 390 days, representing the 390 years of Israel's covenant unfaithfulness from the time of Solomon's apostasy in 931 B.C. (1 Kings 11:31-36) to the end of the Babylonian exile in 539 B.C.[2] Following this, he was then called upon to lie on his **'right side'** for forty days (4:6). The exact period represented here is not so easy to evaluate. It may refer to the years of Judah's punishment from the day of Jerusalem's destruction (in 587 B.C.) until its end in 539 B.C.[3] In both instances he was to be tied with ropes **'so that you cannot turn from one side to the other'** (4:8). Two interesting features emerge.

1. The cloud of judgement has a silver lining

Although the actions of the prophet spoke initially of the doom of Judah, and particularly Jerusalem, the judgement would come to an end. The number 430 stirred memories of Egyptian bondage, which ended in a powerful display of God's love and reclamation. And at the end of Babylonian servitude, another exodus was to take place. Over a century earlier, Isaiah had predicted the coming of Cyrus the Great, the founder of the Persian empire (Isa. 41:2-7; 44:28; 45:1-13). In just over twenty years from now, in 549 B.C., Cyrus was to displace his overlord Astyages as king of the small state of Anshan near the Persian Gulf. His rise to power would spell the end of Babylon; the mighty empire fell without a struggle to the Persians in 539 B.C. Cyrus immediately issued a decree allowing the Jews to return to Jerusalem (Ezra 1:1-4). Those who knew their Bibles in Ezekiel's day had cause to rejoice in the prophet's behaviour for it spoke of judgement followed by mercy.

2. The symbolism of substitution

God instructed Ezekiel to lie down, and in dramatic symbolism to **'put the sin of the house of Israel upon yourself'** (4:4; cf. 4:6). The language is that of penal substitution. Ordinarily sinners, according

to the Old Testament, were to 'bear their iniquity [or sin]' (AV) or
'suffer for their sins' (NIV).⁴ But the possibility existed that some-
body else might bear the sinner's penalty. Thus Moses told the
Israelites that their children would have to wander in the desert, and
'suffer for your sins' (Num. 14:33-34).

More pertinent to our context is the fact that after the destruction
of Jerusalem in 586 B.C. the remnant who stayed in the otherwise
deserted ruins said, 'Our fathers sinned and are no more, and we
bear their punishment' (Lam. 5:7). These words, written at the same
time as Ezekiel's prophecy, define the possibility of vicarious sin-
bearing, albeit involuntary in these cases. The point, however, had
been abundantly clear in Israel's worship ritual. The sin-offering
was given 'to take away the guilt of the community by making
atonement for them before the Lord' (Lev. 10:17). Similarly, the
ritual of the two goats on the Day of Atonement was loaded with
substitutionary symbolism. One goat was to be sacrificed and its
blood sprinkled in the usual way, while upon the other goat's head
the high priest was to lay both his hands, 'and confess over it all the
wickedness and rebellion of the Israelites' (Lev. 16:21). The goat
was then to be driven into the desert; it would 'carry on itself all their
sins to a solitary place' (Lev. 16:22).

Isaiah had made clear that what all this typified was the coming
of God's suffering Servant who would bear the sin of many (Isa.
42:1-4; cf. Matt. 12:17-21; and especially Isa. 52:13 - 53:12). Jesus
would not only suffer with his people, but incur the penalty that their
sins deserved (Isa. 53:4-6). Only when we realize that Christ was
given, as Luther would say, *pro nobis* ('for us'), do we really
understand what Christ has done for us. As Luther once said, 'The
words *our, me [us]*, ought to be written in golden letters — the man
who does not believe them is not a Christian.'⁵ This, at least in part,
Ezekiel was now to symbolize by his actions.

Famine (4:9-17)

Ezekiel's third symbolic portrayal of events had to do with cooking.
It has to be understood that it is not necessary to expect that Ezekiel
never got up at all during his enforced period of lying down. To
begin with, it is more than likely that this enactment was done during
daylight hours. But the third action informs us that from time to time

the prophet would rise to make himself some food. Publicly at least, the food he would prepare was to be meagre to the point of near starvation! The next chapter records the gruesome detail that some of Jerusalem's inhabitants were reduced to cannibalism (5:10; cf. Deut. 28:53; Jer. 19:9). Ezekiel was to depict the consequences of a long siege on Jerusalem: the food supplies would eventually run out. Jehoiachin had seen it coming when he surrendered after only three months. Zedekiah, however, chose to stick it out with all the terrible consequences that history records (2 Kings 25:1-8).

Nebuchadnezzar's final siege of Jerusalem (for Ezekiel's compatriots still some four years away) was to last for two years. Interrupting as it did two years' supply of harvest, as well as the possibility of cultivating the land close to the city, the ensuing famine brought the people of Jerusalem to the point of starvation: 'By the ninth day of the fourth month the famine in the city had become so severe that there was no food for the people to eat' (2 Kings 25:3).

All this Ezekiel was to depict by his daily diet of **'twenty shekels'** (4:10) (about eight ounces) of bread made from the unpromising grains and legumes of **'wheat and barley, beans and lentils, millet and spelt'** (4:9), and **'a sixth of a hin'** (4:11) (about half a pint) of water!

If this was bad, worse was to follow. Ezekiel is asked to bake the bread using human excrement as the source of heating (4:12). Ezekiel protests, understandably — as a priest, human waste was not only offensive, but ritually unclean (Deut. 23:12-14). During the siege any animal within the confines of Jerusalem was undoubtedly eaten. Human excrement no doubt became the only source of fuel. As an alternative, God allows the prophet to bake his bread using cow dung instead. Though this, too, offends our sensibilities, a visit to the Third World, particularly India and Africa, would reveal this to be a current practice. What is interesting to note is the fact that God asks his servant to do something that Ezekiel finds himself incapable of doing. As a mark of his grace, God concedes. This is the first indication of Ezekiel's unwillingness to obey the Lord's command for his life. The Lord's concession is remarkable for, as Craigie comments, 'The concession meant that something of the power of the symbolic message would be lost. Yet the message was modified for the sake of the messenger. For all the suffering he asked of his servant, God was not unfeeling; he was concerned for his messenger as well as for those to whom the message was sent. Ezekiel had no guarantee of such a response to his outburst, but its receipt was an encouragement of love. And for all who would serve God, and accept the hardships which service brings, this little incident is a source of encouragement.'[6]

Two further truths need highlighting here.

1. The real famine was a spiritual one

The downfall of Israel and Judah was due to the fact that they had refused the bread of life. During the wanderings in the wilderness God had fed them with manna from heaven, but even then he had cause to remind them that man does not live by bread alone, but by every word that proceeds from God's mouth (Deut. 8:3). It is the lesson which Jesus repeats during his own temptations in the wilderness (Matt. 4:1-4). The famine, which in itself was an indicator of cursing under the terms of the covenant (Deut. 28:52-57), was a reminder of their spiritual starvation. They had forgotten God.

2. The judgement is due to their sin

In what appears to be a summary of what the prophet might have said to any who enquired of him what he was doing, Ezekiel 4:16-17 concludes with the words: **'because of their sin'**. Ever since the heady days of Solomon the nation had steadily declined in power and influence. Though periods of blessing can be discerned, in the main the history of God's people had been one of sinful neglect of God's ways. Israel's election had been a great blessing; it had also been a test — one which they had consummately failed. Consequently, God confirms the threat he had made in his covenant and Israel and Judah have no one to blame but themselves (cf. Deut 8:18).

The sword of the Lord (5:1-17)

The fourth enactment prophecy that Ezekiel was called upon to perform took place towards the end of the 430 days of lying on his side and involved shaving off his hair and beard, using a sword as a razor (5:1). A shaved head was a sign of mourning (Job 1:20). Ezekiel was then to divide the hair into three parts which in turn were burnt, cut up with a sword and scattered to the wind (5:2). Though some strands were preserved in the prophet's clothing, some of these too were to be taken out and burnt (5:3-4).

To save us from speculation, the meaning of these actions is given. A third of the people would die from disease during and after the siege (the burning of the hair possibly representing the fever), another third would be killed with the sword (hence the prophet's cutting the hair with the sword) and a further third would be exiled (as the hair was scattered to the winds) (5:12).

We have to imagine Ezekiel, bald and somewhat gaunt after a year on starvation rations, perhaps also hobbling from such a lengthy period of inactivity, throwing bits of hair into the fire, flaying at some with his sword and throwing more strands into the air. What God calls some of his children to do requires much grace and we need to be careful when we complain at our lot!

The message conveyed by this final action is quite clear: disaster is coming. God's patience has run out with his disobedient people. God has grasped his flashing sword of judgement (Deut. 32:41). The principle emerges: from those to whom much is given, much will be required (Luke 12:48). This is precisely the lesson of 5:5-6: **'This is Jerusalem, which I have set in the centre of the nations, with countries all around her. Yet in her wickedness she has rebelled against my laws and decrees more than the nations and countries around her. She has rejected my laws and has not followed my decrees.'** The motive for obedience in the Christian life is to remember who we are. 'This is Jerusalem,' can be translated: 'You are God's children; indwelt by the Holy Spirit!' (Rom. 8:14-15; 1 Cor. 3:16).

> Think what Spirit dwells within thee,
> What a Father's smile is thine;
> What a Saviour died to win thee,
> Child of heaven, should'st thou repine?

Once again, two points are worth highlighting.

1. There comes a point in God's dealings when his patience runs out

Twelve times Ezekiel quotes God as saying, **'I myself am against you'** (5:8).[7] It is the opposite of 'God is for us' (Ps. 56:9; Rom. 8:31). All the confidence of the psalmist and apostle in these two references to God's covenant faithfulness to watch over and protect his children is taken away from Jerusalem in Ezekiel's day. It is summarized this way: **'I myself will withdraw my favour; I will not look on you with pity or spare you'** (5:11).

2. The reality of God's wrath

Those who find the emphasis upon the severity of God's **'wrath'** (5:15) difficult to take are those who have not seen sin as God sees it. We are prone to make light of our sin, but we need to be reminded that this is a sentiment encouraged by Satan (cf. Gen. 3:4).

God must remain true to himself. That means sin has to be judged, and judged fully and completely. Firstly, he uses the language of *provocation*. God is provoked by the **'detestable idols'** (5:9) and **'vile images'** (5:11) of the people of Judah. Secondly, he uses the language of *burning*. His wrath must **'cease'**, **'subside'** (5:13). 'If,' as John Stott suggests, 'a fire was easy to kindle during the Palestinian dry season, it was equally difficult to put out. So with God's anger.'[8] Thirdly, he uses the language of *satisfaction*. His wrath must be 'spent' or 'completed'. It must finish its course. Thus God says, **'and when I have spent my wrath upon them'** (5:13).[9]

In summary, God is provoked by sin, and once provoked, his anger burns and does not easily subside. He spends his anger until it is complete. There is something inevitable about this reaction. God's wrath is his reflex to sin.

3. The evil of idolatry

It is idolatry that sparks off God's anger and causes it to burn against his people (5:9,11). A century earlier, Isaiah had delivered a stinging rebuke to the practice of idolatry by calling idols the worshipper's leftovers (Isa. 44:17). Having made a fire with a piece of wood, the carpenter uses the leftovers to make a god and worship it! This is nothing else than 'residue religion'. John Wesley once wrote, 'In his natural state, every man born into the world is a rank idolater.' The history of God's people in the Old Testament would bear this out. In contrast to the dead and powerless idols, God introduces himself as the sovereign one who lives: **'Therefore as surely as I live, declares the Sovereign Lord ...'** (5:11).[10]

A portrait of Ezekiel

A portrait of Ezekiel has emerged from these opening chapters. Having eaten the scroll which was said to contain 'words of lament and mourning and woe' (2:10), Ezekiel is thrown into a lifestyle that involved the severest trials. God's calling is often difficult. To catch sight of Ezekiel, totally bald, preaching to a miniature model of Jerusalem with a frying pan in his hand, lying down for most of the day outside his house and eating starvation rations, must have encouraged the ridicule of most who witnessed it. Those of us who get weary with what God asks us to do should remember what the prophets were asked to perform in his name. To imagine doing this for even a few days is difficult, but Ezekiel's faithfulness shines through in his willingness to do the same task every day for over a year! There are many tasks that we might be called upon to do that may be regarded as humdrum; others which attract ridicule from an unbelieving world. But God calls us to be faithful, even if that means becoming 'fools' for Christ (1 Cor. 4:10).

Summary

God hates sin. His covenant people have turned their backs on God and his covenant — a covenant that contained the warning that those who disobeyed it would incur its curses (Deut. 27, 28). Those who serve other gods, 'residue religion', are guilty of violating the purpose for which they were created. Jerusalem's destruction, only some five years away (in 587 B.C.), is the direct result of the people's sin.

At the close of John Calvin's lectures he would invariably pray. Both his lectures and his prayers were preserved for posterity. At the conclusion of his fifteenth lecture (covering Ezekiel 5:12-17) he prayed the following prayer: 'Grant, Almighty God, since we are so dull and heavy, that we may awake in time at thy threats, and submit ourselves to thy power, that we may not experience by our destruction how formidable it is, but profit under thy rod when thou correctest us like a father, and may we so become wise, that through the whole course of our life we may proceed in the continual pursuit and meditation of true repentance; and having put off the vices and filth of the flesh, we may be reformed into true purity, until at length we arrive at the enjoyment of celestial glory, which is laid up for us in Christ Jesus our Lord. Amen.'[11]

**Part II
Prophecies of judgement
(Ezek. 6-7)**

4.
The Day of the Lord

Please read Ezekiel 6:1 - 7:27

One of the most beautiful areas of Israel (then and now) is the central mountain range, which runs from Galilee in the north to the Negev highlands in the south. This range, rising in places to more than 3,000 feet (915 m.) is severed in an east-west direction by the Jezreel Valley in the north and the Negev Basin in the south.

When the Israelites first settled in Canaan they found that every mountain and hill had its shrines and altars erected in honour of ancient fertility gods. Though initially these were changed so as to provide local places for true worship, the power of native religions, especially the worship of Baal and Asherah, had reasserted itself, particularly during Manasseh's reign in Judah (695-642 B.C.).[1] During the reigns of King Hezekiah and Josiah, attempts at reform were made with considerable success, but once again the appeal of idolatry returned. A glance westward, in the direction of Israel's central mountain range, might have brought sentiment and nostalgia to many an exiled Israelite along the Kebar River in Babylon. To God, however, it was symbolic of all that was wrong with Israel and her people: they were worshipping idols in the **'high places'** of Israel (6:3), **'on every high hill and on all the mountaintops, under every spreading tree and every leafy oak'** (6:13; 1 Kings 14:23; 2 Kings 17:10). It is this that provides the background to the opening of the sixth chapter of Ezekiel.

Chapters 6 and 7 are largely taken up with predictions of doom and disaster to the nation of Israel; Ezekiel is asked to set his **'face against the mountains of Israel'** and **'prophesy against them'** (6:2), because God says, **'I will stretch out my hand against them'** (6:14). The repetition of **'against'** continues a theme from the preceding chapter: 'I myself am against you, Jerusalem...' (5:8); 'I myself will withdraw my favour; I will not look on you with pity or spare you' (5:11).

Syncretism: the curse of apostate religion (6:1-14)

Whether it is a multi-faith worship service in Canterbury Cathedral in the late twentieth century, or the incorporation of Canaanite deities into the worship of Yahweh, Israel's God, the verdict of God is the same: 'You shall have no other gods before me' (Exod. 20:3). Nor do we need to think of idolatry in terms of formal worship services. People's gods are what they love, see, serve and worship. It may be the unholy trio of 's's: sex, shekels or stomach — all three serving self; or, it may the three 'p's: pleasure, possessions or position, which John describes as 'the cravings of sinful man, the lust of his eyes and the boasting of what he has and does' (1 John 2:16).

Verses 1-7 define for us the nature, judgement of and penalty for idolatry.

1. The nature of idolatry

Ezekiel mentions **'high places'**, **'altars,'** **'incense altars'** and **'idols'** (6:3,4,6,9). The 'altars' were used for the cooking of animal meat devoted to the idol, and 'incense altars' were stands similar in appearance to the altar of incense used in Israel's worship in the tabernacle and later in the temple. Of interest, however, is Ezekiel's use of the phrase **'what you have made'** (6:6) to describe their idols. It reminds us of Isaiah's references to idolatry in Isaiah 44:12-20. He pictures a blacksmith, powerful and strong enough to forge an idol in the fire, who suddenly gets hungry and faint! Or a carpenter who cuts down a tree, makes firewood with some of it to cook his dinner and makes a god out of the rest!

'Half of the wood he burns in the fire;
over it he prepares his meal,
he roasts his meat and eats his fill.
He also warms himself and says,
"Ah! I am warm; I see the fire."

From the rest he makes a god, his idol;
   he bows down to it and worships.
He prays to it and says,
   "Save me; you are my god."
They know nothing, they understand nothing;
   their eyes are plastered over so that they cannot see,
      and their minds closed so that they cannot understand'
                                                    (Isa. 44:16-18).

Preaching at the same time as Isaiah, but in the northern kingdom of Israel rather than in Jerusalem, Hosea depicted the nature of Israel's idolatry in starker terms:

'They sacrifice on the mountaintops
   and burn offerings on the hills,
under oak, poplar and terebinth,
   where the shade is pleasant.
Therefore your daughters turn to prostitution
   and your daughters-in-law to adultery
   ... the men themselves consort with harlots
   and sacrifice with shrine prostitutes'
                                                    (Hosea 4:13-14).

If adultery and prostitution literally characterized what had been happening in their shrines, these terms were also descriptive of their spiritual relationship with God: they had **'adulterous hearts'** and God was grieved (6:9). Pretending to have a personal and loyal relationship with Yahweh, they were intimate with other gods, too.

2. God's assessment of idolatry

Adultery is a violation of the covenant of marriage. It speaks of betrayal and disloyalty. It tells of love that has grown sour. Idols are **'evil'** and idolatry **'detestable'** (6:9; cf. 5:9). It is not morally neutral, or an 'alternative form of worship'. Man is not free to worship as he likes, and when the church fails to record God's opprobrium of idolatry, it fails to pronounce his verdict upon such practices. Idolatry is everywhere represented in Scripture as the greatest insult the creature can offer to the Creator. Man's religions have been his greatest crimes.

3. The penalty for idolatry

The warning of the previous chapter, that idolatry sparks off God's anger and causes it to burn against his people (5:9,11), now explodes with severity: the shrines and their contents will be utterly destroyed and idolaters will be **'slain'** by the invading Babylonian armies (6:5-7). Death was the required penalty for idolatry within Israel's theocratic state (Deut. 28:21), and while it may no longer be considered so in our pluralistic states, spiritual death remains God's threat for habitual, unrepentant idolaters. Idolaters, Paul warned, will not inherit the kingdom of God (1 Cor. 6:9).

The prophet, having been asked to set his face against the mountains of Israel (6:2), is now asked to clap his hands and stamp his feet (6:11). This seems to represent the way Israel's enemies will respond to their downfall. The nation that had known such great privileges would **'fall by the sword, famine and plague'** (6:11), and her enemies would taunt her. No matter where the people might be, they would meet with God's judgement (6:12). Chapter 6 ends with a description of Israel's complete desolation from the southern deserts to a city called **'Diblah'** (6:14) in the north.[2]

The Lord-Attacker (7:1-27)

The theme of judgement continues throughout chapter 7. Referring to himself as the Lord-Attacker, **'the Lord who strikes the blow'** (7:9), Ezekiel warns of God's judgement on **'the land of Israel'** (7:2; cf. 6:2), using the refrains: **'The end has come'**, **'The end is now upon you,' 'Doom has come upon you'**, **'The time has come, the day is near'** and **'The day is here!'** (7:2,3,6, 7,10,12).[3] God's **'anger'** burns against them (7:3,8); his **'wrath'** is kindled (7:8,12,14,19); he comes to **'judge'** his people (7:8); he threatens to **'turn [his] face away from them'** (7:22; cf. 6:2). Ezekiel's listeners were no doubt used to referring to God as *'Jehovah-jireh'* (The Lord will provide', Gen. 22:14) and *'Jehovah-nissi'* ('The Lord is my Banner', i.e. the Lord who protects, Exod. 17:15); it must have come as a shock to hear Ezekiel refer to God as *'Jehovah-makkeh'* (**'the Lord who strikes'**, 7:9).

It is all reminiscent of Isaiah's predictions a century earlier (Isa. 13), which warned that the 'day' of Babylonian invasion was coming (Isa. 13:6). Constant repetition here in Ezekiel 7 of **'the day'** underlines for us how difficult it was for the Israelites to believe that Jerusalem could be destroyed. Amos, too, was greeted with incredulity when he prophesied: 'Will not the day of the Lord be darkness, not light?' (Amos 5:20).

It is this sense of shock that lies behind the assertion in verse 7: **'Doom has come upon you — you who dwell in the land.'** Having known the prophecy for over a hundred years, they still do not believe that they — of all people — deserve to be treated in this way! They had believed, rightly, that God's plan and purpose are invincible; but they had believed, wrongly, that his plan and purpose included every Israelite, no matter how they lived. The covenant curses were an integral part of God's message (Deut. 27, 28) — a fact which the Israelites had conveniently forgotten. Moses had reminded them in the wilderness that God confirms his covenant (Deut. 8:18). That meant that he would keep his promise to save his people and cause them to enter into the richness of his blessing. But it also meant that those who became unfaithful to his covenant would discover that they had rejected his blessing. Their hardness of heart would lead to judgement. Even as Ezekiel speaks these words, the rumbling of a Babylonian army approaching for battle is barely three years away!

Four features of these judgement pronouncements are worth noting.

1. God's anger is personal

Stressing the use of the first person singular in Ezekiel 7:8-9 makes a telling point: **'*I* am about to pour out *my* wrath on you and spend *my* anger against you; *I* will judge you according to your conduct and repay you for all your detestable practices. *I* will not look on you with pity or spare you; *I* will repay you in accordance with your conduct and the detestable practices among you. Then you will know that it is *I* the Lord who strikes the blow.'** It was the same message that Amos had preached with faithfulness about Israel's God:

'When a trumpet sounds in a city,
   do not the people tremble?

When disaster comes to a city,
    has not the Lord caused it?'

                                            (Amos 3:6).

There is more at work here than some impersonal cosmic law to the
effect that sin is always followed by disaster. God himself is angry
with his people because of their sin.

2. God's anger is not capricious or arbitrary

It is made clear that God's judgement is due to Israel's sin: **'I will
judge you according to your conduct and repay you for all your
detestable practices'** (7:3; cf. 7:4,8,27). The God of Israel is
different from the pagan deities to which Israel had succumbed; he
is different in his wrath. He is angry with reluctance. He is slow to
wrath (Ps. 103:8) and unwilling to afflict (Lam. 3:33). As he makes
clear later in Ezekiel, he takes no pleasure in the death of the wicked
(18:23,32). It is sin, and only sin, that causes God's anger to burn.
As George Swinnock put it, 'Sin is the weight on the clock which
makes the hammer to strike.'[4]

3. God's anger is related to his covenant

God's anger is different in kind from that of the pagan deities, whose
anger was malicious and vindictive. They were characterized by
unpredictability. At any moment they might 'see red'. Their anger
was no different from that of human beings whose anger is due to
temper and loss of control. This is seen in the way some fathers
discipline their children, 'as they [think] best' (Heb. 12:10). Their
egos are bruised and they lash out. God never behaves in that way.
His wrath is always in response to sin and always in proportion to
the sin committed.

    The threefold use of the word **'repay'** (7:3,4,9) suggests a
principle: sin receives what it deserves from God—no more and no
less. When God judges he does so with equity. His dealings with
man are always in terms of his covenant. He has made clear the
penalty for infringement and he never once operates outside of these
parameters.

4. God's anger is not partial

Priests, elders, even **'the king'** and **'the prince'**, will suffer the judgement of God (7:26-27). God is no respecter of persons. One's station in life is no safety against God's wrath when it ignites against sin. From the highest to the lowest, there will be no escape when invasion and war strike Judah in a few years' time.

Spiritual amnesia: a deadly disease

We are prone to forget God! **'Those who escape will remember me,'** God says (6:9), suggesting that they had forgotten him. This had been Moses' theme in the sermon he preached to Israel in the wilderness (Deut. 8). Then, as now, Israel had forgotten what God had done for them in bringing them out of Egypt (Deut. 8:2-5). They had also become proud, thinking that, somehow, they deserved God's favours because they were special (Deut. 8:10-18). They had forgotten God!

It was the same lesson that caused the downfall of King Uzziah in Isaiah's day (2 Chron. 26:5-16). And once again, it is spiritual amnesia that now lies behind Judah's downfall. They, too, had forgotten what they once were (16:22,43). The exile, however, will cause them to remember their sins (20:43; 36:31). Despite their forgetfulness, God does not forget. The remnant have cause to be thankful that he remembers his covenant (16:60).

Expanding on this theme at length, chapter 7 suggests that a fourfold problem lay behind their deadly amnesia.

1. An arrogant heart

Ezekiel portrays a rod that has blossomed (7:10). It is a rod of pride! When we note that the Hebrew for **'rod'** *(matteh)* can also mean 'tribe', the allusion to Judah's arrogance becomes apparent.[5] God **'will put an end to the pride of the mighty'** (7:24). Despite all that they had received from God, the Israelites had been guilty before of spiritual pride, boasting in the wilderness: 'My power and the strength of my hands have produced this wealth for me' (Deut. 8:17). Those of us who are acquainted with our own hearts know

how prone they are to pride. Solomon's warnings are salutary:
'When pride comes, then comes disgrace' (Prov. 11:2). 'Pride goes
before destruction, a haughty spirit before a fall' (Prov. 16:18).

2. Self-confidence

Arrogance is quickly followed by confidence in one's own ability
to accomplish anything. In the past when enemies threatened, Israel
had matched them with superior power. Once again, when Babylon
comes, they will **'blow the trumpet and get everything ready'**
(7:14), forgetting that unless the Lord fights for them they will be
surely defeated. But they will find their strength is gone: **'Every
hand will go limp, and every knee will become as weak as water'**
(7:17). What God said to King Jehoshaphat is a lesson we need to
remember at all times: 'Listen ... This is what the Lord says to you:
"Do not be afraid or discouraged because of this vast army. For the
battle is not yours, but God's"' (2 Chron. 20:15). God is the Captain
of our salvation. The battle is the Lord's. Following the crossing of
the Red Sea, Moses sang, 'The Lord is a warrior; the Lord is his
name' (Exod. 15:3). Israel had forgotten it.

3. The snare of wealth

When the Babylonians arrive their wealth will be thrown into the
streets, perhaps in hope of saving their lives. Their idols, adorned
with precious jewels and stones, will be carried off. Wealth, Ezekiel
suggests, **'has made them stumble into sin'** (7:19).

Affluence and prosperity can often prove to be a snare. Jesus
spoke of this danger in the parable of the sower and the soils. Some
soil failed to produce fruit because of the presence of thorns, which
he interpreted as 'the worries of this life, the deceitfulness of wealth
and the desires for other things' (Mark 4:19). 'Prosperity is a gift,'
Sinclair Ferguson writes. 'It can be a blessing; *it is always a test.*'[6]

The love of money is the root of all kinds of evil (1 Tim. 6:10).
Martin Luther once suggested: 'There are three conversions necessary: the conversion of the heart, mind, and the purse.'[7]Jesus made it
clear that *mammon*, an Aramaic word meaning 'wealth', is a rival
god (Matt. 6:24). It was the principal cause of the rich young ruler's
doom (Matt. 19:21). Jesus, in the Sermon on the Mount, pointed out
that living for wealth is *daft*— because earthly treasures do not last;

dangerous — because it makes us focus on things 'below'; and *disastrous* — because serving Master Mammon ends in shipwreck (Matt. 6:19-24). If, as Dietrich Bonhoeffer once said, 'Our hearts have room only for one all-embracing devotion, and we can only cleave to one Lord,'[8] then perhaps far too many of us need to cry out, 'Lord, forgive me; money has captured my heart.'

4. The curse of delay

In the ensuing disaster that comes upon Jerusalem some will turn to the prophets, priests and elders for guidance (7:26). But these people will have nothing to say. It is too late: **'When terror comes, they will seek peace, but there will be none'** (7:25).

This is the curse of procrastination. Had they sought peace with God earlier they would have found it; God's arms were ready to enfold them. But now it was too late.

The message of these two chapters has been to show that sin cannot go unpunished. Though the 'day of the Lord' in view in these verses has consistently referred to the Babylonian invasion, it must be remembered that this event, like the Assyrian invasion of Israel earlier, was a precursor of the coming of another 'day': an eschatological day at the end of time when the whole world will appear before God's judgement throne (Isa. 2:12,17; Zeph. 1:14-15). It is a scene that Ezekiel depicts, too (30:3). It is a day for which we need to be ready. Faith in God's Son, Jesus Christ, is the only way to meet it.

The possibility remains that we may be brought to face the judgement, only to find that it is too late for us to make peace with God. We may, like these inhabitants of Jerusalem in Ezekiel's day, wake up to find that the *Jehovah-makkeh* has broken through the fortifications of our lives and all attempts to find a way out are gone (cf. 7:9).

The remnant

But all is not doom in these chapters! God has an inviolable purpose which nothing can destroy — not even the unfaithfulness of Israel! What emerges in this chapter of judgement is a theology of grace, and we must not lose sight of it. A remnant will be saved despite

their adultery (6:8). What explains the fact that God perseveres with
the incessant grumblers of Moses' day, or the apostate and thankless
people of Israel of the seventh and eighth century? It is his covenant
of grace!

The covenant of love explains why, time and again, God steps in
and rescues a remnant from among those whom he judges for their
sin (Deut. 7:7-9). God has determined to save his true church, and
nothing will gainsay it. This had been Isaiah's word of encouragement when Assyria threatened northern Israel (Isa. 1:9; 6:13; 8:16-
18; 17:6; 30:17; 41:8-9; 42:18 - 44:5). It now becomes Ezekiel's
hope when Babylon threatens southern Judah, a century later (6:8-
10). Some, by means of the trial of exile, will have cause to see the
error of their ways and acknowledge their sins (6:7,10). God's
purpose is to save a people for himself; saved sinners know God.

But some, even then, will have cause only to acknowledge that
God is Judge. Even though Ezekiel speaks of these too coming to
'know' God (6:13,14) he is addressing here even those who perish.
'Such was the character of this knowledge', Calvin comments, 'that
it only frightened them, and did not bend them to humility.'[9]

The same discipline hardens one and softens another. It was the
same with the experience of execution suffered by Jesus' companions on either side of him at Calvary. For one the cross brought about
a spirit of repentance, causing him to cry out for pardon. In the life
of backslidden Christians, affliction, as Martin Luther once said, is
the best theologian. This was the secret that George Matheson
knew:

> O joy that seekest me through pain
> I dare not ask to fly from thee.[10]

But equally, the same experience in the other criminal at Calvary
hardened him further. Doubtless the same was true of some who had
survived the Babylonian invasion.

Summary

These two chapters have focused principally upon the reality and
nature of God's wrath. God is angry with Israel because of their sin,
particularly their idolatry. There can be no truce between God and

sin. Where he sees lawlessness and godlessness, he cannot but react with holy aversion. It is his very nature to react in wrath against sin and its perpetrators. Were God to be without anger towards sin, the world would have no meaning. Though these chapters are tough and unrelenting, the message of grace shines through in a remnant that God, and God alone, rescues. This is, of course, not just the story that Ezekiel tells; it is the gospel itself that threads its way from Genesis to Revelation.

Focus

Covenant violation and the book of Deuteronomy

Just before the Lord's people entered Canaan, Moses gathered them together on the plains of Moab and declared to them the Word of God. He spelled out in detail the requirements of discipleship in the kingdom of God. In summary, it was this: 'Love the Lord your God with all your heart and with all your soul and with all your strength' (Deut. 6:5).

A generation later, Joshua, giving his final address before he died, encouraged the settled Israelites in Canaan to do the same: 'So be very careful to love the Lord your God' (Josh. 23:11). But Joshua did more than encourage the Lord's people to love God. He warned them of the consequences of not doing so. In a sermon that includes three marks of discipleship: humility (i.e. putting God first by acknowledging his power in our lives, Josh. 23:3), obedience to God's Word (23:6) and separation from the world (23:7-8), Joshua also includes a fearful note as to what those who fail to comply with these requirements can expect: defeat, discomfort and disgrace (23:12-13,15-16).

Joshua was, in fact, repeating something Moses had made clear: that the covenant of God is a two-edged sword. There are promises, to be sure, and Joshua is adamant that God will keep them: 'You know with all your heart and soul that not one of all the good promises the Lord your God gave you has failed. Every promise has been fulfilled; not one has failed' (23:14). No doubt some of Joshua's listeners were ready to sing, 'Great is thy faithfulness' and go home after that! But Joshua is not finished. Being true to the covenant means being true to its sanctions as well its blessings. God promises to bless those who walk in his ways; but equally, he promises to punish those who do not. 'But just as every good promise of the Lord your God has come true, so the Lord will bring on you all the evil he has threatened, until he has destroyed you from this good land he has given you. If you violate the covenant of the Lord your God, which he commanded you, and go and serve other gods and bow down to them, the Lord's anger will burn against you, and you will quickly perish from the good land he has given you' (23:15-16).

To use a modern phrase, this is 'the down-side' of the covenant. It is what Moses had called the 'vengeance' of the covenant (Lev. 26:25). God will be true to what he has promised — for good or ill!

This is something that Moses highlighted in a remarkable chapter in Deuteronomy where he outlines the blessings and the curses of the covenant (Deut. 28). A knowledge of this chapter (as well as chapters 29-32) is crucial if we are to make sense of Ezekiel, for the prophet is ministering during a time of national and spiritual collapse — a judgement brought about because the Lord has found his people guilty of violating his covenant: 'I will deal with you as you deserve, because you have despised my oath by breaking the covenant' (Ezek. 16:59). We have therefore included a summary of the kinds of things Israel were to expect for covenant violation, together with their fulfilment in Ezekiel.

Curse	Deuteronomy	Ezekiel
War	28:25,49,52-57; 32:23,25,30,42	4:1-2
Famine	28:53-57, 32:24	4:9-17; 14:13
Sword	32:41-42	5:1;11:10; 21:3-17
Danger from wild animals	32:24	5:16-17; 14:15,21; 33:27
Bloodshed	32:42	5:16-17
Cannibalism	28:53-56	5:10
Desolation of cities	28:52; 29:23	6:14; 12:20;14:15 21:18-27; 33:28
Fire	28:24; 32:22	20:47; 21:32
Fear, helplessness	28:65	21:15
Exile	28:36	12:11
Suffering	28:52-57	22:17-22
Terror	28:66-67	23:46
Rejection by God	31:17-18; 23:20	10:1-22; 13:8-9

Part III
The second cycle of prophecies
(Ezek. 8-19)

5.
Revelations of the temple

Please read Ezekiel 8:1- 9:11

Strange things happened to prophets. Fourteen months have passed since Ezekiel received his first vision (8:1; cf. 1:2).[1] Comparing the opening verses with what we are told in 4:4-8, some 420 of the 430 days of lying down outside his house have passed. Ezekiel has just over a week to go on lying on his right side and, with shorn head, preaching at a clay model of Jerusalem.

We saw in an earlier chapter that Ezekiel did not spend his entire time lying down; for one thing, he had to get up to make his food — sparing as it was! Elders have gathered in Ezekiel's house, perhaps to get a detailed explanation of what Ezekiel was doing. As they talk, Ezekiel suddenly becomes the recipient of a vision.[2]

The detailed account of what Ezekiel saw in Jerusalem and, in particular, the temple, in chapters 8-11 may lead us to forget that it was a vision. Like books enclosed between book-ends, chapters 8-11 are bounded at each end by reminders of the unusual nature of these descriptions: **'The Spirit lifted me up between earth and heaven and in visions of God he took me to Jerusalem'** (8:3). 'The Spirit lifted me up and brought me to the exiles in Babylonia in the vision given by the Spirit of God. Then the vision I had seen went up from me' (11:24).[3]

A meeting of elders

It is now the end of summer in the year 592 B.C., fourteen months after the first vision. In only just over a year the first rumblings of the Babylonians would threaten Jerusalem; it surrendered in 597 B.C. Life in exile was not as harsh as it is sometimes depicted.

Ezekiel obviously had a house to live in and freedom to associate with the exiled community of elders (8:1). An elders' meeting is taking place in Ezekiel's home.

This no ordinary meeting; the elders are seeking the Lord's word about their future. Ezekiel is conscious of the **'Sovereign Lord'** who appears, just as in the opening chapter, as **'a figure like that of a man'**, aglow with fire and brightness (8:2). Suddenly, Ezekiel is lifted up by his hair (now regrown!) and transported (in a visionary way) to Jerusalem (8:3). In a fascinating comment on this phenomenon of transportation, Meredith Kline suggests that it provides us with a clue as to what our glorified bodies will be capable of in the next life! These events are, he suggests, 'promissory samples of the powers and capabilities to be enjoyed by those re-created in God's image when, through their physical endowment of glorification, they will have attained to the consummation of their dominion over the creation'.[4]

Readers of Scripture should pause, every now and then, and just think over what it is that lies in store for those who know God! We can, of course, only anticipate with wonder what awaits us; it is, we are assured, beyond what we imagine it to be (1 Cor. 2:9).

Abominations in the temple

The temple is going to feature a great deal in the closing chapters of Ezekiel, where it depicts how things ought to be (40-48). The temple that Ezekiel now 'visits' is altogether different: it is one riddled by sin and pollution. Ezekiel is placed in the outer court of the temple next to the northern gate, one of three entrances from the outer to the inner court of the Jerusalem temple. What happens next is a description of four abominations which Ezekiel sees in the temple.

A debate exists as to whether these abominations were actually present in the temple. Taylor, for example, comments: 'It seems preferable to regard the four abominations as symbolical, or rather typical, of the religious deviations of different sections of the Jerusalem community.'[5]

1. The 'image of jealousy' (8:1-6)

At the gate was some kind of idol which is referred to as an **'idol that provokes to jealousy'** (8:3), possibly an image of Asherah, the lustful, Canaanite goddess of love. This had happened in the past (2 Kings 21:7). Jeremiah's denunciation of the 'Queen of Heaven' may also refer to this same idol (Jer. 7:18; 44:17-30).

All idols provoke jealousy in God. The sanction to the second commandment 'inscribed by the finger of God' (Exod. 31:18) was this: 'I, the Lord your God, am a jealous God' (Exod. 20:5). Even more pertinent are God's words to Moses a little later: 'Do not worship any other god, for the Lord, whose name is Jealous, is a jealous God' (Exod. 34:14).

What these revelations are meant to convey is that God demands of Israel exclusive devotion, the jealous love for which marriage is a type and symbol. His people are to love him with all their heart, soul, strength and mind. Not to do so is spiritual adultery. It is a jealousy which seeks to protect a relationship and which expects loyalty in that relationship. (This is something which will come into a shocking focus in chapters 16 and 23.)

Evidently this image in the temple provoked God to jealousy. It was symbolic of the nature of Israel's worship: disloyal and adulterous. Calvin commented upon it in this way: 'God very commonly takes on the character of a husband to us. Indeed, the union by which he binds us to himself when he receives us into the bosom of the church is like sacred wedlock, which must rest upon mutual faithfulness ... we are not to yield our souls to Satan, to lust, and to the filthy desires of the flesh, to be defiled by them... The more holy and chaste a husband is, the more wrathful he becomes if he sees his wife inclining her heart to a rival. In like manner, the Lord, who has wedded us to himself in truth, manifests the most burning jealousy whenever we, neglecting the purity and his holy marriage, become polluted with wicked lusts.'[6]

We need to ask, 'What idols are we wedded to?' Whatever they are, they are a denial of our covenant vows and provoke God to jealousy.

While gazing at this idol, Ezekiel is conscious of God's **'glory'** and then of God's voice saying, in effect, that Israel's sins are driving him out of his own house! (8:6). Just as oil and water do not mix, so the Lord will not share his glory with another. We are the temples of the Holy Spirit, and as such Paul tells us to 'flee from idolatry' (1 Cor. 10:14). 'Better to remove the false presence,' comments Craigie, 'than have the true presence depart.'[7]

2. The idolatry of art (8:7-13)

Ezekiel is led from beside 'the idol that provokes jealousy' to the door of the inner court. Seeing a hole in the wall beside the door, he digs through it only to find a secret door to a closed room. Upon entering this secret chamber Ezekiel discovers that it is full of paintings, or murals depicting all kinds of creatures (probably unclean according to Israel's dietary laws). But it was not so much the art that aroused God's indignation as the idolatry associated with it. Seventy of Israel's elders, led by **'Jaazaniah son of Shaphan'**, were offering worship to these paintings (8:11).

Jaazaniah came from a distinguished family in the Old Testament. His father had been secretary of state in the cabinet of Israel's reforming king, Josiah (2 Kings 22:3), and one of his brothers was a defender of Jeremiah, Ezekiel's contemporary in Jerusalem (Jer. 26:24).

The tragedy of this episode is that the leaders of Israel are wholly given over to idolatry. They, of whom much was rightly expected, are themselves guilty. This is what Isaiah had predicted (Isa. 3:1-3).

They performed their idolatry **'in the darkness'**, saying to themselves, **'The Lord does not see us'** (8:12). How many sins are committed 'in the dark', where it is imagined that no one can see them! Little children play games of 'hide and seek' covering their faces in the vain hope that no one can therefore see them. This childishness is excusable, even laughable. But sinners play games of this sort too: games of stupidity and wilfulness, thinking no one observes — not even God! It is neither excusable, nor funny: but tragic!

In the opening chapter of this prophecy, the Lord was depicted riding upon a chariot which itself was **'full of eyes'** (1:18). God sees all that we do and it is a powerful motive to holiness. But, as John Owen suggests, those who need the threat of punishment to motivate them to holiness are in a bad way: 'If a man be so under the power of his lust that he hath nothing but law to oppose it withal, if he cannot fight against it with gospel weapons, but deals with it altogether with hell and judgement, which are the proper arms of the law, it is most evident that sin hath possessed itself of his will and affections to a very great prevalency and conquest.[8] Sin ought to be mortified because of its detestability; if this is not perceived then God threatens his judgement. There are no secrets from God.

3. The worship of Tammuz (8:14-15)

Returning to the point where the prophet had arrived at the temple, Ezekiel observes a group of women sitting on the ground and weeping. They are involved in the worship of Tammuz, the Sumerian-Babylonian god of plant-life, whose death was mourned every autumn when the leaves fell. In the spring, Tammuz came to life again when leaves began to sprout. That they should have mourned the death of this god in the very temple of the living God adds to its abomination.

4. The worship of the sun (8: 16-18)

The fourth and final abomination takes place in the inner court of the temple, where only the priests were allowed to go. Here Ezekiel observes **'twenty-five men'**(priests) bowing down and worshipping the sun to the east.

Each abomination highlights Israel's decline: the worship of the image at the north gate revealed the idolatry of the people in general; the secret chamber with its artwork told of the leadership's decline; the worship of Tammuz told of the fall of the women, and even the priests were corrupt. Idolatry had taken hold of Judah's last days. Furthermore, Asherah was Canaanite, the murals were probably Egyptian, Tammuz was of Sumerian-Babylonian origin and the worship of the sun originated from the Near East. Their worship was syncretistic (an attempt to unify differing schools of thought) and eclectic (selecting whatever pleases from whatever source).

Is idolatry trivial?

'Is it a trivial matter for the house of Judah to do the detestable things they are doing here?' the Lord asks Ezekiel (8:17). To many, undoubtedly it did seem trivial. To us, from the sophistication of the twentieth century, these ancient deities are strange. But substitute football colours, a flag, a swastika, or even a pair of jeans, and we are back in the seventh century B.C. On their own these things mean nothing, but they represent a set of beliefs about life itself. We have our own idols today. Nor are they that far removed from those in Ezekiel's vision.

Darwinian evolution is worshipped as the explanation for all reality; it is in essence a worship of nature's powers, differing little from what the women bewailed beside the north gate of the temple. The 'need' for a summer holiday in the sun has also a powerful set of belief systems behind it which differs little from what Ezekiel's priests were doing in the inner court. One of the most powerful forces in our time is astrology; it is nothing short of a devotion to the powers of astral bodies. And behind the art of our time lies another philosophy of existence that reveals the idolatry of contemporary man.

Enough!

Whatever the idol, God finds it **'detestable'** (8:6,9,10,13,15,17). They are a stench in his nose.[9] Consequently, the Lord promises swift punishment. Though they have cause to cry out in prayer under their punishment, God declares that he will not hear them: **'Therefore I will deal with them in anger; I will not look on them with pity or spare them. Although they shout in my ears, I will not listen to them'** (8:18). 'For what is more formidable,' asks Calvin, 'than to have God hostile, and to be verily without any hope of pardon? As often as God withdraws his mercy he shows us material for trembling...'[10]

God has been *provoked* to anger (8:17; cf. 16:26; 20:28). His jealousy has been aroused (8:3; cf. Deut. 32:16,21; Ps. 78:58). God is 'compassionate and gracious ... slow to anger, abounding in love and faithfulness' says Moses. 'Yet he does not leave the guilty unpunished' (Exod. 34:6-7). Though God's anger is not a fit of irrational temper, and though his judgement is not a ruthless and mechanical fate, nevertheless his anger is real. His judgement is real, and to prove it, there comes a point when he says, 'Enough!' If evil did not provoke God to anger he would forfeit our respect, for he would no longer be God. There comes a point when evil is so great that God's patience runs out.[11]

There will come a day when God's patience will run out with the world. It might be considered a pleasant thing if this were not so, but that would be to deny any moral order in the universe. There is a sin which leads to death and which no prayer can absolve (1 John 5:16).

There is a decree which condemns to hell from which no deliverance is possible. If this were not so we could never speak of God's patience at all, only of his total indifference!

Peter tells us that the Lord is not slack about the Day of Judgement: 'He is patient with you, not wanting anyone to perish, but everyone to come to repentance' (2 Peter 3:9). God holds back from summoning us to immediate judgement, as would be his right! And this he does for one reason only: to provide us with an opportunity to repent of our sin. Whatever our idols might be, we need to flee from them to Christ without delay. Paul asks, 'Do you show contempt for the riches of his kindness, tolerance and patience, not realizing that God's kindness leads you towards repentance? But because of your stubbornness and your unrepentant heart, you are storing up wrath against yourself for the day of God's wrath, when his righteous judgement will be revealed' (Rom. 2:4-5). God is patient — but his patience is not without limit! There comes a time when he will say, 'Enough! I can stand it no longer.'

The executioners (9:1-11)

When God's patience runs out, his judgements are fearful (Heb. 10:31). Ezekiel, having been shown the idolatry in the Jerusalem temple, is now witness to a scene of execution. With a **'loud voice'** God summons six **'guards'** (angels), **'each with a deadly weapon in his hand'** (9:1-2). Following the same route that the prophet had taken earlier, they make their way into the inner court of the temple. They are accompanied now by another, dressed in white linen. His task is different from that of his six companions (9:4,11). Instead of a weapon, he is carrying a **'writing kit'**, a small box containing a quill, ink, a small knife and some parchment.

God's glory, normally seen at the ark, in the holy of holies, has now shifted to the front of the building (later the glory will leave the temple altogether, ch. 10). Then the linen-clad angel is commanded to go through the city, placing a **'mark on the foreheads of those who grieve and lament over the detestable things that are done in it'** (9:4). The six executioners are then told to follow him through the city, executing on the spot all those who do not bear the mark on their foreheads — men, women and children alike (8:5-6).

Having witnessed the slaughter in the temple, the executioners leave for the city and Ezekiel is left alone. He is overcome with grief. He begins to think, 'What if everyone is slain?' Falling down on the ground he tries to pray, asking God at least to spare a remnant within the city. God's reply is less than encouraging. Judgement has begun and its course seems inevitable. Just then, the man clothed with linen returns and says: **'I have done as you commanded'** (9:11). There seems some hope.

Several matters call for comment.

1. The executioners are to have no pity

They are to kill men, women and children **'without showing pity or compassion'** (9:5). Israel was called upon to wage war with those upon whom God's judgement had fallen. In the case of the Israelites themselves, they were God's people and were bound to him in a way that a modern secular society is not. In Israel, idolatry, blasphemy, divination and profanation of the Sabbath were all made punishable by death (Lev. 20:2; 24:13; Exod. 22:18; Num. 15:32-36).

We have to believe that in this instance the sinfulness of the Israelites had reached such a proportion that God's judicial punishment was the only course left. If we object that this could not possibly be fair in the case of children, we are making an assumption based on principles other than those found in Scripture (Ps. 51:5). Ezekiel was being shown a vision of what would befall Jerusalem during its war with Babylon. In another war that Jerusalem would face, this time against Emperor Titus of Rome, Jesus warned — citing the oft-denigrated words of Psalm 137 — that even their children would be killed (Luke 19:44; cf. Ps. 137:8-9). Jerry Bridges comments: 'One great problem today is that most of us really don't believe we're all that bad. In fact, we assume we're good. In 1981, a book addressing the difficult subject of pain and heartache was published and rapidly became a best seller. Its title: *When Bad Things Happen to Good People*. The book is based, as the title reveals, on the assumption that most people are "good". The definition by author Harold Kushner of good people is, "ordinary people, nice friendly neighbours, neither extraordinarily good nor extraordinarily bad". By contrast, the apostle Paul said we are all bad.'[12]

2. The judgement begins with Jerusalem's leaders

The principle is vindicated elsewhere: 'For it is time for judgement to begin with the family of God; and if it begins with us, what
will the outcome be for those who do not obey the gospel of God?'
(1 Peter 4:17). 'From everyone who has been given much, much will
be demanded; and from the one who has been entrusted with much,
much more will be asked' (Luke 12:48). The leaders, who had
thought that their actions were unseen (8:12), are visited first of all.
Nothing is hidden from God!

3. A remnant is saved

Grace operates even in God's judging work. Whether the **'mark'**
(9:4) — in Hebrew, *taw*, the last letter of the alphabet — is meant
to convey anything at all of the cross of Christ is highly suspect,
though commentators have made much of it.[13] It may well be that, as
H. L. Ellison remarks, 'This is one of the many examples where the
Hebrew prophets spoke better than they knew.'[14] What is certain is
that this is a further demonstration of God's covenant of grace in
operation. He has determined to save a people for himself and even
now he is at pains to secure them as his own.

A clear connection is made with the book of Revelation at this
point. With Jesus standing on Mount Zion, by his side are 144,000,
the elect of God, each one bearing the name of God the Father and
of Christ written on their foreheads (Rev. 14:1-5). Not one of God's
people is missing, just as Christ had promised (John 6:39). By
contrast, those bearing the mark of the beast are punished (Rev.
14:9,11; cf. 13:16-17; 16:2; 19:20).

4. The prophet's concern

Ezekiel's intercessory prayer for the true people of God emerges as
typical of the prophets. They were men who felt deeply for souls.
They were messengers of doom, but that in no way prevented them
from praying for mercy. Amos, a hundred years earlier, had done
much the same (Amos 7:2-6). So had Abraham on behalf of Sodom
(Gen. 18:23-33) and Moses on behalf of the Israelites who worshipped the golden calf (Exod. 32:9-14). It was, so it seems, a
recognized part of a prophet's duty to intercede on behalf of others.

'He is a prophet,' God said concerning Abraham, 'and he will pray for you' (Gen. 20:7).

Every Christian should have a burden for souls as Ezekiel had. The certainty of the coming judgement should make us fall down and plead that souls be gathered into God's kingdom. Ezekiel laid hold, not of God's reluctance, but his willingness and promise to save. The return of the seventh angel, having accomplished what he had been asked to perform, indicates that wrath is tempered with mercy. It is a further incentive for us to pray, knowing that, unlike the prayers of the unbeliever (8:18), God hears the prayers of his saints.

Summary

Ezekiel has been taken from the banks of the Kebar River in Babylon to the temple in Jerusalem, where he has been shown how far the Israelites have fallen from the true faith. Their worship has become thoroughly idolatrous. God's patience has now run out. Executioners have done their work, first amongst the elders and then in the city itself. They have shown no pity. The Day of Judgement has arrived. And what a day it is! Ezekiel has prophesied the death of Judah; this has been Judah's obituary — in advance! When a newspaper mischievously published in advance an obituary of Mark Twain, he wrote in the paper the following day, 'The news of my death was an exaggeration.' Judah's obituary is no exaggeration. The fall of Israel in the eighth century B.C. and that of Judah in the sixth century B.C. are both foretastes of the coming of another day. John saw this day and warned of it: 'If anyone's name was not found written in the book of life, he was thrown into the lake of fire' (Rev. 20:15).

6.
The chariot of God

Please read Ezekiel 10:1 - 11:25

Readers unfamiliar with Ezekiel's prophecy may, by now, be growing weary of its message of doom and condemnation. 'It's all judgement' is a typical response by the first-time reader. But that is a mistake. Already we have caught a glimpse of the remnant that God will save (6:8-10; 9:5-8). And here, in chapter 11, Ezekiel will preach a prolonged address of hope to his exiled compatriots; they will not only return to Canaan, but they will also experience God's favour and blessing once more (11:14-25).

But before Ezekiel can preach this, he must first preach a message of doom which surpasses anything he has so far delivered. God's greatest judgement is to leave people to the consequences of their sin. When God departs, hell begins. When the apostle Paul declares that unbelievers 'will be punished with everlasting destruction and shut out from the presence of the Lord and from the majesty of his power' (2 Thess. 1:9), he underlines the nature of hell as being that of separation from God.

Jesus also warned of this: 'Then I will tell them plainly, "I never knew you. Away from me, you evildoers!"' (Matt. 7:23). As Matthew Henry says, commenting upon this passage, 'They that would not *come to* Him to be saved must *depart from* Him to be damned. To *depart from* Christ is the very hell of hell; it is the foundation of all misery of the damned, to be cut off from all hope of benefit from Christ and His mediation.'[1]

It is to this theme that Ezekiel now turns and we need to brace ourselves!

Ichabod (10:1-22)

Chapter 10 is very similar to the first chapter: it is a vision of God in his glory. Ezekiel is still standing in the inner court of the temple looking at the ark of the covenant with its two carved cherubim. Presumably, the slain bodies of the idol-worshipping elders and priests lie within view. Suddenly, a sapphire-like throne appears above the cherubim (cf. 1:26). It is from here that God appears to speak to the man clothed in linen (10:2). He is now assigned a very different task.

Among the wheels of the chariot that carried God's throne (10:2; cf. 1:15-21) was a raging fire. The linen-clad scribe is now asked to take some of these coals of fire and **'scatter them over the city'** (10:2). Fire is often a symbol of God's holiness in Scripture and it would appear that by this action the scribe is being called upon to portray symbolically God's wrath upon the city (Gen. 19:24; Deut. 28:24; 32:22).

The unnamed creatures of the first chapter are now identified as **'cherubim'** (10:3). They were to be found above the mercy-seat, supporting the throne of God (Exod. 37:7-9) and elsewhere in temple carvings (1 Kings 6:29,35; 7:29,36). The psalms often portray God as borne by cherubim or enthroned among them (Ps. 18:10; 80:1; 99:1). Suddenly, as Ezekiel focuses on the cherubim, with their close association to God, God's glory begins to move. God is departing from the temple.

What needs to be grasped is that this is worse than any of his judgements thus far. 'For the judgement of God who is present, however terrible, is surely preferable to the absence of God,' says Craigie.[2] The culminating tragedy of a broken marriage occurs when one of the partners leaves. It is a heart-rending moment. Sin has forced God to evacuate his own home!

God's presence is his most treasured gift. It is at the heart of what he promises, or covenants, to his people. 'You are with me,' David says, and one senses that it was the truth he treasured most (Ps. 23:4). Other Bible writers echo it: God is with us (Matt. 28:20), around us (Ps. 34:7; 139:5), in us (John 14:17), in the midst of us (Ps. 46:5), underneath us (Deut. 33:27), near us (Ps. 148:14) and before us (John 10:4). He never forsakes the believer (Josh. 1:5).

Even so, some aspects of God's presence may well be withdrawn even from God's own people. He may withdraw all sense of his love, so that even though he may be present, we may not know it. He may decide to withdraw his help — as Samson discovered with Delilah. But what happens here in Ezekiel 10 is of a different order. Here, God is withdrawing from his church.

Following the warnings of Revelation 3:12-17, where God threatens to fight against the Pergamum church because of their moral and spiritual deviances, and Revelation 3:14-22, where God threatens to 'spit' the Laodicean church out of his mouth and appears to be standing outside the door of the church, the Westminster divines made it clear that the possibility exists that some 'churches' are not churches at all but 'synagogues of Satan'.[3] In such cases, where the church has become no longer a church in the true sense, God departs.

This was the judgement that temporarily fell upon Israel in the time of Samuel when the Philistines captured the ark and took it away, effectively taking God's presence away with it. When Eli heard of it he fell backwards from his chair and died. And when his daughter-in-law heard of it, together with the news of the death of her husband and brother-in-law, she died in childbirth. Before her death she named the child Ichabod, meaning 'The glory has departed' (1 Sam. 4:21).

Once again, the name of Ichabod will be written over Jerusalem when the Babylonians finally overthrow the city. They may lament over the loss of their city; they ought to lament even more over the loss of God's presence.

There follows a description of God's throne almost identical to the one found in the opening chapter (10:9-22). Commentators have been puzzled at its repetition, and many give credence to the idea that this is a later editorial addition. But the solution cannot be that difficult. It is in order to emphasize the magnitude of God's departure that a description of his glory is repeated. It surely makes the point infinitely more distressing to be reminded that it is this glorious God who is leaving.

At the close of this description God's glory, which had briefly lifted away from the chariot (10:4), now rejoins the chariot (10:18) and the entire glory-chariot makes its way to the east gate of the temple, the very edge of the entire temple complex (10:19), ready to depart altogether (which it does in 11:23).

God had finished with those in Jerusalem — apart from the remnant marked by the scribe. When the exile is over, it will be returning exiles who are entrusted with building God's Old Testament church, men like Zerubbabel, Joshua, Ezra and Nehemiah. God chooses faithful people to carry on his work no matter what their status. Poor and despised believers will take precedence over unfaithful bishops and archbishops.

Arrogance (11:1-13)

As we noted in the introduction to this chapter, Ezekiel will shortly have something wonderfully encouraging to say to his fellow exiles, but not just yet. Ezekiel has something to say to the self-righteous leaders who are still in Jerusalem. When Nebuchadnezzar engaged in his policy of deportation into captivity he took away the most able of Jerusalem's leaders. But that was not how the leaders that remained in Jerusalem saw it. They believed that they were 'the favoured few'. Confident that the city was invincible, they boasted openly about their building programme: **'Will it not soon be time to build houses?'**, adding an odd-sounding expression: **'This city is a cooking pot, and we are the meat'** (11:3).

This appears to mean that, just as meat belongs in a cooking pot, so they belonged in Jerusalem. It is an arrogant claim, as God later remarks: they will be hurled out of the pot (11:11). The arrogance and self-confidence of this remark are further exemplified in the fact that the people of Jerusalem had by now grown openly cynical of their blood-brothers and sisters in exile, claiming that the land belonged to them only (11:15).

Standing at the east gate of the temple, Ezekiel sees these Jerusalem elders in his vision, represented by twenty-five men (11:1) and led by two leaders: Jaazaniah[4] and Pelatiah (11:2). This is where God's chariot throne was currently residing (10:19). This is also where Ezekiel hears them making their arrogant, self-confident claims.

Man's arrogance can never ultimately stand; it is invariably followed by a fall (Prov. 16:18). So it will be for these dwellers of Jerusalem. Many, including its leaders, will be slaughtered by their enemies (11:6-9). It is now 592 B.C. In just over two years from now, the first indication of a large-scale Babylonian attack would come upon Jerusalem. By 597 B.C. Jerusalem had fallen and many of its occupants died in the ensuing battle. Leaving a few peasants to keep the land cultivated for the benefit of Babylon,

Nebuchadnezzar marched about seventy religious, political and military leaders in chains to Riblah in Hamath, his headquarters, and executed them (2 Kings 25:18-21). Prophecy was once again fulfilled.

Suddenly, as Ezekiel watches and listens to these elders, Pelatiah collapses and dies as a foreshadowing of the mass executions that would take place at Riblah. As he did previously, when confronted by the 'angels of death', God's sword-bearing executioners who went through the city slaying 'without showing pity or compassion' (9:5), Ezekiel responds to Pelatiah's death with grief, fearing that God's judgement might mean that no one would be saved: **'Ah, Sovereign Lord! Will you completely destroy the remnant of Israel?'** (11:13; cf. 9:8).

Every Christian should be similarly affected. 'I am afraid,' remarked Spurgeon in a sermon on Ezekiel 9:8, 'that it does not cause some people much anxiety when they see sin rampant around them. They say that they are sorry, but it never frets them much, or causes them as much trouble as would come to a lost sixpence or a cut finger. Did you ever feel as if your heart would break over an ungodly son? I do not believe that you are a Christian man if you have such a son, and have not felt an agony on his behalf. Did you ever feel as if you could lay down your life to save that daughter of yours? I cannot believe that you are a Christian woman if you have not sometimes come to that.'[5]

The Lord gives two reasons why he has **'drive[n] them out of the city'** and handed them over **'to foreigners'** (11:9): they **'have not followed my decrees or kept my laws but have conformed to the standards of the nations around [them]'** (11:12).

1. They had disobeyed God

Sin is lawlessness and lawlessness is sin (1 John 3:4). God has laid down what he expects of those whom he has created; sin is man's rebellion against these laws. 'The plain truth is', wrote Bishop Ryle at the end of the last century, 'that a right knowledge of sin lies at the root of all saving Christianity.'[6]

2. They had also become worldly

They had adopted the lifestyle of the 'Gentiles' (**'the nations'**, 11:12). God's people are called to be different. They were meant by their lifestyle to be set apart from the other nations. They were to be holy (Lev. 11:44-45; 19:2; 20:7,26). But it was manifestly obvious that they were no different at all! They had assimilated the gods of the Gentiles. They behaved like pagans; they were pagans! Since they had abandoned his covenant, God was about to leave them.

God's new work (11:14-25)

Having asked God whether any would be saved (11:13), Ezekiel now receives an answer. And what an answer it is! The dwellers in Jerusalem and Judah who have so far escaped exile are to suffer death and exile; while the exiled ones are to be restored to Jerusalem and experience blessing from the Lord. What emerges in these verses is a key that unlocks the book of Ezekiel. Far from being 'all about judgement', Ezekiel is 'all about grace'! 'The prophecy,' comments Hengstenberg, 'is essentially Messianic.'[7]

The key is *God's determination to save his people.* Ever since the Fall in Eden, God's plan and purpose to gather for himself a people redeemed by his power is evident. Looking to their recent past history in exile, God states that he has 'been a sanctuary for them' (11:16). He is not about to leave them, as he most certainly is leaving the temple in Jerusalem. In contrast to those Jews in Jerusalem and Judah, many of the exiled Jews were true believers who were able to meet together and worship (as the exiled elders were currently meeting in Ezekiel's house). God had provided them with a prophet to speak to them and warn them of things to come. But even better things are in store for his people, for he promises to restore them to the land of Israel again (11:17).

Following Nebuchadnezzar's victory over Judah and Jerusalem in 587 B.C., and his death in 562 B.C., the power of the Babylonian empire waned and was quickly swallowed by the rising power of Persia, led by Cyrus, who inherited the throne in 559 B.C. In 539 B.C., 'the troops of Cyrus entered Babylon without battle'. The Babylonian empire was finished.

During the Babylonian reign of power, Judah and its capital were attacked in a three-stage period spanning the years 605, 597 and 587 B.C. During the first of these stages, Daniel and his three companions had been taken into captivity. Daniel would have been in his mid-twenties as these prophecies of Ezekiel were being delivered.

It is also possible that the leaders of the return to Jerusalem, Zerubbabel and Joshua (who returned following Cyrus' decree issued the year after the collapse of Babylon in 538 B.C.) were already born at the time Ezekiel spoke these words. But in the future, not yet born, there would be a host of other believers including Ezra and Nehemiah. These were the people among whom God made his sanctuary during this period of exile when he had left Israel because of their sin.

But looking even further into the future, the Lord gives expression to an anticipated day in which God will put a **'new spirit'** within his people (11:19). This is a theme which will receive much elaboration in chapter 36, but several matters are worth noting here.

The first point of interest is just how God promises to dwell with his people throughout the ages. Following a period when he dwelt in the tabernacle, we may summarize it this way:

1. The temple in Jerusalem: from Solomon to exile.
2. With his people as a 'temporary sanctuary' in exile.
3. The temple in Jerusalem: 516 B.C. - A.D.70.
4. The new heart — the New Testament temple.
5. The eternal temple — New Jerusalem — the new heavens and new earth.[8]

1. God promises to do something 'new'

The language of 11:18-20 implies that what will take place in the future (the verbs are all in the future tense) will be a break with the past. It is a 'new' spirit that they are to receive. Instead of hearts of stone, they will have hearts 'of flesh'. Other prophets, too, employ the concept of 'newness' to characterize their anticipation concerning God's future dealings with his people. Isaiah speaks of 'new things' (Isa. 42:9; 43:19; 48:6; 62:2; 65:17; 66:22). Jeremiah speaks in similar fashion (Jer. 31:31-32). A new covenant will replace all of God's previous covenant dealings.

2. The 'new' is not altogether an abandonment of the 'old'

Though Ezekiel points out the 'newness' of God's future dealings with his people, he nevertheless points out lines of continuity. Though the law will be followed by his people under the new covenant, or as Ezekiel's contemporary, Jeremiah, was to put it, God will write his law on their hearts (Jer. 31:33), the substance of the law is the same for both covenants. Furthermore, Ezekiel states that the essence of the new covenant relationship can be summarized in this way: **'They will be my people, and I will be their God'** (11:20; cf. 2 Cor. 6:16; Rev. 21:3). But this had always been the pattern of God's covenant with his people from the very start (Gen. 17:7-14; Exod. 19:4-6; Lev. 26:12; Deut. 7:6; 14:2).

The essence of the promise is contained in the words: **'I will give them an undivided heart and put a new spirit in them; I will remove from them their heart of stone and give them a heart of flesh'** (11:19). The promise is repeated again in Ezekiel 36:26 where the matter receives a lengthier analysis. God promises that under the new state of things, his people will be renewed. They will be in possession of a new spirit. Later, he makes it clear that this new spirit is brought about by God's Spirit (36:27). The giving of a heart of flesh in place of a heart of stone is the language of regeneration. As B. B. Warfield says, 'The re-creative activity of the Spirit of God is even made the crowning Messianic blessing...'[9] But this, too, was not unknown under the old covenant administration. What is patent in the new is latent in the old. 'Circumcise your hearts, therefore, and do not be stiff-necked' (Deut. 10:16; cf. 30:6). No one can reasonably draw the conclusion that folk like Abraham, Moses, Joshua, David, Elijah, Naomi or Ruth were not regenerate!

Sovereign grace

Emphasis falls on God's power and grace in accomplishing this renewal in men's hearts: '*I* will give them... *I* will remove from them...' Man is wholly unable to accomplish this for himself because, to use the analysis given by Ezekiel's contemporary in Jerusalem, 'The heart is deceitful above all things and beyond cure. Who can understand it?' (Jer. 17:9). As John Murray puts it, 'There is a change that God effects in man, radical and reconstructive in its nature, called new birth, new creation, regeneration, renewal — a change that cannot be accounted for by anything that is in lower terms than the interposition of the almighty power of God. No combination, permutation or accumulation of earth-born forces can explain it or effect it.'[10]

We are not to think of the difference between God's old and new covenant dealings as absolute. 'It is the speciality of the measure of grace under the New Covenant that is stressed,' says Murray. 'It is not a denial of regeneration or forgiving grace existing in the Old.'[11]

As to when all this is to take place, the immediate reference is to the days, some half a century later, when the Persian leader Cyrus would give permission for exiled Jews to return to Jerusalem and begin the work of rebuilding the city. Over a century and half later, in the time of Ezra and Nehemiah (c.458-420 B.C.), returning Jews found that religion in Jerusalem was still corrupt. God had in part fulfilled his promise to give the returning Jews a new spirit and it was through their reforming effort and zeal for God that Jerusalem's worship was cleansed according to the pattern described in these verses. However, these verses signify the dawning of a greater day, as later chapters in Ezekiel make clear. What is in view is the dawning of the New Testament era.

Having prepared God's faithful people in exile for what lies ahead for them, Ezekiel's vision once more returns to the covenant retribution that is to be inflicted upon the covenant-breakers of Jerusalem. God's glory-chariot, having already moved from the inner court (above the ark of the covenant) to the very edge of the temple complex (10:19), now takes off and leaves the temple altogether. Ezekiel could see it clearly outside the city limits (11:22-23). The God of glory has departed! The vision is over. Ezekiel perceives himself back in his own house in the company of gathered elders (11:24; cf. 8:1).

By any standard, this has been an uncomfortable passage; preaching on judgement always is. Ezekiel is, in part, inducing in the hearts of his hearers a sense of fear at what lies ahead of them unless they repent. Some object that this has no place in evangelism. 'You cannot frighten people into the kingdom of God,' they argue. This is true, up to a point. Nevertheless, as Jonathan Edwards has written, 'Some talk of it as an unreasonable thing to think to fright persons to heaven; but I think it is a reasonable thing to endeavour to fright persons away from hell. They stand upon its brink, and are just ready to fall into it, and are senseless of their danger. Is it not a reasonable thing to fright a person out of a house on fire?'[12]

Faithful preaching will always follow this course: 'I warn you, as I did before, that those who live like this will not inherit the kingdom of God' (Gal. 5:21). 'Do not be arrogant, but be afraid'

(Rom. 11:20). 'Since you call on a Father who judges each man's work impartially, live your lives as strangers here in reverent fear' (1 Peter 1:17).

Summary

The vision which began in chapter 8:1 is now over. Ezekiel has been transported to Jerusalem to see for himself the extent of the idolatry that had infiltrated their worship. In scene after scene, God shows him how corrupt they have become. Having witnessed the executioners perform their terrible work, in chapters 10 and 11 he has continued with more pronouncements of judgement. But no judgement can compare with God's departure. This is the ultimate sign of his rejection. When the glory-chariot left the temple and the city of Jerusalem it was a sign of their doom.

But all is not doom and gloom. In the midst of the tunnel shines a light: it is the grace of God towards his faithful remnant. There had been those in Jerusalem who had received the mark of his favour; now there was yet another indication that God would not abandon them completely. God promises that the exiled Jews would return to Jerusalem and experience his blessings again. It would be a foretaste of the New Testament era itself when the Holy Spirit would be poured out upon his church.

7.
False prophets and prophetesses

Please read Ezekiel 12:1 - 14:23

Warnings about the future often go unheeded. For many years we have become familiar with forecasts of doom for Planet Earth unless mankind curbs its present wastefulness and misuse of natural resources. It is not disputed that emission of poisonous gases from fuel consumption by the petrol-driven motor car contributes heavily to the poisoning of the planet. Yet there are few, if any, indications of a willingness by the nations of the world to do anything significant about it. The technology exists for radical changes, but they would be hugely unpopular. We prefer to live for today, quietly ignoring the forecasters of doom. Isaiah had cried out, 'Who has believed our message?' (Isa. 53:1). Things were no different in Ezekiel's day.

A hasty departure (12:1-16)

'Men display great ingenuity in making excuses for rejecting the message of God's love,' Spurgeon said. 'They display marvellous skill, not in seeking salvation, but in fashioning reasons for refusing it; they are dextrous in avoiding grace, and in securing their own ruin. They hold up first this shield and then the other, to ward off the gracious arrows of the gospel of Jesus Christ, which are only meant to slay the deadly sins which lurk in their bosoms.'[1] This was precisely Ezekiel's experience.

Having **'returned'** from Jerusalem (in spirit, not in body), Ezekiel is reminded of something he had been told two years earlier: that the Israelites were **'rebellious'** by nature (12:2 (twice),3,9; cf.

2:3 - 3:11). They were not disposed to listen to his words of doom! No doubt some of the exiled Jews took refuge in the message of a remnant that would be delivered and assumed they would be part of it. Perhaps some took the view that because Ezekiel's message largely concerned folk in Jerusalem, with whom they had little sympathy, it was not designed for them at all. And those who did believe that it had relevance for them saw it as being so far in the future that it need not concern them just yet; they could get on with living their lives.

To overcome this apathy, Ezekiel is once more asked to engage in one of his enactment rituals. He is told to gather his belongings as though he were about to make a journey (12:3). This apparently took all day (12:4), though his belongings — those that could reasonably be carried — would have been few. In the evening, when a crowd had gathered, he dug through a hole in the wall (of his house, or the courtyard outside), and left with his face covered (12:5-6). The following day, having returned, Ezekiel has to give an account of himself (12:8).

The ritual has all been about Israel's **'prince'** (King Zedekiah, the current, and last, monarch of Judah and Nebuchadnezzar's 'puppet' following the surrender of Jehoiachin), together with the people of Jerusalem who survive the conquest of Nebuchadnezzar; they will be taken into captivity (12:10). What Ezekiel has performed is a **'sign'** of this deportation (12:11).

The whole pathetic story is recalled in 2 Kings 25, where Zedekiah made an attempt to leave at night, disguised so as not to be seen. The Babylonians captured him and he was led away to Riblah, Nebuchadnezzar's headquarters. There his sons, together with seventy other leaders of Jerusalem, were executed before him. Zedekiah was blinded and led off to Babylon where, following a period in prison, he too was executed (Jer. 52:7-11). Ezekiel's prophecy was fulfilled. And it was only four years away (c. 588 B.C.). Those deluding themselves that these events were far away were entirely wrong.

Alive, but disgraced!

Once more Ezekiel has a word about some who will survive the defeat of Jerusalem. Despite the **'sword, famine and pestilence'** —

the signs of God's judgement — God assures Ezekiel's hearers: **'I will spare a few of them ... so that in the nations where they go they may acknowledge all their detestable practices. Then they will know that I am the Lord'** (12:16). But he does not mean to imply that all those who survived the fall of Jerusalem were true believers. On the contrary, as Calvin observes, 'Although some remained alive and unconcerned by either the sword, or famine, or pestilence, yet they were cursed, since their expulsion to a distance served no other purpose than that of spreading their disgrace and rendering them detestable, so that the profane Gentiles acknowledged that they deserved vengeance for their wickedness.'[2] It seems as though it might have been better if these poor folk had not survived at all! Ezekiel is warning his obstinate hearers, before it is too late, that since God has acted towards them as a Father, and they have not acknowledged his favour, they will one day be compelled to meet him as their Judge — to their eternal destruction.

Afraid of God? (12:17-20)

Is it ever right to be afraid of God? Most Christians would say that it is right for unbelievers, but not for believers. John Murray was more careful in his reply: 'The only proper answer is that it is the essence of impiety not to be afraid of God when there is *reason* to be afraid.'[3] Professing believers in Judah had every reason to be afraid!

Having already conveyed a message foretelling a food shortage during the siege of Jerusalem by the meagre rations which he had been eating over the last year, the prophet now adds a further dimension, in the *way* that he eats his food. His hands are to tremble as he eats and his face is to portray a fearful expression (12:18). It should be noted that the word 'tremble' is used elsewhere to describe an earthquake! (Amos 1:1). Those who watched him must have been revolted to witness the soiling of his garments and generally embarrassed by his 'table manners'!

But what they should have felt was not embarrassment but fear. For the explanation of Ezekiel's actions is altogether distressing: **'Say to the people of the land: "This is what the Sovereign Lord says about those living in Jerusalem and in the land of Israel: They will eat their food in anxiety and drink their water in**

**despair, for their land will be stripped of everything in it because
of the violence of all who live there'"** (12:19).

Violence generates violence! In the part of the world where I live
violence is a fact of everyday life. It is a grizzly spiral of despair as
one atrocity calls for another in retaliation. Judah was going to reap
what they had sown. When the forces of Babylonian darkness came
down upon them they would have no one to blame but themselves.
'Do not be afraid of those who kill the body but cannot kill the soul,'
Jesus said. 'Rather, be afraid of the One who can destroy both soul
and body in hell' (Matt. 10:28).

Three times in chapter 12 we discover the expression: 'Then you
[or 'they'] **will know that I am the Lord'** (12:15,16,20). It has
already occurred eight times in the first eleven chapters and will
occur forty-three more times before we finish with Ezekiel. Clearly,
it is an important expression. God is concerned to demonstrate his
power and glory. The 'LORD' (with capital letters in the NIV text)
always refers to God's covenant name: YAHWEH (occasionally,
though inaccurately, rendered, in the Authorized Version by the
time-honoured 'Jehovah', Exod. 6:3; Isa. 12:2). When Moses asked
the name of the one who spoke to him from the burning bush, he was
told God's name was 'I AM WHO[OR WHAT] I AM' (Exod. 3:13). God
was revealing himself to Moses as sovereign, self-sufficient and
self-consistent. Later, 'I AM' is identified with Yahweh (Exod.
3:15), thus further revealing that 'the Lord' whose name appears
some 6,700 times in the Old Testament is invincible, inexhaustible
and limitless in his power. For believers, he is safe to trust at all times
and in all places. For unbelievers (those to whom Ezekiel mainly
refers) he is greatly to be feared. If men will not acknowledge him
as sovereign, and bow the knee in worship, they will have cause to
confess his power and tremble.

Popular proverbs (12:21-28)

What did his hearers make of Ezekiel's preaching? Seemingly there
were two responses. One section of the community derided it as
nonsense. Ezekiel cites a popular proverb, seemingly encouraged
by false prophets (12:24): **'The days go by and every vision comes
to nothing'** (12:21). Ezekiel replies by changing the sound of a few
of the Hebrew words, thus making the proverb say, **'The days are
near when every vision will be fulfilled'** (12:23).

Ever since the eighth century, people had grown accustomed to predictions of Judah's downfall. Amos had preached in the prosperous northern kingdom of Israel some thirty years before its downfall. They had the temerity to look forward to the 'the day of the Lord' even when Amos had warned them it was a day of darkness and not light (Amos 5:18).[4] Amos had warned quite specifically about the fall of Jerusalem (Amos 2:4-5), but around 170 years had passed since then and Jerusalem was still standing. Why should they listen to prophets of doom any more?

Peter encountered a similar scepticism about the Second Coming of Jesus Christ. 'Where is this "coming" he promised?' they asked (2 Peter 3:4). Peter's reply is a fascinating study in answering questions like this one. It is all a matter of faith, of trusting what the Bible — the Word of God — says about certain matters, Peter says. 'Dear friends, this is now my second letter to you. I have written both of them as reminders to stimulate you to wholesome thinking. I want you to recall the words spoken in the past by the holy prophets ...' (2 Peter 3:1-2). 'In other words,' Dr Martyn Lloyd-Jones comments, 'in this letter, as indeed in all central matters of the Christian faith, we either accept the revelation or we do not; and the Bible itself tells us that revelation is something which is definitely beyond reason. That is perhaps the great watershed that divides men into two groups at this moment — those who are prepared to accept the revelation of this Book and those who reject it.'[5] Most of those who dwelt in Jerusalem in Ezekiel's day had decided to reject it.

If one section of the community derided his message as nonsense, another section postponed its relevance to another generation. They believed that what Ezekiel said was true enough, but it bore no relevance to them. Ezekiel cites another proverb: **'None of my words will be delayed any longer'** (12:28). We saw earlier that some who did believe the words of the prophet hoped that their fulfilment would be in another era, and not their own. When Isaiah warned Hezekiah of his foolishness in showing Babylonian envoys around the treasures of the palace, teling him, 'The time will surely come when everything in your palace, and all that your fathers have stored up until this day, will be carried off to Babylon,' Hezekiah responded with some measure of relief that at least he was safe! (2 Kings 20:12-21, especially verse 19). This is the way many live their lives — with no regard for the future. There is ample evidence that this philosophy lies behind the current state of our planet. Future generations will reap the consequences of man's avarice in this century, but who cares? It is the way many respond to God's warning about spiritual matters, too.

These two responses more or less summarize the reaction given to the Word of God by many today. Some are quite open in their hostility to it. They look around and suggest that the Bible has no relevance to their way of life. Its warnings and threats are rejected. Others are loath to be so openly hostile. They give lip-service to the truthfulness of what the Bible says. But they are careful not to believe it in such a way that it affects the way they live. They keep its teachings at arm's length. They are not prepared to reject it entirely; they dismiss the Bible by giving it faint praise. Of the two conditions, the latter is probably the worst.

But is it fair that the Israelites should have to suffer this way? That is a question to which the next two chapters will respond. In case some of Ezekiel's listeners might be entertaining the idea that God's ways were in some sense in violation of what they deserved, Ezekiel underlines the false prophecy and idolatry that pervaded their lives.

Preaching to preachers (13:1-16)

Along with true prophets were false ones, and it was part of the faithfulness and courage of men like Ezekiel and Jeremiah to denounce them (Jer. 23:9-40), to **'prophesy against the prophets'** (13:1). It takes courage and care to preach against preachers. It must never be done out of envy or spite, but always and only out of regard for the truth of God's Word.

Why do false prophets come under such heavy criticism?

1. False prophets are 'liars'

False prophets prophesy **'out of their own imagination'** and **'follow their own spirit'** (13:2-3). They guess as to what may happen, but their predictions are **'false'** and **'a lie'** (13:6-7,9). In contrast, Ezekiel brings to them **'the word of the Lord'** (13:2). He delivers what **'the Sovereign Lord says'** (13:3).

God said to Moses, the archetypal Old Testament prophet, 'I will help you speak and will teach you what to say' (Exod. 4:12; cf. 24:3). Later, God spoke to Moses about a similar process with another prophet (which is, in fact, a reference to Jesus the Prophet): 'I will put my words in his mouth, and he will tell them everything I command him' (Deut. 18:18). God gives the same assurance to Jeremiah: 'Now, I have put my words in your mouth' (Jer. 1:9).

This emphasis on the actual words given to the prophet by God meant that the prophets were given more than just ideas and impressions, to be formulated into their own words; the very words they spoke were from God. The words a prophet used are even referred to as coming from the Lord. Elijah's words in 1 Kings 21:19 are referred to in 2 Kings 9:25-26 as the oracle that 'the Lord made'.

2. False prophets are distinguished by their attitude towards God's people

They are like **'jackals among ruins'** (13:4). Jesus called them 'ferocious wolves' (Matt. 7:15). Foxes are known to forage litter bins at night in our modern cities. In certain cities in America they are rapidly becoming a major concern. They inhabit the ruins left by others, but are incapable of repairing them. They are only interested in what they can attain for themselves. They are like Diotrephes, who instead of promoting the peace and unity of the flock of God, destroyed it — all for the sake of his own reputation (3 John 9-10). True prophets, on the other hand, repair the **'breaks in the walls'** and thus prepare them for **'the battle on the day of the Lord'** (13:5).

3. False prophets are untrustworthy

False prophets told people what they wanted to hear. They were like stonemasons who covered the defects in their construction by applying a liberal amount of whitewash (13:10-16). What appeared to be a building of some strength was in fact nothing of the sort. It was a sham. The merest push and the wall would come crashing down. The people wanted to hear a message of peace, that all was well; this is what they heard. But God's wrath would come **'against'** (13:15, twice) the wall and those who whitewashed it, and the wall would collapse.

The image of violent winds, hailstones and torrents of rain is reminiscent of the illustration Jesus used to close his Sermon on the Mount. Having warned of false prophets, he went on to describe the

foolish man who built his house on sand. With no foundations, he
had made the 'wise' man look foolish. But when the storm came,
the house built on sand came crashing down. Its builder was
untrustworthy.

4. False prophets are identified by their priorities

They prophesy **'"Peace", when there is no peace'** (13:10). Jeremiah had obviously heard them too (Jer. 6:14). These were prophets who preferred the easier path of appeasement to the costly walk
of obedience to the will of God. They placed their own advantage
before the true needs of the flock of God. 'They dress the wound of
my people as though it were not serious,' Jeremiah said of them.

False prophets prefer to tell people that even if they are sinners,
it does not matter a great deal. They speak of God's love and ignore
his righteousness. They assure their listeners that even if hell exists,
it is in this world and not the next. And they do all this to ease their
own consciences.

5. False prophets deserve judgement

Any prophet who spoke words which did not come 'from the mouth
of the Lord' (Jer. 23:16) was a false prophet. Their judgement was
to be severe: 'But a prophet who presumes to speak in my name
anything I have not commanded him to say, or a prophet who speaks
in the name of other gods, must be put to death' (Deut. 18:20). God
says to them: **'I am against you'** (13:8, cf.15). They will have no
part in the new Israel (13:9). Stuart helpfully observes that in the
same way as impersonating a police officer is a crime in our society
because it 'harmfully defrauds people who trust and obey the
police,' so 'Impersonating a true prophet of the Lord was, by God's
law, a fraudulent misleading of Israelites in Ezekiel's day.'[6]

It would prove a valuable exercise to apply the fivefold assess-
ment of false prophets to the so-called 'prophets' today. In the first
place, we can ask of modern-day preachers, are they speaking what
the Bible teaches, or are they delivering the ideas of their own
minds? Is their concern to build up the flock of God in holiness, or
are they simply endeavouring to line their own pockets? Are they
faithful to God's message, despite the audience to whom they

speak? When King Ahab revealed his insecurity by suggesting to King Jehoshaphat that he hated the prophet Micaiah, he inadvertently testified to the prophet's greatness: he could not be bribed into speaking what the king wanted to hear (2 Chron. 18). 'As surely as the Lord lives,' Micaiah said, 'I can tell him only what my God says' (2 Chron. 18:13) It is to preachers like Micaiah that we should give heed.

Prophetesses too! (13:17-23)

In the Old Testament, women could not be priests, but they could be prophetesses and queens. The Old Testament also claims one woman judge.[7] Ezekiel's denunciation of prophetesses here is not due to the fact that they were women; like the preceding section, it is *false* prophetesses, those who have turned to magic and divination, that he denounces. Like the false prophets, they had given false counsel, giving encouragement to evil-doers, while discouraging the righteous (13:22).

Ezekiel points out two areas for comment: firstly, they attached some kind of **'magic charms'** to their arms (13:18,20), and, secondly, they wore **'veils of various lengths'** (13:18,21). The veils not only looked like nets, their name sounded a little similar in Hebrew. Ezekiel therefore likens the prophetesses to bird-hunters trapping their unsuspecting enquirers with their witchcraft. Once more, God is **'against'** them (13:17,20).

A couple of points are worth noting about magic. The prophetesses, by dabbling in magic, had essentially **'profaned'** God (13:19). They had used God's name in vain in their incantations. They had broken the third commandment (Deut. 5:11). They had used the name of God lightly and with disrespect. They had also **'ensnare[d]'** the people (13:20). Magic, because it is essentially an evil thing, has a certain power. The 'prince of this world' uses it to capture the minds and hearts of his subjects (John 12:31).

Ezekiel, faithful preacher that he was, pronounced God's judgement on the frauds, liars and exploiters of his day — even if they did wear religious clothes. Those who tell lies about the future can expect, one day, to find the future has caught up with them. God's Day is coming and then his power will be seen as a force to be reckoned with. **'Then you will know that I am the Lord'** (13:23).

One factor that this chapter points up is the real danger of self-deceit. It is possible for someone to have a 'temporary faith'. Calvin makes the point that 'There is a great likeness and affinity between God's elect and those who are given a transitory faith.'[8] Hence the need for self-examination.

'The Holy Spirit admonishes us,' Calvin comments on Ezekiel 13:9, 'that it is not sufficient to suppose men members of the Church because the greater number seem to excel others, just as chaff lies above the wheat and suffocates it: thus hypocrites bury the sons of God whose number is small... Hence let us learn to examine ourselves, and to search whether those interior marks by which God distinguishes his children from strangers belong to us, viz., the living root of piety and faith.'[9]

The elders (14:1-11)

Ezekiel has denounced idolatry as the root cause of Israel's demise in previous chapters (e.g. 5:9-11; 6:1-14; 8:7-14). Once more he takes up the theme, this time castigating the elders of Israel for their shameful worship of idols.

Once again, Ezekiel receives a visit from some of the exiled elders in Babylon (14:1; cf. 8:1). We might assume that these elders would be in better spiritual shape than their counterparts in Jerusalem, but that would be a false assumption. They, too, worshipped their idols, even though it was in secret, **'in their hearts'** (14:3). No doubt, living in Babylon brought with it its own sources of temptation to idolatry. In addition to what we have already learnt about idolatry, some further truths are now underlined.

1. Idolatry can never be hidden from God

He sees into our hearts (1 Sam. 16:7). He reads us like an open book. When secret idolaters came to Ezekiel for a word from God he knew what was in their hearts. And what was the prophet to say when such secret idolaters came to him for spiritual counsel? The answer Ezekiel was to give them was that God would answer them **'in keeping with'** their idolatry (14:4).

Imagine a quarrelsome child who is arguing with his brother over some trifling object and says, 'Give it to me. It's mine!' The brother refuses, so he comes to you, his parent, and cheekily says,

'Tell him to give it to me!' 'I'll give it to you,' you say in reply and promptly scold him for his cheeky behaviour. We get what we ask for.

This is a principle we need to learn quickly. And those who ask guidance and direction from an idolatrous god can expect to receive the folly that such an idol will speak. The purpose behind this was to bring them to repentance (14:6).

2. Idolatry is covenant violation and is cursed

Idolaters are guilty of **'separating themselves'** from God (14:7). This is the counterpart to what God had done in covenanting to be their God. He had separated them to be his people. He had made (literally, 'cut') a covenant with them. Now, the idolater was to be **'cut off'** from God's people; God's face would be **'set ... against that man'** (14:8). 'If a person turns away from God to seek idolatrous aid,' says Craigie, 'God in turn will avert his face from that person. When the idolater turns aside, it is sin; when God turns aside, it is death.'[10]

And what if a true prophet is enticed into a accepting the bribe which the idolater offers? He, too, is to be cut off (14:9-10). Even true prophets could be enticed away by the lure of money. Many a Christian worker's usefulness has been curtailed by the love of the idol's bribe. No wonder Paul addresses young Timothy: 'For the love of money is a root of all kinds of evil. Some people, eager for money, have wandered from the faith and pierced themselves with many griefs' (1 Tim. 6:10).

God is purifying his church so that his true people might emerge bearing the covenant relationship of fellowship: **'They will be my people, and I will be their God'** (14:11). Amos had likened the process to sifting grain: 'As grain is shaken in a sieve, and not a pebble will reach the ground...' (Amos 9:9). Only the grain drops through, the refuse being screened out to be discarded. Anyone who has eaten rice only to find some pieces of grit in it will know how painful a thing it can be.

Deception and responsibility

Occasionally God is represented as leading people into some delusions. Speaking of false prophets, God says, **'And if the**

prophet is enticed to utter a prophecy, I the Lord have enticed
that prophet, and I will stretch out my hand against him and
destroy him from among my people Israel. They will bear their
guilt...' (14:9-10 cf. 1 Kings 22:22-23; 2 Chron. 18:21-22; Jer.
20:7).

Several matters come into focus.

1. God is never the author of sin

This principle must always be kept at the forefront of every discussion of providence and sin.

2. God's providence is 'the determinative principle for all human plans and works'[11]

This passage in Ezekiel teaches us, so Calvin assures us, 'that
neither impostures nor deceptions arise without God's permission'.[12] If we find this difficult to grasp, he adds: 'Soberly,
therefore, and reverently must we judge of God's works, and
especially of his secret counsels.'[13]

3. It is not God himself who actually performs the deception

God, in his sovereign control of all things, 'sends forth Satan to fill
them with his lies'.[14] God himself cannot deceive: 'God is not a man,
that he should lie' (Num. 23:19). 'He who is the Glory of Israel does
not lie...' (1 Sam. 15:29). 'God is truthful' (John 3:33; cf. Rom. 3:4;
2 Tim. 3:13; Titus 1:2; Heb. 6:18; 1 John 1:5).

4. This is not a mere permission

In the hardening of Pharaoh's heart, God does not merely permit it
to happen: 'But I will harden his heart so that he will not let the
people go' (Exod. 4:21). The psalmist speaks of those whose 'hearts
he turned to hate his people' (Ps. 105:25). Likewise God sends the
Assyrians against Israel with the express command 'to seize loot
and snatch plunder, and to trample them down like mud in the
streets' (Isa. 10:6).' From this,' comments Calvin, 'it appears that
they had been impelled by God's sure determination.'[15] Thus God
'directs his voice to them but in order that they may become even

more blind; he sets forth doctrine but so that they may grow even more stupid; he employs a remedy but so that they may not be healed.'[16] Jesus indicated that his parables had a similar purpose (Matt. 13:11).

5. The sinner is still responsible for his sin

'They will bear their guilt' (14:10). God's use of means to execute his overall plan and purpose in no way reduces human responsibility. The prophets are never forced contrary to their inclination to deceive. 'However much obscurity there may be in the Word, there is still always enough light to convict the conscience of the wicked.'[17] So why are these prophets not converted? Calvin cites Augustine and says, 'God could ... turn the will of evil men to good because he is almighty. Obviously he could. Why, then, does he not? Because he wills otherwise. Why he wills otherwise rests with him.'[18]

Noah, Daniel and Job (14:12-23)

The chapter ends with yet another prediction of judgement upon Jerusalem, culminating in the, by now, familiar phrases of doom and destruction: **'For this is what the Sovereign Lord says: How much worse will it be when I send against Jerusalem my four dreadful judgements — sword and famine and wild beasts and plague — to kill its men and their animals!'** (14:21).

Included in this prophecy are the names of three Old Testament heroes: **'Noah, Daniel** [or Danel], **and Job'** (14:14). Though Daniel, Ezekiel's contemporary in Babylon, would have been around twenty-five years old at the time of this prophecy and had probably already risen to chief administrator in Babylon, it seems unlikely that he is the Daniel Ezekiel has in mind. Since he links the name with two men who lived in the days of the patriarchs, Noah and Job, it seems probable that it is a Daniel of around 1500-1200 B.C. and famous in Ugaritic literature. All three men stood out as godly men in an age of wickedness (cf. Gen. 6:5-12; Job 1:1,22).[19]

The point of mentioning these three men is to declare a sobering truth: that even if they were to be present in Jerusalem when God's wrath fell upon it, only they would be saved, despite merciful deliverances in the past in Sodom, through Abraham's intervention (Gen. 18:20-33), and in Judah by King Josiah's pleas (2 Kings 22:16-20). Judah and Jerusalem were believed to be invincible. And the presence of folk like Jeremiah, Obadiah and Habakkuk within the city made it, so they surmised, even more so. But though Noah and his family were saved, his generation perished, and Job's righteousness proved of no help to his companions (Job 42:7-8). And, ultimately, the intercessions of Abraham and Josiah proved futile, too.

Even if Ezekiel's listeners were at present sceptical as to the fairness of God's actions upon Judah, when the second wave of exiles came among them in the early 580s B.C., they would see, by the prevailing ungodliness of these people, that God's punishments had been right. They would be **'consoled'** (a word which can also mean 'to change one's mind') **'regarding the disaster'** (14:22). They would testify to the rightness of God's actions (14:23).

Summary

Much of these three chapters has been concerned to point out the evil work of false prophets and the judgement they can expect. Once more Ezekiel's warnings are falling on deaf ears. Instead of being afraid of the righteous judgements of God, they are complacent, hoping that either Ezekiel is exaggerating his message, or else the prospect of doom is so far into the future they need not be afraid. In reality it was barely four years away. God was already standing at the door and in a moment his wrath would burn against their wicked idolatries. But even in his judging work, God will be glorified: one way or another, they would know that he is the Lord (12:15,16,20; 13:14,21,23; 14:8).

8.
Grapes, a wayward woman and two eagles

Please read Ezekiel 15:1 - 17:24

Every Bible teacher knows the value of a really good illustration. It can be a humbling (and irritating) experience that people remember illustrations far better than they do the point of doctrine that is being taught. The Bible uses several kinds of illustration, including allegories — stories in which the meaning of something is symbolically portrayed, similar in kind to Bunyan's *Pilgrim's Progress,* which describes the Christian life as a journey to heaven. In the following chapters (17-23) a wide variety of allegories are used. They begin with a grapevine.

The vine (15:1-8)

A gigantic golden vine decorated the temple gates and had grape clusters over six feet long. It was a reminder that Israel was the true vine that God had taken out of Egypt and planted in a choice land (Ps. 80:8-14; Isa. 3:14; 5:1-7). No fewer than five parables of Jesus relate to the figure of a vine: the fig in the vineyard (Luke 13:6-9); the labourers in the vineyard (Matt. 20:1-16); new wine in old wineskins (Matt. 9:17); the two sons (Matt. 21:28-32); and the wicked tenants (Matt. 21:33-41; Mark 12:1-11; Luke 20:9-18). Of even greater significance is Jesus' own allusion to himself as the true vine (John 15:1-7). Despite the cultivation Israel had received as God's vine, they had produced only bitter fruit and were now fit only to be cut down and burned (John 15:6).

Ezekiel puts it even more bluntly. Instead of comparing Israel to the grapes themselves, he points out the wood of the vine. Apart from the fact that it is not producing any fruit, the vine itself has no value except for firewood, and even then its value is limited (15:4). Following the devastation of the Assyrian invasion of Israel in 722 B.C. and the Babylonian invasion of Judah in 605 and 598 B.C., 'Israel' was already similar to a piece of charred wood (15:5). If the wood of a vine is too pliable even to be made into a peg (15:3), a half-burnt piece of vine has no use whatsoever. Soon the fire will rekindle (in the third Babylonian siege of Jerusalem in 586 B.C.) and the rest of the wood will be consumed (15:7) The allegory (for the use of the word 'allegory', see 17:2) was particularly apt for the Babylonians did practise a scorched-earth policy, burning everything in the city once it had been plundered of its treasures (2 Chron. 36:19).

'I am the vine; you are the branches,' Jesus said (John 15:5).[1] What had been pictured in the Old Testament in such passages as Psalm 80:8-9 and Hosea 10:1 was meant to convey a truth that has now emerged in full flower in the New Testament: that Christ together with his people comprise the vine from which the fruit of the Spirit should emerge — the nine graces which make the Christian believer Christ-like (Gal. 5:22).

The pathetic sight presented by Israel in the sixth century B.C. was a violation of this beautiful image. It had been no different a century and a half earlier:

> 'I will sing for the one I love
>   a song about his vineyard:
> My loved one had a vineyard
>   on a fertile hillside.
> He dug it up and cleared it of stones
>   and planted it with the choicest vines.
> He built a watchtower in it
>   and cut out a winepress as well.
> Then he looked for a crop of good grapes,
>   but it yielded only bad fruit'

(Isa. 5:1-2).

Two things are essential in producing fruit from a vine: the vine needs to be pruned (John 15:2); and care is also needed to make sure none of the branches are bruised or severed so as to prevent the sap from getting to the growing tips of the branches. In other words, the branches need to abide in the vine (John 15:4-5).

Pruning is what Ezekiel has in mind in verse 3, where dead wood is cut away. This is what he has been talking about in the previous chapters (6:8-10; 7:16; 9:5-8; 11:13-25; 12:14-20). True believers were not spared the temporal judgements God inflicted upon the Israelites. But they were assured that the knife was wielded by a loving Father who would eventually bring his people back to their land.

Pruning can be a ruthless exercise, but its purpose is to promote new and healthy growth from vigorous new shoots. Job spoke about the effect of pruning on a tree:

'There is hope for a tree:
   If it is cut down, it will sprout again,
   and its new shoots will not fail.
Its roots may grow old in the ground
   and its stump die in the soil,
yet at the scent of water it will bud
   and put forth shoots like a plant'

(Job 14:7-9).

And yet in his own life the pruning had been so severe that he despaired of ever rising again: 'My spirit is broken, my days are cut short...' (Job 17:1).

Many of God's people can echo similar thoughts when severe trials have come into their lives — divorce, death, a handicapped child. Perhaps a fallen tree has more hope than such as experience these trials. God's pruning shears can be severe. It seems as though nothing lies outside the cutting edge of his will. And yet even Job was to know a time when new life emerged from the broken stump of his life: 'All his brothers and sisters and everyone who had known him before came and ate with him in his house. They comforted and consoled him over all the trouble the Lord had brought upon him... The Lord blessed the latter part of Job's life more than the first...' (Job 42:11-12). Pruning encourages new growth!

As for *abiding*, Ezekiel has also alluded to this. The vine branches of Israel were **'not useful for anything when it was whole'** (15:5). It is a picture of canes that have withered. They produce nothing; they are fit for nothing. And the reason? **'They have been unfaithful'** (15:8). They did not abide, or remain, in the covenant relationship. It is this allusion to unfaithfulness which prepares us for the next allegory — one of the longest in the Scriptures — the unfaithful bride. 'Remain in me, and I will remain in you' Jesus said. 'No branch can bear fruit by itself; it must remain in the vine. Neither can you bear fruit unless you remain in me. I am the vine; you are the branches. If a man remains in me and I in him, he will bear much fruit; apart from me you can do nothing. If anyone does not remain in me, he is like a branch that is thrown away and withers; such branches are picked up, thrown into the fire and burned. If you remain in me and my words remain in you, ask whatever you wish and it will be given you... As the Father has loved me, so have I loved you. Now remain in my love. If you obey my commands, you will remain in my love, just as I have obeyed my Father's commands and remain in his love' (John 15:4-10). Abiding, or remaining, in Christ involves focusing on the grace of God in the gospel ('As I have loved you...'), obedience to God's revealed will ('If you obey my commands...'), and being 'at home' in God's Word ('My words remain in you...'). These are features that were evidently lacking in the Israelites of Ezekiel's day.

The unfaithful bride (16:1-63)

This lengthy chapter is mirrored in chapter 23; both make use of blunt words to convey the imagery of Israel's prostitution. Indeed, so graphic is the language that C. H. Spurgeon felt that, in Victorian England, 'A minister could scarcely read it in public.'[2]

It was the words, **'I said to you, "Live"'** (16:6) that God used to convert the Puritan Thomas Goodwin, the leader of the Dissenting group within the Westminster Assembly and a prominent member of the Savoy Assembly of Congregational elders. Having been brought under conviction of sin by a sermon preached at a funeral, he confessed that he 'saw no way to escape: but together with the sight of all this sinfulness, hell opened his mouth upon me, threatening to devour and destroy me...' A few hours later, God gave him a 'speedy word' from Ezekiel 16:6: 'I said unto you, "Live.".'. Goodwin testifies of the occasion: 'So God was pleased on the sudden, and as it were in an instant, to alter the whole of his former dispensation towards me ... as he created the world and the matter of all things by a word, so he created and put a new life and spirit into my soul...'[3]

Though the chapter comprises a single unit, and should be read as such, it is possible to perceive that Israel — here referred to by its capital city, Jerusalem — is being viewed from the three time dimensions : past, present and future.

1. The past

Ezekiel receives this word from the Lord (16:1); it is a word about Jerusalem's **'detestable practices'** (16:2). Jerusalem's father and mother are described as 'Amorites' (16:3,45), Canaanites who inhabited the city before it was finally conquered by David (2 Sam. 5:6-9), and the 'Hittites', non-Semitic residents of Canaan who had flourished in Asia Minor during the second millennium B.C. (Gen. 23:1-20; 26:34; 1 Sam. 26:6; 2 Sam. 11:2-27).

Jerusalem is compared to an abandoned baby girl, with umbilical cord still attached and having been denied the rudiments of care: salting (a primitive form of disinfectant), rubbing or washing. But God decreed that she should live (16:4-6). God chose the city as his place of residence (16:7-8). He made it a city of great beauty and magnificence. She was like an attractive young woman in the prime of life (16:9-14). This is how things used to be. When a relationship turns sour, partners often reminisce about better days, about how things used to be.

2. The present

Jerusalem's conduct is described as prostitution. She used her **'fame to become a prostitute'** (16:15). It began in the days of Solomon, when he introduced sites for idolatrous worship into Israel (1 Kings 11:1-10). Thereafter, Jerusalem slid further and further into idolatry (16:17-19), even to the point of participating in ritual child sacrifice (16:20-21; 2 Kings 23:10; Jer. 32:35). As time went by, she forgot God altogether and turned to foreign nations to protect her (16:22-29). In so doing she lost much that the Lord had given her (16:31-34). What, then, is her present condition? **'How weak-willed you are, declares the Sovereign Lord, when you do all these things, acting like a brazen prostitute!'** (16:30). Unrepentant adulterers, the apostle Paul assures us, will not inherit the kingdom of God (1 Cor. 6:9-10).

3. The future

This kind of behaviour in a marriage cannot be overlooked. Once it is out in the open, the consequences for the marriage are grave and often terminal. So it is here. God will cause Jerusalem's enemies to attack because of her unfaithfulness (16:35-37). She will be left **'naked and bare'** (the Hebrew word for 'naked' is the same as that for 'exile'); it will mean the loss of her wealth (16:38-41). The Lord's fury will mean the desolation of Jerusalem (16:42-43). Jerusalem had forgotten **'the days of [her] youth'** (16:43); consequently, God says to her, **'Then my wrath against you will subside and my jealous anger will turn away from you; I will be calm and no longer angry'** (16:42).

Jealousy is an integral part of any commitment. There are in fact two kinds of jealousy and only one of them is a vice. 'Vicious jealousy,' says J. I. Packer, 'is an expression of the attitude, "I want what you've got, and I hate you because I haven't got it." It is an infantile resentment springing from unmortified covetousness, which expresses itself in envy, malice, and meanness of action. It is terribly potent, for it feeds and is fed by pride, the taproot of our fallen nature.'[4] But there is another kind of jealousy, a 'zeal to protect a love-relationship, or to avenge it when broken'.[5] As R. V. G. Tasker puts it, persons 'who felt no jealousy at the intrusion of a lover or an adulterer into their home would surely be lacking in moral perception; for the exclusiveness of marriage is the essence of marriage'.[6]

It is this jealousy, the jealousy of God to protect the marriage-relationship, that is now threatened by this unfaithfulness on Jerusalem's part. She is compared to the cities of Sodom and Samaria (16:46-52). Their downfall had been brought about by materialism, arrogance and exploitation of the poor (16:49). Jerusalem in copying them and thereby justifying their behaviour, had broken the covenant and must face God's rejection (16:52-54).

Several observations are now relevant.

1. *God's relationship to his people is described in this chapter as that of a husband.* Marriage is an exclusive relationship. The love that joins husband and wife is necessarily a jealous love. That adultery is a violation of this covenant relationship is a principle enunciated in the Ten Commandments, when God gives his

covenant law to his redeemed people (Exod. 20:14). Later, God underlines it by revealing himself to Israel as a jealous God; his name is 'Jealous' (Exod. 34:14). When Solomon, who had built the temple and dedicated it to the service of the Lord, ascended the Mount of Olives, immediately to the east of the Temple Mount, and dedicated an offering to Chemosh, the god of the Moabites, he broke the covenant relationship. In pleasing his Moabite wives, he displeased his Father in heaven. In bringing security to Israel by making treaties with foreign nations, he further provoked the Lord.

The exclusive relationship of marriage is an idea that comes to full expression in the New Testament: '"Nor is there salvation in any other, for there is no other name under heaven given among men by which we must be saved"' (Acts 4:12, NKJV). 'Jealousy' and 'zeal' are two possible translations of a single word in both Hebrew and Greek. God is zealous to protect his marriage and avenge any violations. This is why holiness on our part is so important. We are to stop behaving like 'brazen prostitutes' by constantly yielding to our sinful hearts.

2. *The subtlety of Jerusalem's decline into unfaithfulness* is worth noting; it is instructive of the way sin takes hold of our lives. Her fall was not sudden. It did not transpire overnight. It was her success that became her snare. She became more interested in the gifts than the Giver. It is interesting to recall that it was in Solomon's time, when Israel was at the height of her powers, that idolatry gained a foothold. It is humbling to think that immediately after the Refor-mation the church fell prey to superstition and idolatry. The same is true of the period following the Great Awakening. It is also true in our personal lives. Sin creeps up and entraps without announcing its presence loudly. Sin is shy to make any claim for itself. It is often the case that we realize our liaison with sin too late. Sin is deceitful (Heb. 3:13; Eph. 4:22; 1 Tim. 2:13-14). We are warned again and again 'not to be deceived' (Luke 21:8; 1 Cor. 6:9; 15:33; Gal. 6:7; Eph. 5:6). 'Sin ... will use a thousand wiles to hide from it the terror of the Lord,' said John Owen.[7]

3. *To whom much is given, of him much will be required.* Israel had received the very finest of the Lord's blessings. She had responded with indifference and even contempt. Jesus warned the cities of Chorazin and Bethsaida that they too had shown remarkable

ingratitude, seeing they had witnessed many of his miracles. On the Day of Judgement, it will be more tolerable for the pagan cities of Tyre and Sidon than for Bethsaida and Chorazin, Jesus warns them (Matt. 11:20-24). We are accountable for what we have received. Moreover, the more we know, the more accountable we become. When God asked Ezekiel to make a clay model of the city of Jerusalem, shielding his face with an 'iron pan' to display God's displeasure at the city, he says, 'This is Jerusalem, which I have set in the centre of the nations, with countries all around her. Yet in her wickedness she has rebelled against my laws and decrees...' (5:5). Those who have been given a trust must prove faithful (1 Cor. 4:2).

4. *God gives us our hearts' desire.* Israel had desired the attention of the gods of the world and this is what she received! It is humbling to realize that in spiritual things, we receive what we set our hearts on. Those who set their hearts on the Lord will find that the Lord reveals himself to them in his Word. But those who set their hearts on nothing of any spiritual significance will discover that this is precisely what they receive — nothing of any spiritual significance. God gave them over to a reprobate mind (Rom. 1:28). The pleasure they craved became a curse which destroyed them.

Today the gods of materialism, alcohol and sexual pleasure are what millions crave for. What they inherit is loneliness, disease and death. There is a chilling passage in Psalm 106:13-15 which describes this very thing. Following a description of what God had done for Israel in leading them through the wilderness, we read that

'They soon forgot what he had done
    and did not wait for his counsel.
In the desert they gave in to their craving;
    in the wasteland they put God to the test.
So he gave them what they asked for,
    but sent a wasting disease upon them.'

This was what Moses had warned them to expect (Deut. 8:19-20).

We need to think about where our lives have been leading us. We need to ask ourselves what it is that we are aiming at. Are we surprised that our lives are so worldly if, in fact, it is the world that we live for? Humble yourselves or be humiliated!

5. The question has to be asked, *how God can give up on the church*. We might not need to ask it if Scripture did not indicate to us over and over again God's promise never to abandon his people. After all, we take refuge in such promises as: 'I will never leave you nor forsake you' (Josh. 1:5); 'No one can snatch them [God's sheep] out of my Father's hand' (John 10:29); and the assurance that absolutely nothing 'will be able to separate us from the love of God that is in Christ Jesus our Lord' (Rom. 8:39). How can such promises be made when clearly passages like Ezekiel 16 — indeed the greater part of the entire prophecy — are designed to stress the very opposite?

The answer lies in understanding that the promises of God are made to God's *true* people. They are not made to the entire membership of the professing church. It is possible to give some indication of belonging to the people of God, and to continue in that profession for a while, and then to fall away. It is also possible to profess one thing and display another in one's lifestyle. It is also possible for this to be true on a collective basis, for the entire church to move so far away from its moorings that it is no longer a church at all. This was how the Reformers perceived it: 'The purest Churches under heaven are subject both to mixture and error; and some have so degenerated, as to become no Churches of Christ, but synagogues of Satan.'[8]

God will always remain true to his covenant, though men and nations depart from it, either temporarily or in complete apostasy. Commenting on a remark made earlier by Ezekiel in 3:20, where 'A righteous man turns from his righteousness and does evil', Calvin foresees an objection: 'How can the just turn aside, since there is no righteousness without the spirit of regeneration? But the seed of the Spirit is incorruptible (1 Peter 1:23), nor can it ever happen that his grace is utterly extinguished; for the Spirit is the earnest and seal of our adoption, for God's adoption is without repentance... But we must here mark, that righteousness is here called so, which has only the outward appearance and not the root: for when once the spirit of regeneration begins to flourish ... it remains perpetually. And we shall sometimes see men borne along with a wonderful ardour of zeal for the worship of God, and to be urged to promote his glory beyond even the very best men; indeed we shall see this, but, says Paul, God knows those who are his own (2 Tim.2:19).'[9]

The covenant was capable of violation in a number of ways: the want of faith and obedience, forgetfulness of God's works, a spirit of ingratitude for God's goodness (Ps. 78:11; 89:31-34; 132:12; Jer.11:6-8, 22; 22:9, etc.); such action was regarded as **'breaking the covenant'** (16:59). The violation of the covenant by man would not ultimately affect the fulfilment of God's side of the covenant. 'For', as Calvin further explains, commenting upon 16:61, 'a contrast must be understood between the people's covenant and God's. He had said just before, I will be mindful of my covenant. He now says *not of thine*. Hence he reconciles what seemed opposites, namely, that he would be mindful of his own agreement, and yet it had been dissipated, broken and abolished. He shows that it was fixed on his own side, as they say, but vain on the people's side.'[10]

When God 'gives up' on the church, it must always be understood that it is the outward, professing church that is meant. The true people of God who have experienced the grace of salvation are never cast away, though they, too, may experience the outward forms of punishment (Ezekiel, after all, found himself in exile). The outward church, at any time, is composed of those who are true believers and those who are merely hypocrites or those who are in possession of what the Reformers called 'temporary faith'. When such are deemed to be the majority, God brings down the rod of discipline in order to refine his church. Those who are truly his remain faithful; but those whose faith is only a mirage will be revealed for the hypocrites that they are. It is precisely this that Ezekiel was witnessing in Judah at the beginning of the sixth century.

6. *God has a remnant.* Though the church may become so corrupt that it no longer deserves to be called a church, the Reformers added an important rider: 'Nevertheless, there shall be always a Church on earth to worship God according to His will.'[11] That is something to bear in mind as we read this chapter, for after fifty-two verses exposing Jerusalem's sins, the chapter ends with a note of resounding triumph. Once again, God is going to spare a remnant of his people. He will not reject Jerusalem for ever: her captivity will end (16:53) and God will re-establish the covenant with her (16:60-62), making her pure and secure (16:61), forgiven and righteous (16:63).

Perhaps the most striking illustration of God's intentions was indicated by Ezekiel's fellow-prophet, Hosea, who was asked to take back his adulterous wife in demonstration of God's love for the remnant of apostate Israel (Hosea 3). Israel had broken God's covenant, but God says he will **'remember'** it (16:60).This calls to mind what God had said 800 years earlier when Israel had cried out to God under Egyptian bondage (Exod. 2:24).

7. In describing Jerusalem as an abandoned, newly-born, child, Ezekiel has not only used the figure of a betrayed husband, but also that of *a forsaken father*. It is interesting that Hosea, too, used this figure, suggesting that God leads his little son, Israel, out of Egypt, holding him by the hand and teaching him to walk (Hosea 11:3). His son's rebellion brings judgement, but the Lord cries out:

> "'How can I give you up, Ephraim?
>   How can I hand you over, Israel?
> How can I treat you like Admah?
>   How can I make you like Zeboiim?
> My heart is changed within me;
>   all my compassion is aroused.
> I will not carry out my fierce anger,
>   nor will I turn and devastate Ephraim.
> For I am God, and not man—
>   the Holy One among you.
>   I will not come in wrath'
>
>   (Hosea 11:8-9).

These prophetic pictures were meant to indicate an enormous privilege that God's children receive: that as sons, we are recipients of the Father's tender care and compassion. This is what we are meant to see at the heart of these otherwise harsh chapters. Though God is angry now, it is because of Israel's sin. They have despised God's promise to be gracious by 'breaking the covenant' (16:59). Palmer Robertson suggests that another translation is suitable here: 'They have *nullified* the covenant.' The point is 'not so much that the counsel offered is "broken", but that it is "frustrated" or "voided" because its promised success is not realized.'[12]

They had spurned God's love at every turn. Consequently, God has threatened punishment even though this means that his own true children will suffer. That is a lesson we need to learn very quickly. God seems to be saying in this and previous chapters that he will use the Babylonians, as he had used the Egyptians and Assyrians in the past, to discipline his own children. As we have noted already, Jesus, in describing the way God works in the lives of his people, used the analogy of the Father as a vine-dresser pruning the branches of the vine in order to make a rich harvest. Martin Luther suggested that God even uses Satan for this very purpose. He wrote that the Father says, 'Devil, you are indeed a murderer and an evildoer; but I will use you for my purpose. You shall be my hoe; the world and your following shall be My manure for the fertilization of My vineyard.'[13]

8. Five times in verses 59-63 the *covenant* is alluded to, sometimes referring to the 'old covenant' (as in 16:59) and sometimes to the 'new', as in **'I will establish an everlasting covenant with you'** (16:60). But had not David in his old age centuries earlier expressed his own sense of assurance in God's 'everlasting covenant'? (2 Sam. 23:2-5). If that covenant had been everlasting, how can God create another covenant which is also to be 'everlasting'? The answer seems to lie in the fact that *essentially* it is the same covenant that is being referred to. God's ultimate intention for his true people, the remnant, could hardly be clearer: it is that he might forgive their sins, by making **'atonement for'** them (16:63).

This is at the heart of what God has been doing since the very beginning, when he promised our first parents that he would send a Deliverer (Gen. 3:15). Throughout history, God has been showing us that his intention is to save a people through an atonement that he will provide — namely his own Son, Jesus Christ. God's promise will be kept, despite all the changes and vicissitudes of life. God 'loved us from the first of time, he loved us to the last'.

9. What is startling in Ezekiel's prophecy is the mention of *Sodomites and Samarians who are to be included within the covenant* (16:61). If Sodom and Samaria had been corrupt, Judah was worse (16:47-48). Sodom and Samaria will be first in the restoration (16:53,55). Ezekiel sees the nations of the world flocking into the kingdom of God. This is what God had promised to Abraham (Gen. 12:2-3; 17:5), and what David had expressed in many of his psalms (Ps. 67; 87; 117; 148). Isaiah had talked about a highway from Egypt and Cush and Assyria running right through to Jerusalem (Isa. 19:23-25; cf. Jer. 12:14-17; 46:25; 48:47). The next chapter also alludes to this theme (17:23). No wonder this prophecy was to have the effect of shutting their mouths! (16:63).

Two eagles and a vine (17:1-24)

What we have in chapter 17 (as in chapters 15 and 16) is an **'allegory'** or a **'parable'** (17:2). Though commonly referred to as 'earthly stories with a heavenly meaning', essentially, parables cover a range of sayings and stories of all sorts. Commonly associated with the teaching ministry of Jesus, the parables have roots stretching back into the Old Testament. One entire Old Testament book is called 'Parables', though we know it as 'Proverbs' — the Hebrew word for proverb is the same word that is translated elsewhere in the Old Testament as 'parable'. Here, the words 'parable' and 'allegory' are meant to convey the same thing.

The allegory in Ezekiel tells the story of Judah's history from the time of the first exile in 598 B.C. to the second exile — still some four or five years in the future — in 586 B.C. The parable itself covers verses 3-10 and the explanation, verses 11-21.

The allegory (17:3-10)

Ezekiel tells of a huge eagle, with gorgeous plumage, which comes to Lebanon, landing in a cedar tree. The eagle promptly breaks off the topmost shoot of the tree and carries it away **'to a land of merchants, where he planted it in a city of traders'** (17:3-4). The eagle is King Nebuchadnezzar, the 'land of merchants' is Babylon, and the 'shoot of the tree' is Jehoiachin. **'The king of Babylon went to Jerusalem and carried off her king and her nobles, bringing them back with him to Babylon'** (17:12). [14]

The parable continues by saying that the eagle (Nebuchadnezzar) took **'some of the seed'** and planted it in **'fertile soil'** (17:5). The seed sprouted and grew into a **'spreading vine'** of some size and health (17:6). The 'seed' represents King Zedekiah (17:13), whom Nebuchadnezzar established as his puppet king in Jerusalem.

'Another great eagle' now comes into the story; the vine is attracted to it (17:7). It represents the Egyptian Pharaoh (either Psammetichus II (595-598 B.C.), or Hophra (589-570 B.C.), with whom Zedekiah sought an alliance to rebel against Babylonian imperialism (17:15), and thereby break **'the covenant'** with Babylon (17:18). History seems to record that Egypt proved a poor ally, managing only to sell Judah some **'horses'**, which proved useless against a siege of Jerusalem. The **'large army'** which

Zedekiah had hoped to get did not materialize. When the Babylonians came against Jerusalem, **'the east wind'** of verse 10, and laid siege against the city (17:17), the vine was easily uprooted and destroyed.

But Zedekiah was not merely rebelling against Nebuchadnezzar; he was, in effect, rebelling against God (17:19). Nebuchadnezzar, indeed the entire Babylonian empire, was merely a tool in God's hand to chastise and punish Judah for their sins. Breaking the covenant with Nebuchadnezzar was only a symptom of the problem: Zedekiah had broken the covenant with God (17:19). There is no escape when God decides that our days are numbered. He throws out a net to capture Zedekiah (17:20) and his pathetic army (17:21). These defeated rebels would now join the rest of the Judeans in exile in Babylon.

But God's work is not finished. The chapter ends with a reference to God taking **'a shoot from the very top of a cedar'** (17:22), and planting it on the mountains of Israel, where **'It will produce branches and bear fruit and become a splendid cedar. Birds of every kind will nest in it; they will find shelter in the shade of its branches'** (17:23). Who is meant by this shoot? That it must refer to a representative of the royal house of David is clear (17:3-4,12). It is not King Jehoiachin, for he died in Babylon. It cannot be King Zedekiah, who is described as the 'vine' that withered in Babylon. Who, then, is the 'shoot' from the very top of the cedar of Israel, under whose sprouting branches the 'birds' will make their nests and find shelter and refuge? 'This prophecy without doubt refers to Christ,' writes John Calvin, 'because ... what is here written was never fully exhibited except under Christ.'[15] Since God had promised in the previous chapter that Israel's captivity would end and that he would remember his covenant with his people and re-establish it, providing a means whereby their sins were atoned for (16:59-63), it was always necessary to enquire how this might be brought about.

What is the essence of the covenant that God makes? How is it possible for rebellious sinners to find peace with God? What possible hope was there for Judah as she wept in Babylon? (cf. Ps. 137). The answer to all these questions is in the provision of a Saviour, God's only begotten Son, Jesus Christ! He it is who will be planted in Jerusalem and in his death and resurrection will draw sinners to himself from the four corners of the globe! Ezekiel's message, far from being one of mere 'doom and gloom', is a message all about the coming of Jesus Christ into the world to save sinners.

All this shows us that in the midst of all the comings and goings of this world, the Lord takes a peculiar interest in the establishment of his kingdom. In the last resort it is only his kingdom that will last: **'All the trees of the field will know that I the Lord bring down the tall tree and make the low tree grow tall. I dry up the green tree and make the dry tree flourish'** (17:24). God is in control of history; nations rise and fall at his behest. This had been the source of encouragement to those in exile: '[God] changes times and seasons; he sets up kings and deposes them.' 'The God of heaven will set up a kingdom that will never be destroyed... It will crush all those kingdoms and bring them to an end, but it will itself endure for ever.' 'The Most High is sovereign over the kingdoms of men and gives them to anyone he wishes' (Dan. 2:21; 2:44; 4:25).

The key to understanding history is not military or economic, but rather a moral and spiritual one. What we see happening all around us is all part of God's great plan that will culminate in the return of Christ in triumph and glory. Seeing God at work in this way is a wonderful encouragement.

Commenting upon this passage in a sermon , John Owen said, 'I know no better way of praising God for any work, than the finding out of his design therein, and closing with him in it.'[16]

These chapters, which emphasized the enormity of Judah's sin, have ended by highlighting the magnitude of God's grace! The poet George Herbert once wrote:

Philosophers have measured mountains,
Fathomed the depths of seas, of states, and kings,
Walk'd with a staff to heaven, and traced fountains,
But there are two vast, spacious things,
The which to measure it doth more behove:
Yet few there are that sound them: Sin and Love.

Sin and love: that is what these chapters have been about.

Summary

In these three chapters (15-17), three allegories have been presented: a vine, a wayward woman and two eagles. In all three the rebellious nature of Judah has been portrayed, together with their consequent judgement by the Babylonians. What Ezekiel has been presenting here was less than five years away; the wrath of God was imminent. What was the cause of this? God's people had 'nullified' the covenant. They had chosen to live for this world and their own selves. In doing so, they had turned their backs on God and would face the consequences.

But throughout the impending judgements, Ezekiel has spoken of a remnant according to the election of God's grace who will be brought back to Jerusalem. And further into the future still, he sees the coming of Christ himself and the kingdom of God which will grow as a result of his coming. If Ezekiel warns of the outcome for the apostate church, he also assures his listeners that the true church has a wonderful and secure future. The future is as bright as the promises of God to those who live according to his Word!

Calvin, following his comments on these verses in his fifty-third lecture on Ezekiel — given a few months before his death and when he was in great discomfort and pain — offered the following prayer: 'Grant, Almighty God, since thou hast not only created us out of nothing, but hast deigned to create us again in thine only begotten Son, and hast taken us from the lowest depths, and deigned to raise us to the hope of thy heavenly kingdom — Grant, I say, that we may not be proud or puffed up with vainglory; but may we embrace this favour with becoming humility, and modestly submit ourselves to thee, until we become at length partakers of that glory which thine only begotten Son has acquired for us. Amen.'[17]

Focus

The nature of the covenant

Covenant violation

As far back as Abraham, God had entered into a covenant with his people. The promised inheritance of a land in which to dwell was a gift on God's part. It was not a reward for good behaviour. Nevertheless, God asked of Abraham that he walk in the ways of God, as an example to all who followed him of what God expects from his people (cf. Gen. 17:1).

The history of Israel, however, is a history of covenant unfaithfulness. One thing emerges quite clearly in the opening chapters of Ezekiel: the people have sinned grievously against God's covenant. 'This is what the Sovereign Lord says: I will deal with you as you deserve, because you have despised my oath *by breaking the covenant*' (16:59, emphasis added). Israel had committed spiritual adultery; she had violated a marriage bond between God and his people (16:32).

The people were to blame for this violation. The exile which they currently experienced was not due to any shortcomings in God's administration or provision for his people. Their plight could not 'be charged against the covenant'.[1]

God would, however, always remain faithful to his covenant, though Israel chose to depart from it, either temporarily or, as now, in complete apostasy (3:20; cf. Isa 31:6; 54:8-9; 55:3; Jer. 21:11-12). Covenant violation would not ultimately affect the fulfilment of God's side.[2]

The nature of God's covenant

Being in covenant with God involves certain conditions. On God's side, he binds himself to his people in grace and mercy — to those whom he has chosen to bless. He pledges himself to be the God of his chosen people. But that does not negate the requirement laid on his people faithfully to keep God's covenant. Israel thought that God's promise to Abraham secured them in the land of Israel for ever, no matter how they lived! But as Calvin comments on Micah 2:10, 'False confidence deceives you, as ye think that ye are inseparably fixed in your habitation. God indeed has made such a promise, but that condition was added, "If ye will stand faithful to his covenant".'

God's covenant, on the one hand, is a gratuitous, unilateral promise; on the other hand, there is a conditional (bilateral) element involved. If the covenant depends upon man's fulfilling certain requirements in some way, does this mean that salvation is no longer a matter of grace, but of works? Are we saved as a reward for our obedience to the requirements of the covenant? The solution to this problem lies in noting that the obedience that God requires is the evidence of a work of grace already brought about by his Spirit working in our hearts. The obedience he requires, as evidence of faith, is an obedience which God himself gives! Even the good works that are necessary on our part are those that 'God prepared in advance for us to do' (Eph. 2:10). The kingdom that God establishes is of grace from beginning to the end. The faith and obedience which are a necessary part of participation within the covenant are evidences of life.

Those who fail to obey God's law, like so many of Ezekiel's companions in exile, identify themselves as not being children of God, even though they may have been brought up within the sphere of the covenant community and be what Calvin calls 'flesh sons of the saint', who 'idly boast of the fatherhood of God on that account'.[3] This is one of the clearest warnings in Ezekiel: that it is possible to belong to the outward community of God's people and yet be a hypocrite.

The election of Israel

If God's election of Israel was an irrevocable predestination to life, and Israel was 'chosen as his special people', the problem is raised as to how they can be spoken of by the prophets as having fallen. Ezekiel does not mince his words about the matter: 'I will deal with you as you deserve, because you have despised my oath by breaking the covenant' (16:59).

Calvin's response to this was to affirm 'two degrees' in the election of God. There is a general election of Israel as a nation and as a people, and with them God's covenant is made. But within this people was God's 'hidden' elect, 'individual persons whom God not only offers salvation but so assigns it that the certainty of its effect is not in suspense or doubt'.[4] Commenting upon Ezekiel 16:21, Calvin adds: 'There was a twofold election of God, since speaking generally he chose the whole family of Abraham. For circumcision was common to all, being the symbol and seal of adoption ... this was one kind of adoption or election. But the other was secret, because God took to himself out of that multitude those whom he wished: and these are the sons of promise.'[5] Thus those chosen may suffer the general chastisement of the nation (Ezekiel found himself in exile) but be exempt from the ultimate punishment of separation from God. The elect within the elect were spiritually regenerated and given new hearts and received the spirit of adoption. Others, who had shown ingratitude, were rejected and disowned as children.[6]

All this can be applied to the New Testament church. There are those who grow up in the covenant community. They share in the privileges of worship. Nevertheless they are hypocrites. They are, in one sense, members of the visible church, and yet they are not members of the invisible church of true believers who may be assured of eternal glory (cf. Rom. 10:16) These can be one of three categories: children of believers who have grown up to despise the true nature of the covenant and are content with external things only; those who have joined the church by feigning piety; or those who are sincere enough but only have temporary faith. All these will slip away from the covenant. The difference between these and backsliders (genuine believers who temporarily stray) is that in the latter case their inner seal remains (2 Tim. 2:19) and they are restored to repentance. Their fall is not permanent.

9.

'I am, Yours sincerely...'

Please read Ezekiel 18:1 - 19:14

Following a prolonged discussion in the newspapers about the possible causes of society's ills, the public were invited to write with their own opinions as to what might be the root cause of all the trouble. G. K. Chesterton wrote the simple lines: 'Dear Sir, I am, Yours sincerely...' It could hardly have been more effective. The root cause lies within each one of us: it is indwelling sin. It is something for which each one of us is responsible. This is the theme that Ezekiel now takes up in chapter 18. People then, as now, were muddled over the nature and consequences of individual sin.

Sin is one of the first things we need to learn about ourselves. Without this knowledge, the Bible will make no sense; for its message from beginning to end is an exposition of God's answer to the problem of human sin. The self-excusing instinct is a strong one: it was, after all, what Adam and Eve both did in Eden — Adam blaming Eve, and Eve blaming the serpent (Gen. 3:12-13). It was, apparently, what the exiles were doing too. Citing a proverb which they must have learnt during their days in exile, they blamed their present troubles on the errors of previous generations — not on anything that they themelves had done:

> **'The fathers eat sour grapes,**
> **and the children's teeth are set on edge'**

(18:2).

Perhaps they cited the words added to the second commandment: 'For I, the Lord your God, am a jealous God, punishing the children for the sin of the fathers to the third and fourth generation' (Exod. 20:5), which taught that children certainly are affected by their parents' sin. Children often repeat what they see their parents doing. But each child is responsible for his or her own actions. Ezekiel's companions, on the other hand, had drawn a quite different conclusion. The fault, they concluded, lay entirely with their forefathers; it had nothing to do with them.

There is nothing new here. Each one of us attempts to wriggle free from personal responsibility for our actions. Politicians, workers, schools, parents, even the church — all attempt to shun their accountability. But blame-shifting is something God will not allow; he holds us personally responsible for our actions. It was true that previous generations had sinned and brought about the judgements of God, including the present exile in Babylon.[1] Nevertheless, the ones who endured the exile were not guiltless. They, too, were sinners and they must face up to it. God therefore forbids them to use this proverb any more (18:3). What follows is a carefully reasoned account of the individual's responsibility.

The principle of individual responsibility illustrated

1. The case for individual responsibility

The penalty for sin is death, no matter who it is that has sinned. God will not treat father and son differently: if both have sinned, both will die (18:4). But other computations are possible.

Taking three generations — grandfather (18:5), son (18:10) and grandson (18:14) — the prophet imagines the case of a 'righteous' grandfather who has 'a violent son'. Notwithstanding the father's righteousness, the son will **surely be put to death and his blood will be on his own head**. His father's righteousness will not save him; the son remains responsible for his own actions (18:10-13).

But if, in turn, the violent man has a son who turns out to be honest, this son will live because of his integrity. He will not suffer the penalty that his father's sins deserved. His father, though, will be called to account for his actions (18:14-18).

In each case individual responsibility is being underlined: **'The son will not share the guilt of the father, nor will the father share the guilt of the son. The righteousness of the righteous man will be credited to him, and the wickedness of the wicked will be charged against him'** (18:20).

2. The ultimate penalty for sin is death

'The soul who sins is the one who will die' (18:4, 20). Throughout
the Bible death, in both its physical and its spiritual aspects, is
viewed as God's penalty for sin. Sin's employees are paid with the
wages of 'death', Paul tells us (Rom. 6:23). When God told Adam,
'When you eat of it [the tree of knowledge] you will surely die'
(Gen. 2:17), the primary reference was to physical death (see Gen.
3:19), a threat which was confirmed in Adam's eventual death (Gen.
5:5). All of us share in this curse by virtue of our solidarity with
Adam (1 Cor. 15:22). However, when Paul speaks, in Romans 5:12-
21, of the 'many' being delivered from the death in which Adam had
involved them, he has something wider in mind: justification (vv.
16-19) leading to a restoration of 'life' (vv. 17-21). In other words,
the death which Adam received included a spiritual dimension: he
died to fellowship with God — a fact confirmed by his eventual
expulsion from the garden in Genesis 3:23.

3. Sin is a state of condemnation

Every sinner — and that means everyone! — stands under a death
sentence. The catalogue of sins listed in these verses, which include
sexual immorality (18:6,11), robbery and exploitation (18:7, 12-
13), false religion (18:11) and indecency (18:8), is similar to those
which the apostle records in Romans 1:29-31, and of which he says,
'Those who do such things deserve death.' Unless a way of forgiveness can be found, every sinner is condemned to die, both physically
and spiritually.

4. There is a way for man to avoid the condemnation

It is to walk in accordance with God's ways. **'But if a wicked man
turns away from all the sins he has committed and keeps all my
decrees and does what is just and right, he will surely live; he will
not die'** (18:21). Repentance to a life of obedience to God's
covenant is something Ezekiel has stressed before (3:19) and will do
so again (18:23,27; 33:12,14,19).
    It must be made clear that in all these examples, Ezekiel is not
suggesting that the 'righteous' man obtains the reward of life on the
basis of what he has done alone. In order to follow a life of

obedience, Ezekiel makes it clear that man needs a **'a new heart and a new spirit'** (18:31). Before Jesus ever told Nicodemus that he needed to be born again, or 'from above', in order to obtain the life that the kingdom of heaven offered, the Old Testament prophets had spoken of the very same necessity. The fact is that those who demonstrate a life of obedience, and are therefore assured of the life of glory, are those who have 'turned' from their sin to God (18:21). 'When we discuss the cause [of salvation],' adds Calvin, ' we must look nowhere else but the mercy of God, and there we must stop.'[2]

An insight into the heart of God

All this talk about the punishment of the wicked might create the wrong impression. For a start, it might imply that God might take some pleasure in their destruction. This is emphatically not the case. Putting the matter in both a negative and positive form, God says, **'Do I take any pleasure in the death of the wicked? declares the Sovereign Lord. Rather, am I not pleased when they turn from their ways and live?'** (18:23); **'For I take no pleasure in the death of anyone, declares the Sovereign Lord'** (18:32; cf. 33:11). The translation of verse 23 misses something of the force of the original, which could be rendered: 'Taking pleasure in, do I take pleasure in?' The answer is equally emphatic: 'I do not by any means desire the death of a wicked person.'

1. The sovereignty of God in Ezekiel

Although the doctrine of predestination does not figure very prominently in Ezekiel, it does occur at various points. In the preceding chapters, Ezekiel has underlined the point that Israel's salvation was nothing to do with any merit in themselves (16:1-8). Indeed, the covenant that God entered into with Israel was a sovereign one from beginning to end (16:8). B. B. Warfield, citing this verse together with Ezekiel 17:22, comments: 'No means are left unused to drive home the fact that God's gracious election of Israel is an absolutely sovereign one, founded solely in his unmerited love, and looking to nothing ultimately but the gratification of his own holy and loving impulses, and the manifestation of his grace through the formation of a heritage for himself out of the mass of sinful men, by means of

whom his saving mercy should advance to the whole world.'[3] Added
to this is the fact that the opening chapter, with its vision of the throne
of God, was designed to reinforce the truth that God has a plan, one
which he is determined to fulfil.

Ezekiel's God is the 'Sovereign Lord', something that Ezekiel
points out 217 times! If, then, all things do in fact happen under the
direct dominion of God — the coming of the Babylonians to destroy
Jerusalem, the return of the remnant in the time of Cyrus the Persian,
the coming of the Saviour as promised at the end of the previous
chapter — does this not have a bearing upon the identity of those
who will be saved and those who will not? After all, if God is
sovereign, does he not already know the identity of the 'remnant'?
And if God does know their identity, as he most surely does, then
how can he express a desire for all men to repent and live?

There is a sense in which it is right to let passages such as these
speak for themselves, without the encumbrance of other passages
which might seem to convey another point of view. Certainly, we
must not allow other considerations to dilute the force of what is
being said here. Equally, however, the fact that we believe the *entire*
Scriptures to be inerrant means that we must not interpret one
passage so as contradict another. What is said here may well *appear*
to be at odds with sovereign election; but it only appears to be so.
There are doctrines in the Scripture which cannot be reconciled by
a finite mind: God's sovereignty and man's responsibility being two
such truths. No amount of reasoning can fully understand how both
can be true; and yet both *are* true. Like the twin tracks of a railway
line, they lie alongside each other, stretching out into the foreseeable
distance. We tamper with either one at our peril.

2. God's desire and his secret decrees

Since it is evident that some will not repent, does this not pose a
problem — that God longs for something that will not happen; that
God sometimes expresses a desire for the fulfilment of certain
things that he has not decreed in his inscrutable will to come to pass?
'This means,' comments John Murray, 'that there is a will to the
realization of what he has not decretively willed, a pleasure towards
that which he has not been pleased to decree. This is indeed
mysterious, and why he has not brought to pass, in the exercise of
his omnipotent power and grace, what is his ardent pleasure lies hid

in the sovereign counsel of his will.'[4] Is God sincere when he expresses such emotions? This dilemma comes into sharp focus in the incarnate ministry of God's Son, for when Jesus beheld the city of Jerusalem, he longed to gather them under his protection 'as a hen gathers her chicks under her wings' (Matt. 23:37). 'But,' he adds, 'you were not willing.' He longed for the conversion of Jerusalem's inhabitants, but this evidently did not occur. Jesus' will seems in opposition to the will of God's decree.

It might be objected that these words form merely the *human* desire of Christ, and not the desire of God himself. But it is erroneous to set the human will of Christ against his divine will. These words, as all of Jesus' words, were spoken in his capacity as Messiah. Jesus spoke these as the God-man, the incarnate Lord. They are a reflection of the pathos and sadness in God himself at the death and condemnation of the unrepentant. 'My teaching,' he asserts, 'is not my own. It comes from him who sent me' (John 7:16).

The same teaching is to be found in 2 Peter 3:4, where Peter recalls scoffers who say, 'Where is this "coming" he promised?", to which the answer is given: 'The Lord is not slow in keeping his promise, as some understand slowness. He is patient with you, not wanting anyone to perish, but everyone to come to repentance' (2 Peter 3:9). The word Peter uses, 'patient' *(makrothymei),* means 'long-suffering' (AV). The apparent delay of Christ's Second Coming, Peter says, does not mean that the Lord is slow or forgetful of his promise, but rather that he is long-suffering towards us; it is evidence of his grace that he gives us time to repent and believe upon his Son. The Lord does not wish *any* to perish.

Calvin hears someone asking, 'Then why do any perish, if God desires that they be saved?', to which he replies: 'No mention is made here of the secret decree of God by which the wicked are doomed to their own ruin, but only of His loving-kindness as it is made known to us in the Gospel. There God stretches out His hand to all alike, but He only grasps those (in such a way as to lead to Himself) whom He has chosen before the foundation of the world.'[5]

What Jesus desires, God desires. Jesus is the 'Word' of God. He who has seen him has seen the Father. 'No one has ever seen God, but God the One and Only, who is at the Father's side, has made him known' (John 1:18). Jesus 'has made him [God] known' (literally, *exegetes*). Everything that we see and hear in Christ is an expression of what God is essentially like. There is no unchristlikeness in God.[6]

We must not therefore dilute the longing expressed in these verses: God desires the repentance of those whom he has not decreed to save. He yearns for them to be saved. It is partly this that gives us the warrant to preach the gospel to everyone. We are entitled to say to everyone, whoever they may be, 'God longs for you to be saved.' The grounds upon which Christ is offered to the world have nothing to do with election. Four reasons tell us why we should call upon everyone to repent and believe the gospel:

1. Everyone is sinful and needs him (Rom. 3:19-26; Acts 4:12).
2. Christ is a perfect and sufficient Saviour for everyone who believes in him (John 3:16; Acts 13:39; Rom. 1:16; Heb. 7:25).
3. Christ invites all who are needy to come to him (Matt. 11:28; John 6:37)
4. God commands that everyone who hears the gospel should repent and believe in Christ (Acts 17:30; 1 John 3:23). Evangelism is not be carried out under speculative notions of whether folk are elect or not. That is something we are not given to know. We evangelize because God tells us to. If someone asks: 'How can such an invitation on our part, or for that matter a desire on God's part, be *bona fide*?', the answer, in brief, is that we do not know. The truth of God's sovereignty should not affect the necessity, or the urgency, of evangelism on our part. The secret will of God is, to put it bluntly, but truthfully, none of our business. And if election does not affect the role of the evangelist, neither ought it to affect the responsibility of the one being evangelized.

The whole point of this chapter is to underline the fact that each man is accountable for his own actions. 'Everywhere in Scripture,' writes J. C. Ryle, 'it is a leading principle that man can lose his own soul, that if he is lost at last it will be his own fault, and his blood will be on his own head. The same inspired Bible which reveals this doctrine of election is the Bible which contains the word, "Why will ye die, O house of Israel?" — "Ye will not come unto me that ye might have life" — "This is the condemnation, that light is come into the world, and men loved darkness rather than light, because their deeds were evil" (Ezek. 18:31; John 5:40, 3:19). The Bible never says that sinners miss heaven because they are not elect, but because they "neglect the great salvation", and because they will not repent and believe. The last judgement will abundantly prove that it is not the want of God's election, so much as laziness, the love of sin, unbelief, and unwillingness to come to Christ, which ruins the souls that are lost.'[7]

Calvin further comments: 'We hold, then, that God wills not the death of a sinner, since he calls all equally to repentance, and promises himself prepared to receive them if they only seriously repent. If anyone should object — then there is no election of God, by which he has predestined a fixed number to salvation, the answer is at hand: the Prophet does not here speak of God's secret counsel, but only recalls miserable men from despair, that they may apprehend the hope of pardon, and repent and embrace the offered salvation.'[8]

Who, then, is to blame if a person is not saved? The answer is not God but the sinner! The following passage underlines the fact that no one can blame God's sovereignty for his or her lost condition.

It's not fair!

Suppose a man lives a blameless life and then, at the end, commits evil. Will he be condemned for that evil? For Ezekiel's listeners the answer must surely have seemed to be negative; but they are mistaken. **'Because of the sin he has committed he will die'** (18:26). Suppose, then, that a really wicked person lives a life of evil for the duration of his life, and then repents at the end of it. Will he be accepted by God? Again, Ezekiel's listeners expect the answer to be negative, and once again they are mistaken. **'He will surely live; he will not die'** (18:28). This seems to Ezekiel's hearers inherently unfair: **'The way of the Lord is not just,'** they object (18:25).

The problem with Ezekiel's listeners is a failure to comprehend the nature of grace! The point about our salvation is that it is wholly undeserved. Neither person in these two illustrations deserves salvation. The fact that the one who repents gains life is due to the fact that he acknowledges the fact that his acceptance is nothing to do with him, or what he does. His works do not come into it. He is a sinner and he knows it. All he does is to plead for mercy — something that the Lord is only too pleased to grant to those who ask him. Salvation is not simply an inventory of the good deeds we have accomplished. The fact is that no one has lived 'a blameless life' — none that is, apart from Jesus Christ (Heb. 7:26). Nor is this contradicted by the assertion in verse 30 that God will judge each man **'according to his ways'**. This judgement includes the appraisal of whether the man has repented and turned to the Lord for salvation.

Repentance

The fact that all are equally guilty calls forth the response that all men need to repent. This chapter of the Old Testament provides us with the evidence that genuine repentance had taken place. The first fruits of repentance were to be obedience to the ways of the covenant. Included within this was the notion that they had rejected the ways of ungodliness. This was a truth that Ezekiel has already preached so powerfully (3:19) and now repeats again (18:21,23,27; cf. 33:12,14,19). If a man turns from his wicked ways he will discover that repentance leads to life (18:21-23). What is of interest is to note the basis upon which Ezekiel issues his appeals: **'Rid yourselves of all the offences you have committed, and get a new heart and a new spirit. Why will you die, O house of Israel?'** (18:31). When Jesus upbraided Nicodemus for his ignorance of the Old Testament teaching on the new birth, saying, 'You are Israel's teacher, and you do not understand these things?' (John 3:10), he undoubtedly had passages such as Ezekiel 18 in mind.

As though to underline the fact of individual responsibility, the next chapter of Ezekiel contains a funeral dirge lamenting the decline and fall of Judah. If the Babylonian exiles were not to blame previous generations of Judeans for their condition, neither were they to look to present Judeans to rescue them. In a sense they were on their own before God. They were responsible for their condition; they were equally responsible to turn and seek the Lord's mercy. No help would be forthcoming for their deliverance from Judah. She was already as good as dead.

A funeral song (19:1-14)

Chapter 19 is different from the preceding chapters. It is written in the style of a song. Actually it is a dirge lamenting the state of things in the royal household during the final days of Judah's decline before the nation succumbed to Babylonian take-over. Three kings are considered in turn: Jehoahaz, Jehoiachin and Zedekiah. Songs such as these, revealing a distinctive pattern, were often composed and sung at funerals (cf. David's funeral lament for Saul and Jonathan in 2 Sam. 1:19-27).

The poem begins in melancholy mood with a command to lament (19:1). Though Ezekiel suggests this poem is going to be about princes of **'Israel'**, specifically, it is understood that he has Judah in mind. It is quite probable that Ezekiel sang this song in the hearing of his audience. It would soon become obvious to his listeners that he was speaking about Judean kings. The dirge begins with a reference to King Jehoahaz II, who had ruled for just three months in 609 B.C.

Lions (19:1-9)

The story of how King Jehoahaz II was captured and exiled into Egypt where he eventually died (2 Kings 23:21-34) is told in the form of an allegory of a mother lion (Israel, i.e. Judah) who gave birth to two young whelps. One of them (Jehoahaz) grew to be a young lion, with all the typical features of ferocious lions (19:3-4). The reference to Jehoahaz is unmistakable from the line: **'And they brought him with chains to the land of Egypt'** (19:4, NKJV). The history behind this tale involves Pharaoh Necho, who led an expedition into Palestine to regain Egypt's once great empire. Having removed Jehoahaz out of the way, he was then able to install Egypt's puppet king, Jehoiakim, in his place.

Passing quickly by the story of Jehoiakim, and his successor, Jehoiachin, Ezekiel now mentions the other lion cub: **'She took another of her cubs'** (19:5). This section of the poem probably refers to Zedekiah, who was, of course, still alive and reigning in Jerusalem at the time Ezekiel spoke these words.[9] The lament forms a prediction of Zedekiah's downfall. The fact that both Zedekiah and Jehoahaz had the same mother, Hamutal (2 Kings 24:18) further makes sense of this song with its mother lion and two cubs (19:2,3,5). This funeral dirge was then somewhat different: it was a funeral song for someone who had not yet died! Zedekiah's days are numbered. Make no mistake about it, he too will be brought to Babylon.

What this dirge did was to remove from Ezekiel's companions

any hope that they were going to be rescued by their companions in
Judah. All hope in man's ability to deliver them is taken away. They
are being systematically closed in to the mercy of God alone to
deliver them from their captivity. This may, at first sight, appear to
have been cruel on Ezekiel's part. Surely we need hope in difficult
times and to remove it like this was harsh. But this is a short-sighted
way of looking at things. Only when all false avenues are closed off
can we be sure of finding ourselves on the true road. Israel's young
lions may have appeared to have great strength, but in reality they
were mice! To place all our confidence in human resources is always
a mistake. It is not Judah's lions, but the Lion of Judah who will
deliver these people from their bondage.

A vine and its branches (19:10-14)

These verses continue the lament, but with a different image: that of
a vine and its branches: **'Your mother was like a vine in your
vineyard'** (19:10). (The reader should note that the theme is quite
different from the allegory of chapter 17 and the transplanted vine.)
The mother of the last kings of Israel, literally Hamutal, though
Judah is probably is in mind, was like a vine planted **'by the water'**
(19:10). The vine grew abundantly, sprouting branches and tendrils
and bearing fruit. These branches represent the twenty-two kings
that appeared from David's day to Zedekiah's day. But this vine has
been pulled up and left lying on the ground, its roots exposed
(19:12). Dried by the east wind from the desert, its strongest
branches shrivelled and were burnt. The fact that grape wood was
used for firewood was something Jesus alluded to, warning his
disciples of the consequence of not 'remaining' in him (John 15:6).

What happened next to this vine, now only ashes, seems impossible: it was planted in a **'dry and thirsty land'** (19:13), that is,
Babylon. Even assuming that such a thing might be possible, any
vestige of hope is removed at a stroke; the vine catches fire,
consuming its fruit. Zedekiah's rebellion against the Babylonians in
the late 590s B.C. brought about the collapse of Judah (2 Kings
24:20); the nation was defeated. Ezekiel was giving a glimpse of
what lay ahead for Judah in the not too distant future. In a few short
years, Judah had fallen. This dirge was her song of lament.

To place one's hope in the royal family of Judah was misguided.
God's message to his people in this chapter is designed to make sure

that their confidence is in him alone. We are reminded of the psalmist's words:

'Do not put your trust in princes,
    in mortal men, who cannot save.
When their spirit departs, they return to the ground;
    on that very day their plans come to nothing.
Blessed is he whose help is the God of Jacob,
    whose hope is in the Lord his God,
the Maker of heaven and earth,
    the sea, and everything in them
    the Lord, who remains faithful for ever'

(Ps. 146:3-6).

What can we conclude from this chapter? At first glance it appears cruel to tell these exiles that Judah is going to be destroyed in a few short years. We tend to want to reassure folk that some hope remains, no matter how dark the circumstances might be. Few of us would tell a friend suffering from terminal cancer that he has no hope. That would be cruel. So why does Ezekiel rob his hearers of what was to them the only source of comfort? The answer lies in the fact that this was not their only source of comfort! Their delivery lay, not in the power of Zedekiah or anyone else in Judah; it lay in the power of God to rescue them from their bondage. Sovereign grace was the source of their deliverance, and nothing else! This is a lesson that needs repeating again and again. For what saves us from our sin is not ourselves; nor is it the combined resources of other sinners. It is the power of God in the gospel, the operation of the sovereign Spirit of God at work in our hearts (cf. Rom. 1:16). We need to be shut in to the utter futility of every other means of rescue so that we might turn to the Lord and seek his mercy. That is what Ezekiel was doing here. Far from being cruel, it was an act of mercy in itself.

There was no other good enough
To pay the price of sin;
He only could unlock the gate
Of heaven and let us in.[10]

Summary

The exiles blamed their situation on the sins of others rather than their own. They also sought for deliverance from the wrong source. Ezekiel has to correct both these errors, for both were fatally flawed. Before we can be made right with God we must learn and acknowledge that we are sinners and that we are morally culpable. It is equally essential to know that Christ alone is the source of our deliverance from sin's curse and bondage. These basic truths have been behind these two chapters.

On President Harry S. Truman's desk was a hand-lettered sign which read, 'The buck stops here.' Blame-shifting could go no further than the president himself! When it comes to our sins, we have no one to blame but ourselves. And when it comes to our salvation we have no one to whom we may turn but Christ. The knowledge of these truths, together with that of God's wonderfully yearning heart, should drive us into his arms for mercy. That is precisely what the evangelist Ezekiel was of a mind to do.

Part IV
The third cycle of prophecies
(Ezek. 20-24)

10.
Dumb idols

Please read Ezekiel 20:1- 44

Since Ezekiel had clearly made the point in the previous chapter that no hope of deliverance for the exiles could come from the Judeans led by Judah's last king, Zedekiah, it may well have occurred to his companions to wonder if deliverance was possible at all. To answer that question, Ezekiel turns to one of Israel's most spectacular deliverances, the Exodus from Egypt, to illustrate what the Lord can do for them. God is going to perform a second exodus — something which other prophets allude to, too (Isa. 41:17-20; 43:16-21; Jer. 23:7-8; Micah 7:15-17).

Once again, Ezekiel provides us with a date: **'In the seventh year, in the fifth month on the tenth day'** (20:1), that is, July/August in the year 591 B.C. Almost a year has passed since the last dated reference (8:1), suggesting that everything that took place from chapters 8-19 occurred in the eleven months from late summer of 592 B.C. to mid-summer 591 B.C.

The elders have once more gathered to hear what Ezekiel has to say (cf. 8:1; 14:1). The reason for their coming together was **'to enquire of the Lord'**. Perhaps they were anxious to know the length of the exile; or perhaps they wished to know if Zedekiah's fall, predicted in chapter 19, was now imminent and how this might affect relatives and friends back home. It is possible that some of them were anxious to make a deal with their captors and were seeking Ezekiel's support for it. Whatever the precise reason for their coming together, the tables are turned: the Lord does not allow the elders to set the agenda for discussion; he has an urgent, and highly critical, word for them to hear.

Calvin comments that the reason for God's refusal to answer

their enquiry was that they were insincere in their desire to know God's will for their lives. Their minds were already made up: 'And because their hypocrisy was stained by various colours, God swears that their disposition was perverse, and that they did not come with pious and holy affections, and were neither docile nor obedient, nor desirous of making progress, and hence were unworthy of having him for a teacher.'[1] Sincerity is essential if we are to make progress in discerning God's will for our lives. As the Lord said through Jeremiah, currently in Jerusalem: 'You will seek me and find me when you seek me with all your heart' (Jer. 29:13).

What follows is an outline of Israel's history of disobedience from the days when they were in exile in Egypt until the present day.

Israel's disobedience in Egypt (20:5-8)

Israel were God's covenant people. He had chosen them (20:5). With **'uplifted hand'** (20:5) God had promised to deliver them from Egypt and bring them **'into a land [he] had searched out for them, a land flowing with milk and honey, the most beautiful of all lands'** (20:6). As to when this took place, verse 5 refers to **'the day'**. The context of these verses refers to the time when Israel were in bondage in Egypt, and it is true that they were considered to be God's people: 'I have indeed seen the misery of my *people* in Egypt' (Exod. 3:7). But the covenant relationship and the promise of the 'land flowing with milk and honey' go back through the patriarchs to the time of Abraham (Gen. 12:1-2; Exod. 3:8).

The point Ezekiel is now making is that the Israelites in Egypt, far from longing for the fulfilment of this promise, were fully accommodating themselves to their surroundings, even to the extent of needing to be told to get rid of their **'vile images'** (20:7,8). These **'idols of Egypt'** (20:7) were undoubtedly dear to the Israelites, for they refused to forsake them (20:8). God's reaction to these flagrant violations had been to **'to pour out my wrath on them and spend my anger against them'** (20:8). They were to spend 430 years in captivity in Egypt making bricks without straw (Exod. 5:1-20). Nevertheless, God remained faithful to his covenant promise and brought them out of Egypt (20:9-10).

In summarizing this passage we could no better than quote John Calvin's prayer at the close of his sixtieth lecture on Ezekiel covering the section 20:1-8. After commenting on verse 6 of this chapter, with its reference to the way God had delivered Israel out of Egypt with his powerful hand, Calvin closed that day's session with the prayer: 'Grant, Almighty God, since thou hast once stretched forth thine hand to us by thine only-begotten Son, and hast not only bound thyself to us by an oath, but hast sealed thine eternal covenant by the blood of the same, thy Son: Grant, I pray thee, that we in return may be faithful to thee, and preserve in the pure worship of thy name, until at length we enjoy the fruit of our faith in thy heavenly kingdom by the same Christ our Lord. Amen.'[2]

Israel's disobedience in the wilderness (20:10-26)

Israel had been prepared for their existence as a nation by being given a rule-book by which to live (20:11), which included legislation outlawing idolatry (Exod. 20:3-6,23). On at least two occasions, they showed how ingrained idolatry had become in their lives, and how difficult a thing it was to eradicate. Moses, descending Mount Sinai with the stone tablets of the law in his hand, found them worshipping a golden calf (Exod. 32). At Baal-Peor, on the eve of the conquest of Canaan, the men engaged in sexual immorality with certain Moabite women and offered sacrifices to their gods (Num. 25:1) — this despite the warning given by Moses at that time that idolatry would result in death and exile (Deut. 28:64-68).

Israel's rebellion in the wilderness is set forth in terms of their rejection of the covenant given at Sinai. Specifically, three elements of their rejection are noted: **'They did not follow my decrees but rejected my laws ... and they utterly desecrated my Sabbaths'** (20:13). The Sabbath, mentioned six times in this chapter (20:12,13,16,20,21,24) was a sign of God's covenant with Israel (Exod. 31:16-17). Keeping the Sabbath was to be the Israelites' way of demonstrating their identity as the Lord's people. Again and again they rebelled and each time God threatened to pour out his wrath against them (20:13) — 3,000 people were destroyed at the foot of Mount Sinai (Exod. 32:28) and 24,000 at Baal-Peor (Num. 25:9). Nevertheless they were not completely destroyed, either at Sinai or Baal-Peor. God reveals his mercy and forbearance, for the sake of his own name (20:14-16). The entire nation was not destroyed, though an entire generation died without ever seeing the promised land. The new generation born in the wilderness were warned to stay away from idolatry (20:18-20).

If earlier generations of Israelites had to spend 430 years in Egypt for their sins, another generation spent forty years wandering in the desert for theirs. Such is the measure of God's wrath against them (20:21). But once again, instead of obliterating Israel for their sin of idolatry, God shows mercy to them (20:22). Yet his mercy is according to his covenanted warnings: he will scatter them among the nations (20:24). This is what Israel had been told before they crossed into Canaan: 'I call heaven and earth as witnesses against you this day that you will quickly perish from the land that you are crossing the Jordan to possess. You will not live there long but will certainly be destroyed. The Lord will scatter you among the peoples, and only a few of you will survive among the nations to which the Lord will drive you' (Deut. 4:26-27). This was a reference to the exile in Babylon which Ezekiel's companions were currently experiencing. What led to the exile was their idolatry (20:24). Ezekiel singles out its major features.

1. Child sacrifice

Of all the most detestable practices that Israel ever committed, the worst by far was the practice of child-sacrifice (20:26). Stuart explains the reasoning that lay behind it this way: 'A sacrifice as understood by Israel's pagan neighbours was a way of giving desirable things to the gods. Humans were supposed to feed the gods by cooking for them... And if you could send food via smoke to the gods, how about sending them servants that way? How about really impressing a god with your dedication and sincerity by sending that god something more precious to you than anything else — your own firstborn child?'[3] This practice, known to be performed by the Canaanites (2 Kings 3:27) was copied by the Israelites (2 Kings 16:3; 21:6; 23:10).

What is extraordinary about this passage is the way Ezekiel puts it: **'I let them become defiled through their gifts — the sacrifice of every firstborn — that I might fill them with horror so that they would know that I am the Lord'** (20:26). God permitted this terrible thing to occur. But this is not as difficult as it might at first appear, for everything that ever happens in the world comes under the oversight of God's control of human history. Even the death of

God's own Son was, according to Peter, an act perpetrated 'with the help of wicked men' but nevertheless in accordance with 'God's set purpose and foreknowledge' (Acts 2:23).

Ezekiel even seems to imply in verse 25 that the Israelites used one of God's commandments to justify child-sacrifice, perhaps Exodus 22:29: 'You must give me the firstborn of your sons.' There is no limit to the sin men can do; even the Bible is called in to defend it. This is, of course, what Satan did when tempting Jesus to sin, citing passages from the Bible to justify a heinous transgression.

2. *Ritual sex*

Sexual promiscuity has always been a feature of man's rebellion from the beginning. Even the greatest of Old Testament saints fell into this snare. To give it religious justification was only to add to the abhorrence of it in God's eyes. Most of the ancient Near Eastern religions believed that the gods brought things into being through a sexual act. Baal and Asherah, the Canaanite god and goddess of fertility, were believed to be capable of stimulation by sexual acts performed by their worshippers. Consequently the shrines of Canaanite religion had their professional prostitutes with whom sexual acts were performed. It is hard to imagine a more perverted justification of sin. Our own society is guilty of bowing down at this shrine, too.

Rebellion of Israel in the promised land (20:27-29)

Israel were brought into the promised land according to the promise of God. They were delivered **'with a mighty hand and an out-stretched arm'** (20:33-34); they were borne 'on eagle's wings' (Exod. 19:4). They were to experience the mighty power of God at the crossing of the River Jordan in flood. Joshua carefully set up twelve memorial stones on the banks of the River Jordan to serve as a reminder to future generations of the mighty power of God at work among his people (Josh. 4:8-9). They were to see that power at work once more at Jericho (Josh. 5:13 - 6:27). In the execution of Achan, they were to witness a graphic statement of what happens to those who disobey the Lord (Josh. 7:1-26).

One might have thought that Israel would have learnt a lesson or two from these experiences, but they did not. Dwelling as they did in **'the most beautiful of all lands'** (20:6,15), they were to imitate the deviant ways of the Canaanites. In addition to their crimes in the wilderness, Ezekiel now adds another — that of blasphemy (20:27). What is said about blasphemy here is important: God accuses Israel of having **'blasphemed me by forsaking me'** (20:27). 'Blasphemy connotes a word or deed that directs insolence to the character of God, Christian truth or sacred things.'⁴ It is a deliberate attempt to attack the honour of God. It is what the third commandment was directed at (Exod. 20:7; Deut 5:11). The thing to note here is that blasphemy consists in more than words: they blasphemed God by what they did. Once settled in Canaan, the Israelites looked on travelling to Jerusalem as an inconvenient way of worshipping God. Israel had never been content with Jerusalem as the base of religious worship. Travelling to Jerusalem for the great festivals of worship was far too inconvenient. Far better, they thought, to follow the way of the Canaanites and set up shrines on every mountain and hill in the land (20:28-29). In doing so they implied that they knew better than God.

By way of a summary of their unfaithfulness, God refers to Israel as **'lust[ing] after their vile images'** (20:30, 'harlotry' in NKJV). Israel's behaviour is thus characterized as prostitution. In language similar to that of the book of Hosea, Israel's craving for other gods to worship and serve is seen as a violation of her marriage contract with God. She has dishonoured God in the most shameful of ways. This is, in essence, what our sin is: prostitution!

Some matters are now worth remembering.

1. A formula of rebellion followed by wrath reveals itself in verses 8, 13 and 21. In one sense, the history of Israel appeared to be nothing but a continuation of rebellion against God. They had learnt few lessons from the time of their infancy. They had not grown or matured. But along with this repetition, there appears another, one that appears immediately after the mention of God's wrath: that of God's determination to save his people for his name's sake (20:9, 14, 22). 'The mystery, as Ezekiel sees it, is not why God smites, but why he refrains from smiting.'⁵

2. Idolatry always involves a violation of the covenant. Belonging to God's people carries with it responsibilities. In essence, being a believer is likened to having entered into a marriage contract with

God. Ezekiel's contemporary Jeremiah could be heard in the streets of Jerusalem, speaking on God's behalf and saying such things as: '"Return, faithless people," declares the Lord, "for I am your husband"' (Jer. 3:14). Why does he say this? Because 'You have lived as a prostitute with many lovers' (Jer. 3:1). This is a theme Ezekiel has stressed already (16:15-19, 30-34).

3. God acts, not so as to bring us what we deserve, but to bring glory to himself. It is for his name's sake.

It is interesting to note that Israel's downfall at this point in their history was due to a recurring tendency to copy the sins of the nations. Ezekiel rebukes them because **'You say, "We want to be like the nations, like the peoples of the world..."** ' (20:32). At the time of the exodus, God had warned: 'You must not do as they do in Egypt, where you used to live, and you must not do as they do in the land of Canaan, where I am bringing you. Do not follow their practices. You must obey my laws...' (Lev. 18:3-4). God looks for an intensive nonconformity from his people. It is something that he repeats in the New Testament. In spite of the clear commands of Jesus: 'Do not be like them' (Matt. 6:8) and of the apostle Paul: 'Do not conform ... to the pattern of this world' (Rom. 12:2), the constant tendency of God's people was, and still is, to behave 'like the heathen' (1 Thess 4:5; cf. 1 Cor. 5:1; Eph. 4:17). It has not always been so, however. C. S. Lewis said of Athanasius, who maintained the deity of Jesus and the doctrine of the Trinity against fierce opposition: 'It is his glory that he did not move with the times; it is his reward that he now remains when the times, as all times do, have moved away.'[6]

The future (20:33-44)

Ezekiel now turns to the future. What hope do they have? Their sin has provoked God to anger. The curse of the covenant threatened their death and destruction. Already they are in exile in Babylon for their rebellion. But just as God had rescued them 'with a mighty hand and an outstretched arm' in the past, so he will gather them again from their captivity (20:33-34).

What follows in verses 33-38 is assigned by Dispensationalists to the period following the ending of the Battle of Armageddon, when the nation of Israel will have been regathered into Palestine.

When Christ returns 'with the saints' the vast majority of Israelites then living will turn to Christ and be saved. Those who do not will be judged and forbidden to enter into the enjoyment of the millennium where Christ will rule from a throne in Jerusalem. Ezekiel 40-48, with its elaborate portrayals of Jerusalem, is then interpreted as a description of temple worship during the millennium. We shall see in our comments on those chapters that this is a misguided view.[7] Along with Patrick Fairbairn, this commentary takes the view that this vision refers to God's church in the New Testament era. The future in view here is one where a 'new and better state of things [is] introduced through the gospel'.[8]

God has a great future for the church! To confirm it he pronounces it in the form of a covenant oath involving a strange, but reassuring gesture. A binding oath of the covenant might take a variety of forms. Sometimes it was a merely verbal affair (Gen. 21:23-24,26,31; 31:53; Exod. 6:8; 19:8; 24:3,7; Deut 7:8,12; 29:13; Ezek. 16:8). At other times a symbolic gesture was attached to the verbal commitment, such as the granting of a gift (Gen. 21:28-32), the eating of a meal (Gen. 26:28-30; Exod. 24:11), the setting up of a memorial (Gen. 31:44-54; Josh. 24:27), the sprinkling of blood (Exod. 24:8), the offering of a sacrifice (Ps. 50:5), or the dividing of animals (Gen. 15:10,17-18). Here it is an ancient custom of counting sheep by letting them pass, one by one, under a shepherd's staff held over a convenient passageway (20:37). It is a delightful picture: God will 'count-in' his own sheep. It is implied, of course, that none will be lost. However, God warns that some of the flock will be kept out of the promised land (20:38). These are the ones who continue to **'revolt and rebel against me'**, God says.

In an outburst of irony, Israel is told to **'Go and serve your idols'** (20:39), but the time is coming when the Israelites will be restored and will offer pure worship on Mount Zion to the glory of God. It will be a **'fragrant incense'** (20:41). Ezekiel foresees a day when a purified remnant will worship the Lord on God's holy mountain. God will be glorified among them and they in turn will be ashamed of their sins. In that day, they **'will ... listen'** to what God has to say (20:39; cf. 20:8).

It had been Israel's consummate failure from the start that they did not listen to God. Ezekiel had been warned about it at the beginning of his ministry (2:7-8; 3:6-7,10-11, 27). Unlike the heathen idols which, being dead, are dumb, God speaks, and when he does we are meant to listen. We find this theme throughout the Old Testament. Take the Law: 'Love the Lord your God, listen to his voice' (Deut. 30:20). Or the Psalms: 'Today, Oh that ye would hear his voice'(Ps. 95:7, RV). Or the Prophets — God told Jeremiah that Israel's 'stubbornness' of heart showed itself in precisely this way: 'These wicked people ... refuse to listen to my words' (Jer. 13:10).This was the cause of Israel's eventual judgement: 'When I called, they did not listen; so when they called, I would not listen' (Zech. 7:13; cf. Jer. 21:10-11). It is a failure of which we today are often guilty. Ezekiel sees a day of renewal when God's people will adopt the attitude of Samuel: 'Speak, Lord, for your servant is listening' (1 Sam. 3:9).

The lesson of this chapter is that 'We cannot otherwise worship God with acceptance unless we adopt whatever pleases him as pertaining to our salvation. For if we wish to ... consider that he is in the slightest degree indebted to us, we in this way diminish his glory... And since that was said to his ancient people because they returned to the land of Canaan, how much more ought God's gratuitous goodness to be extolled by us, when his heavenly kingdom is at this day open to us, when he openly calls us to himself in heaven, and to the hope of that happy immortality which has been obtained for us through Christ? [9]

Calvin ended the session on this passage with a prayer in which he gave thanks to God for having 'already entered in hope upon the threshold of our eternal inheritance, and know[ing] that there is a certain mansion for us in heaven after Christ has been received there, who is the head and the first-fruits of our salvation'. It was at this point that 'That most illustrious man, John Calvin, the divine, who had previously been sick, then began to be so much weaker that he was compelled to recline on a couch, and could no longer proceed with the explanation of Ezekiel.'[10] Suffering from haemorrhoids, gall-stones and gout he wrote to his physicians at some length about his health. At the close of the letter he thanks them for taking the time to read about 'my trifles'.[11] Three months later, Calvin was dead. Thus, one of God's giants drew assurance of heaven from Ezekiel's words in chapter 20!

Summary

To provide God's true people with hope for the future, Ezekiel has prophesied about a second exodus, this time from Babylon. Having surveyed the history of Israel from the time of their exile in Egypt to his own day — a period of some 1,200 years — Ezekiel summarizes it in this way: it is a history of rebellion against God's covenant. But a light shines in the distance. It is the anticipation of the new covenant era, when Jews and Gentiles will turn to the Lord and serve him. God's church will not be extinguished. His people are reassured of ultimate triumph. Exile has been necessary, but the future, as Adoniram Judson put it, is as bright as the promises of God.

11.
The sword of the Lord and no intercessor

Please read Ezekiel 20:45 - 22:31

A new chapter begins at 20:45 in the Hebrew text, though our English Bibles have followed ancient versions in their divisions of the chapters. The section consists of four passages, all of which have the word **'sword'** in common (the word occurs nineteen times). It begins with a parable of a forest fire with its accompanying explanation (20:45 - 21:7); then follows a 'song of the sword' (21:8-17); next comes a section about Nebuchadnezzar of Babylon (21:18-27); and finally, a judgement against the nation of Ammon (21:28-32).

A raging forest fire (20:45-21:7)

This section is interesting because it throws light on certain aspects of Ezekiel's ministry among his own people. It appears that he was asked to preach messages that they did not, at first, understand. They accused him of **'telling parables'** (20:49). Whether Ezekiel himself understood what it was that he spoke is also in doubt. Once again, it highlights his complete submissiveness as God's servant. In response to the prophet's appeal, the meaning of the parable is then given (21:1-7).

A forest fire is a potent symbol of destruction, now as in Ezekiel's day. The direction of the fire is repeated three times: it is coming southwards (the Hebrew uses three different words, all meaning 'south'). It is not difficult, with hindsight, to see that Babylon is meant. The Babylonians attacked Judah from the north, hence moving in a southerly direction. Though Babylon is the immediate cause of Judah's destruction, it is clear from the parable that the ultimate cause lies with God. It is God who uses the Babylonians in his judging work. To miss that point is to fail to understand the nature of history as 'his story'.

The parable states that every tree, **'both green and dry'** (20:47), will be burned and in the explanation, where the metaphor changes to that of a **'sword'** slashing at its victim (21:3,4,5), the point is made that no one will escape this judgement (21:4). If only a partial conquest had taken place at the time of Ezekiel's exile, this time (in 598 B.C.) the exile will be complete: **'Then all people will know that I the Lord have drawn my sword from its scabbard; it will not return again'** (21:5).

To add significance to the parable, Ezekiel is now to go about **'groaning'** (21:6,7). And in response to enquiries as to what all this meant, he was to say, **'Because of the news that is coming. Every heart will melt and every hand go limp; every spirit will become faint and every knee become as weak as water'** (21:7). God's judgement **'is coming! It will surely take place.'** We must not think that Ezekiel did not feel the pain of what he preached, fulfilling this role merely as an actor. He was deeply troubled in spirit by the thought of God's judgements. 'Streams of tears flow from my eyes' commented the psalmist, 'for your law is not obeyed' (Ps. 119:136). No form of ministry for the Lord should be done without some measure of empathy with those to whom we minister. We are to weep with those who weep. We are even to weep for those who will not weep for themselves.

The song of the sword (21:8-17)[1]

As we have just seen, Ezekiel has used the word 'sword' to characterize the nature of God's judging work (21:3,4,5). Now, in this section, Ezekiel recites a poem about the 'sword of the Lord'. The sword is sharp, polished; its razor-like edge sparkling in the light (21:9-11). We are meant to imagine it cutting through flesh with ease. Next follows a series of actions, including the sharpening and polishing of the sword (21:11). Just as in the first oracle of the forest fire, Ezekiel is once more called upon to **'cry out and wail'** (21:12). The sword is **'against my people ... the princes of Israel'** (21:12). Using various dramatic gestures (which the prophet possibly enacted) Ezekiel warns his hearers that the sword of the Lord is **'for slaughter'** (21:14). It is God's instrument of **'wrath'** (21:17), that will cause the people to **'melt'** in fear (21:15).

Those who find it hard to think of God bearing a sword need only be reminded that when Joshua stood before Jericho contemplating how the city might be taken, he was confronted by a theophany — an Old Testament appearance of God in human form. The appearance came in the form of a soldier with a drawn sword in his hand — appropriately enough, given the fact that Joshua was a soldier himself and preparing for battle. At first it was not clear against whom the sword was drawn, and so Joshua asked, '"Are you for us or for our enemies?" "Neither," he replied, "but as commander of the army of the Lord I have now come"' (Josh. 5:13-14). The Lord who had promised to be with Joshua as he had been with Moses (Josh. 1:5-9) now came to his help as a warrior armed for war. He assumed the very form of a soldier ready to kill and destroy. The cup of Canaanite iniquity was now full (Gen. 15:16; Lev. 18:24-25), and their doom was now about to unfold. What happened at Jericho, when the entire city was destroyed — apart from Rahab and her family (Josh. 6:21-23) — was 'an anticipation in history of God's final judgement'.[2]

Several commentators cite 'the Battle Hymn of the Republic' as evidence that this graphic language is used by hymn-writers too.

> Mine eyes have seen the glory of the coming of the Lord,
> He is trampling out the vintage where the grapes of wrath are
> stored;
> He has loosed the fateful lightning of his terrible swift sword;
> His truth is marching on.[3]

Can we add the words, 'Glory, glory Hallelujah!' as we read this passage in Ezekiel? Those who are following the Lord have no cause to be afraid of God's sword for it has already alighted upon Jesus Christ. For Christians, this passage in Ezekiel is further evidence that a war is being conducted against all that is evil, that will one day end with victory for God and his people. To those whose lives are bereft of the evidence of sonship this sword has terrible consequences.

When John L. Girardeau returned to Charlston, Virginia, after a defeat in the Southern War of Independence, he preached on why God had not heard their prayers. Certain benefits are withheld, he

suggested, 'for the bestowal of greater ... temporary suffering is but
the prelude to everlasting blessing, short-lived disappointment to
the dawn of unfading honour, and ... truth and right go down beneath
a horizon of darkness and an ocean of storms, only to appear in the
morning glory of an eternal triumph.' In other words, God knows
best what is good for us.

'Jesus as an infirm human being,' he continued, 'staggering
under the curse of a world, prayed that he might be delivered from
suffering the second death. His prayer was unanswered and he died;
but his grave was the scene of death's dethronement and the birth of
millions of deathless souls redeemed from Satan, sin and hell.'

'Hold, Christian brother!' he exhorted his congregation, 'Do not
despair because your prayers for certain blessings have a time been
unanswered. Where is your faith? Where is your allegiance to your
almighty, all-wise, all-merciful Sovereign? Collect yourself. Put on
the panoply of God... Look up. God, your Redeemer and Deliverer,
reigns.

'See he sits on yonder throne, and suns and systems are but the
sparkling dust beneath his feet. Thousands of thousands of shining
seraphs minister before him. Infinite empire is in his grasp ... his eye
is upon his afflicted people.

'See, see, he comes riding upon the wings of the whirlwind
wielding his glittering sword bathed in the radiance of heaven,
driving his foes like chaff before his face, and hastening to the
succour of his saints with resources of boundless power and illim-
itable grace.'[4]

Would not these words have encouraged the congregation?

The sword of King Nebuchadnezzar of Babylon (21:18-27)

Pretending to be the King of Babylon, Ezekiel — who is standing at
some imaginary crossroads — has to decide whether to take his
army eastwards and attack Rabbah of the Ammonites, or to go
westwards and attack Jerusalem (21:20). Ezekiel had to mark out the
two routes by drawing a simple map on the ground. Then, using an
elaborate method of divination — something on which the
Babylonians relied a great deal — Ezekiel portrays the King of
Babylon casting lots (dice), shooting arrows and consulting idols to
indicate possible courses of action (21:21). The lot falls upon

Jerusalem (21: 22). Verse 22 outlines the battle plans, including **'battering rams'** to break down the city walls, a **'ramp'** to scale the city wall and **'siege works'** — wooden or stone structures which the enemy would use to gain cover from attack. Those in Judah will not believe it, partly because those left behind after the siege of 598 B.C. made an oath with King Nebuchadnezzar to be loyal to him (21:23). But they were mistaken; Nebuchadnezzar attacked.

Once more the cause of Judah's downfall is reiterated: **'Because you people have brought to mind your guilt by your open rebellion, revealing your sins in all that you do — because you have done this, you will be taken captive'** (21:24). King Zedekiah will be stripped of his crown (21:25) because he is a **'profane and wicked prince'** (21:25). In a threefold repetition, God declares Jerusalem's immediate future: **'A ruin! A ruin! I will make it a ruin!'** (21:27). In a word of hope at the end of this section, we are told that the kingship will not be restored until Israel's rightful king is given the crown by God himself. Who is this 'rightful king'? Many commentators have seen in this passage a reference to the Shiloh prophecy in Genesis 49, with its promise of a future ruler.

When the old man Jacob pronounced his blessings upon his sons before he died, fulsome though he was in his praise of his favourite son, Joseph, it was Judah who received the highest blessing. It is to Judah, not to Joseph, that Jacob sees his eldest sons bowing (Gen. 49:8). He likens Judah to a crouching lion, and continues:

'The sceptre will not depart from Judah,
   nor the ruler's staff from between his feet ,
until he comes to whom it belongs
   and the obedience of the nations is his'

                            (Gen. 49:10).[5]

No doubt Jacob knew of Judah's leadership among the brothers, and of the faithful way in which he had met the test Joseph had given them. When the brothers came to Egypt to buy grain, they did not recognize Joseph. He accused them of being spies, and acquired from them news of his full brother, Benjamin. He then pretended to make the existence of Benjamin the proof of their story, keeping Simeon as a hostage until they would bring Benjamin to him. When the famine forced the brothers to return to Egypt, Judah guaranteed that he would bring Benjamin back. This promise was severely tested when Joseph planted a silver cup in Benjamin's sack of grain and made accusations of theft. It was Judah who offered himself as a hostage in the place of Benjamin. This act of Judah's demonstrated beyond any doubt his repentance for what he had done to Joseph.

Yet Jacob's blessing goes further still. The blessing Judah received from his dying father assigned to him the rule among the tribes of Israel. Jacob, now in exile in Egypt, gave a prophecy about the future of Judah's rule in a land that he did not at present possess. Jacob was claiming the promise of the covenant given by God to Abraham: that though Abraham's descendants must serve a foreign nation for four hundred years (Gen. 15:13), a blessing to the nations must come through his seed. The Ruler of God's own choosing would one day come, and the sceptre would be his.

This prophecy is recalled again in the last book of the Bible. When the apostle John weeps because there is no one who can open the book of God's decrees, one of the elders in the throne room responds: 'Do not weep! See, the Lion of the tribe of Judah, the Root of David, has triumphed. He is able to open the scroll and its seven seals' (Rev. 5:5). Jesus, the Lamb that was slain, is the descendant promised by the dying Jacob. It is from this ancient promise that Ezekiel now draws comfort, too. Zedekiah, the last king of Judah, failed to convey the obedience to the covenant that ought to have been his testimony. Consequently, his **'day has come'**, his **'time of punishment has reached its climax'**. But even though the house of David is to be humiliated, it will rise again when God grants to it its rightful ruler — his own Son, Jesus Christ. Ezekiel has referred to him before (1:25-28; 17:22) and will do so again at the end of the prophecy.

The sword against the nation of Ammon (21:28-32)

Moab and Ammon were the names of the two sons born of the incestuous relationship between Lot and his two daughters in a cave near Zoar (Gen. 19:37-38). The Israelites regarded them as relatives and were commanded to treat them kindly (Deut. 2:9,19). The Ammonites occupied a territory of land to the north and east of the Dead Sea, roughly what we regard as Jordan today. Its ancient capital city, Rabbah, is what we now know as Amman.

The Ammonites always had expansionist ambitions: in the eyes of the prophets, they were terrorists (Amos 1:13-14) who delighted in casting 'insults' at Israel's misfortunes (21:28). During the period of the judges they assisted Eglon of Moab to subdue Israelite territory (Judg. 3:13); when Saul became king, his first task was to drive them out of Jabesh-Gilead, which they had recently taken (1 Sam. 11:1-11; 12:12; 14:47); in Jehoshaphat's time, the Ammonites and Moabites joined together to raid Judah (2 Chron. 20:1-30), and Joash was slain by an Ammonite, Zabad, and a Moabite, Jehozabad (2 Chron. 24:26). And shortly after the time of Ezekiel's prophecy, Baalis, King of Ammon, was to deal a disastrous blow against Judah by instigating the murder of Gedaliah, the chief minister and governor of Judah appointed by Nebuchadnezzar at the fall of Jerusalem (Jer. 40:14; 41:15).

Admittedly, some individual Ammonites were friendly with the Israelites: Nahash and Zelek in David's time (2 Sam. 17:27,29; 23:37; 1 Chron. 11:39); Solomon included Ammonite women in his harem — resulting in his idolatrous worship of Molech, the Ammonite god — and Naamah, the mother of Rehoboam, was an Ammonite (1 Kings 14:21,31; 2 Chron. 12:13). Yet, clearly, in general the relationship between Israel and the Ammonites was a hostile one. The prophets lost no time in condemning them (Jer. 49:1-6; Amos 1:13-15; Zeph. 2:8-11). Ezekiel also joined in the attack, both here and later in chapter 25:1-7.

If God's sword is to come down upon Jerusalem, what is going to happen to Israel's enemies? Is God going to punish them as well? The question is raised because earlier (21:20-21) Nebuchadnezzar was depicted as standing at a cross-roads deciding whether to attack Jerusalem or Rabbah, and deciding upon the former.

It seems a natural concern to enquire as to the fate of our enemies. If the church is going to increase, then the cause of our enemies must decrease. Indeed, it was part of God's covenant pattern that he promised to deal with the church's enemies (Deut. 30:1-10) — something that Jesus himself reiterated when he assured his disciples: 'I will build my church, and the gates of Hades will not overcome it' (Matt. 16:18). When Joshua was confronted by the commander with his drawn sword, he was reassured that the divine presence had come to fight on Israel's behalf. That he had also come to root out sin within Israel becomes apparent as the story of the

conquest moves from Jericho to Ai, and the consequent execution
of Achan (Josh. 7). But the reassurance lay in the knowledge that if
God was *for* his people, then he was *against* Israel's enemies. Every
Christian receives this same assurance by his participation in the
gospel (Rom. 8: 31-38). This explains why the Ammonites are told
by Ezekiel that resistance is futile: they might as well **'return the
sword to its scabbard'** (21:30) despite what their diviners might be
saying (21:29). The Babylonians, **'brutal men ... skilled in destruction'** (21:31), will be God's instrument of **'wrath'** upon the
Ammonites; they will become **'fuel for the fire'** (21:32).

No intercessor!

John Knox, in the final two days of life, and in great physical
discomfort, informed his friends that he had spent the last two days
battling on behalf of the church. He ended his days doing the work
of an intercessor. Intercessory prayer has been practised by all the
best of God's saints. Think of Abraham, the father of the faithful,
praying for his son Ishmael: 'If only Ishmael might live under your
blessing!' (Gen. 17:18); or pleading on the plains of Mamre on
behalf of Sodom (Gen. 18:16-33). Think of many instances in which
we read that Moses and Aaron fell on their faces before the Lord
(Num. 14:5; 16:4,22,45; 20:6). Think, too, of Paul, pleading for
Christians that they might be strengthened with power in Ephesians
3:14-19. These are just a few of God's intercessory giants.

In Ezekiel's day, no intercessors could be found for Jerusalem:
her fall came about because no intercessor was prepared to stand
between the city's sin and God's wrath. There have been times when
the entire course of history has been changed by the prayers of God's
intercessors.

This had been the case some 150 years earlier, too: in Isaiah we
read of a time of trouble when God sought in vain for an intercessor,
but there appeared to be no one who loved the people of God enough,
or who had sufficient faith in his power to deliver, to intercede on
their behalf: 'He saw that there was no man, and wondered that there
was no intercessor' (Isa. 59:16, NKJV). If there had been an
intercessor, God could have given deliverance; without an intercessor his judgements came down:

'No one calls on your name
  or strives to lay hold of you;
for you have hidden your face from us
  and made us waste away because of our sins'

(Isa. 64:7).

The northern kingdom of Israel fell for lack of an intercessor. The southern kingdom of Judah is about to go the same way — and for the same reason.

When Richard Strauss saw Germany destroyed by the wickedness of the Third Reich, and the famous Munich opera house bombed, he composed a work for twenty-three string players which he entitled *Metamorphosen*. It is said to be his greatest work, though tragedy and pain are evident from the opening bars. The fall of Jerusalem must have brought a tremendous sense of shock, too, for God's people in exile. For some, it was their home; and even if they did not live in Jerusalem, they loved the city as the place of worship and festival. All their hopes and aspirations were tied in with the fate of this city.

For several years now, Ezekiel had been predicting its collapse. What was the reason for its demise? Why did God bring such ruin upon that city, which the psalmist had described as 'beautiful in its loftiness, the joy of the whole earth ... the city of the Great King'? (Ps. 48:2). The answer is given in the opening verses of this chapter: it is because of an entire catalogue of sins committed by Jerusalem's inhabitants.

A register of sins (22:1-16)

We all recall days in school when a register was kept indicating our presence at, or absence from, school. Names were meticulously read out each morning, checking on every pupil. God keeps a record of our sins, too. The Great Assize will reveal his marks against our character for each day's actions. The inhabitants of Jerusalem are given a preview of what that day will be like as Ezekiel reads out a directory of shortcomings on their part.

Seven times in this section Ezekiel highlights the words **'blood'** or **'bloodshed'**. The people of Jerusalem are bloodthirsty, violent people. Their behaviour has reached the attention of God and they are now called to account for it. What follows is, perhaps, the longest catalogue of sins anywhere in the Bible. In the style of a legal argument, Ezekiel outlines their sins, general and specific, religious and secular. God is the Judge and Jerusalem the defendant.

The crimes against God include: violence (22:3), idolatry (22:3), dishonouring parents — a violation of the fifth commandment (22:7) — mistreating resident aliens, orphans and widows (22:7), breaking the Sabbath (22:8), slander (22:9), eating sacrifices at various mountain shrines (22:9), sexual deviances, including adultery and incest (22:10-11), bribery, usury and extortion (22:12). As to the extent of this depravity, Ezekiel mentions that even the leaders were engaged in it (22:5). By way of a summary of their condition, they are described as having **'forgotten'** God (22:12).

Back on the plains of Moab, before Israel had ever entered the promised land of Canaan, Moses had warned them not to forget the Lord: 'Remember how the Lord your God led you all the way in the desert these forty years, to humble you and to test you in order to know what was in your heart, whether or not you would keep his commands. He humbled you, causing you to hunger and then feeding you with manna, which neither you nor your fathers had known, to teach you that man does not live on bread alone but on every word that comes from the mouth of the Lord. Your clothes did not wear out and your feet did not swell during these forty years. Know then in your heart that as a man disciplines his son, so the Lord your God disciplines you' (Deut. 8:2-5).

These were very significant words, for they were designed to underline in the minds of the Israelites the importance of remembering who they were and what God had done for them. But the history of Israel is one of 'forgetting God'. They failed to profit from the activity of God in their lives.

As if anticipating this failure and its many causes, Moses goes on to warn them: 'When you have eaten and are satisfied, praise the Lord your God for the good land he has given you. Be careful that you do not forget the Lord your God, failing to observe his commands, his laws and his decrees that I am giving you this day. Otherwise, when you eat and are satisfied, when you build fine houses and settle down, and when your herds and flocks grow large and your silver and gold increase and all you have is multiplied, then your heart will become proud and you will forget the Lord your God, who brought you out of Egypt, out of the land of slavery...

Remember the Lord your God, for it is he who gives you the ability to produce wealth, and so confirms his covenant, which he swore to your forefathers, as it is today' (Deut. 8:10-14,18).

Again and again, then, Israel had been warned to remember God, particularly when they began to increase in wealth. What was said of King Uzziah in Isaiah's day could be written about many in Israel: 'But after Uzziah became powerful, his pride led to his downfall. He was unfaithful to the Lord' (2 Chron. 26:16).

If the register of sins recalls days in the classroom, another gesture is mentioned in verse 13 that also reminds us of a teacher trying to get the attention of disobedient children: **'I will surely strike my hands together'** (22:13). God is calling attention to Israel's sins. He will overcome their stubbornness (22:14) and will send them into exile (22:15). Israel, God says, will once more come to realize, one way or another, that **'I am the Lord'** (22:16).

The melting pot (22:17-22)

It is not that uncommon to see a heap of rusting vehicles, piled up nine or ten high, in a vehicle graveyard. This is the kind of image that Ezekiel now employs to picture Jerusalem. Once God's pride and joy, the city has now become a scrapyard. Israel has become the dross left over after the smelting process has taken place. **'Israel has become dross to me,'** God says (22:17). Ezekiel's hearers must realize that, soon, Jerusalem will be ruined. The exile, God's smelting process, will reduce Israel to dross. Other prophets use the same imagery (Isa. 1:22-25; Jer. 6:27-30; Mal. 3:2-4). While it must be said that the intention of the refining process is to produce something valuable at the end (**'silver'**, 22:20, 22), and this is the emphasis in the other prophets cited, the emphasis here is different. Ezekiel focuses on the worthlessness of the dross. God's **'fiery wrath'** is going to burn against Israel (22:21). When the invasion begins, they will take refuge in Jerusalem for safety (22:20), but far from being a safe haven, they will find that Jerusalem is a furnace. In the **'day of wrath'** (22:24), when Judah will be brought to an end, the land will have **'no rain or showers'** — a sign of God's displeasure (cf. Lev 26:19; Deut. 28:22-24).

The dross (22:23-31)

A society is only as good as its leaders. Various people held power
in ancient Israel, including kings, civil servants, military leaders,
priests, prophets, rich landholders and the wise men. The fall of the
Roman empire is laid at the door of bad government. Roman skill at
government soon gave way to expediency when later emperors tried
to force revenue out of people who could not pay. Bad leadership
explains the fall of Jerusalem, too.

Five particular branches of government are singled out for
rebuke: **'princes'**, that is, kings (22:25)⁶ **'priests'** (22:26), **'officials'** (22:27), **'prophets'** (22:28) and wealthy landholders, **'the
people of the land'** (22:29). This establishment collusion in evil lay
behind Israel's downfall. By imposing heavy taxation, the kings of
Judah have been the cause of many deaths. As a result of imprison-
ment and death many women have been left widows (22:25). The
priests have not taught God's law and have encouraged immorality
and godlessness (22:26). The civil servants, instead of protecting the
people, have made money by dishonest means (22:27). The prophets, false prophets that is, instead of condemning the sins of the
leaders, ignored them and were guilty of **'whitewash'** (22:28). And
the wealthy landowners exploited the poor.

Things have not changed in our own day. It is the cry of people
all over the world that the establishment is guilty of crimes against
humanity and against God. Ezekiel is not suggesting that the
ordinary people were guiltless. Far from it! But leaders have a
particular responsibility for which they must give account. It is these
leaders that he now has firmly in his sights.

Is there any hope for Judah and its capital city? Can anyone save
her from her forthcoming doom? Ezekiel now imagines a man who
could stand in the way of God's wrath and protect the city from
destruction. He looks for someone who might act as a defensive wall
against a landslide of anger: **'I looked for a man among them who
would build up the wall and stand before me in the gap on behalf
of the land so that I would not have to destroy it'** (22:30). He
imagines someone who might intercede on behalf of Jerusalem and
save her from ruin, someone who might 'stand in the gap'.

In Psalm 106, the psalmist recalls how God threatened to destroy
the Israelites in the wilderness because of their rebellious hearts. But
he did not. Why? The answer is due to something Moses did:

'They forgot the God who saved them,
   who had done great things in Egypt,
miracles in the land of Ham
   and awesome deeds by the Red Sea.
So he said he would destroy them—
   had not Moses, his chosen,
stood in the breach before him
   to keep his wrath from destroying them'

                                 (Ps. 106:21-23).

Moses 'stood in the breach'! The story is worth remembering. When the Israelites were found worshipping a golden calf and engaged in an orgy of immoral behaviour at the foot of Mount Sinai, God's anger was kindled and 3,000 people died. But God's anger was appeased by Moses' prayer on their behalf. He acted as an intercessor and saved Israel from destruction in the wilderness. Even before he saw their rebellion in person, he engaged in prayer to God for their rescue and pardon: 'O Lord, why should your anger burn against your people, whom you brought out of Egypt with great power and a mighty hand? Why should the Egyptians say, "It was with evil intent that he brought them out, to kill them in the mountains and to wipe them off the face of the earth"? Turn from your fierce anger; relent and do not bring disaster on your people. Remember your servants Abraham, Isaac and Israel, to whom you swore by your own self: "I will make your descendants as numerous as the stars in the sky and I will give your descendants all this land I promised them, and it will be their inheritance for ever "'(Exod. 32:11-13). Later, Moses went even further in his boldness in prayer. His precise words are deeply moving: 'Oh, what a great sin these people have committed! They have made themselves gods of gold. But now, please forgive their sin — but if not, then blot me out of the book you have written"' (Exod. 32:31-32).

Moses' prayer of intercession, in which he honoured God, pleaded the integrity of God's covenant with Israel and volunteered himself as a substitute of punishment on Israel's behalf, is one of the Bible's most moving and daring prayers. It was by means of this prayer that he moved the heart of Almighty God. An old theologian once said that prayer is the shadow of omnipotence. Mighty things can be accomplished by intercessory prayer. It is not a denial of God's sovereignty to say, 'Prayer changes things,' because it is by prayer that God's mighty will is done.

Another example of intercession is that of Aaron and Hur holding up Moses' arms in the battle against the Amalekites. So long as they held up his arms, the battle against the Amalekites prevailed. As soon as they allowed his arms to fall, the battle waned (Exod. 17:8-13).

The point is, however, that no such intercessor can be found in Ezekiel's day. No one can be found to 'stand in the gap' on Jerusalem's behalf. What the church needs most is someone who will engage in the strategic work of prayer for the defence and advance of the kingdom. If such a person could not be found in Ezekiel's day, in the mercy of God he could be found when the exile came to an end, some fifty years later. Daniel was such a person. We learn that, despite the fact that Cyrus issued a decree allowing the Jews to return home in the first year of his reign (Ezra 1:1-4), Daniel remained in Babylon and was still there some two years later (Dan. 10:1-4). Why? Why did he not return to his beloved Jerusalem? For one thing, he was an old man by now. But the explanation lies elsewhere. Daniel knew of the opposition to the rebuilding programme (described in the book of Nehemiah). Indeed, the work of rebuilding the temple had almost come to a complete stop. What they needed was someone to pray the work through these difficult days: 'At that time I, Daniel, mourned for three weeks' (Dan. 10:2). He was prepared to pray for something he himself would never see. He sacrificed his twilight years in the ministry of intercession on behalf of God's church. He became an intercessor, someone who would 'stand in the gap'.

The sad feature of this chapter is the lack of an intercessor. But behind it lies the shadow of the one whose intercession would be mighty before God. The coming of Jesus Christ into the world was in order to provide sinners with one who would stand 'in the gap' between God and man. We have only to look at him as he appears in John 17, pleading with his heavenly Father on behalf of his people: 'I pray for them ... for those you have given me, for they are yours' (John 17:9). 'Therefore he is able to save completely those who come to God through him, because he always lives to intercede for them' (Heb. 7:25). Where darkness lay over Jerusalem in the late fifth century B.C., a bright light now shines at the right hand of God. There Jesus continually pleads on behalf of his own. We are to intercede on behalf of others knowing that he intercedes on our behalf. The problem with us is that we take our eyes off him. When folk have their eyes on Jesus they intercede with mighty power. God is looking for intercessors and we need to take our Saviour as our example. We need to listen to him as he intercedes for us in John 17. By what right does he intercede? His wounds have won for him the right to come before his Father's presence and plead for us.

In 1863, during the American Civil War, Stonewall Jackson was accidentally shot by his own troops. His body was laid in state in the Capitol in Richmond, Virginia, for two days before his funeral in the Presbyterian Church in Lexington. Tens of thousands of mourning Confederate troops crowded the capitol building during those short days. As the sun was setting on the last day of viewing, the marshal gave orders for the great doors of the state chamber to be closed. Hundreds of sad people would thus be excluded from paying their last tribute. Just before the gates were shut, a rough-looking Confederate veteran in tattered grey uniform pushed and shoved his way forward, tears running down his bearded cheeks. The marshal in charge was about to push the man down the steps when suddenly he lifted up the stump of his right arm and cried out, 'By this right arm which I gave for my country, I demand the right of seeing my general one more time.' The Governor of the Commonwealth of Virginia happened to be standing nearby and ordered the marshal to let the old veteran in with these words: 'He has won the entrance by his wounds'[7] (cf. Rev. 5:6-10).

By faith in Jesus Christ, we too have entrance into the Father's presence. Indeed, Jesus wants us to be intercessors. Teaching his disciples to pray, he said, '*Our* Father ... Give *us* this day *our* daily bread...' (Matt. 6:9,11).

One such was Jeremiah Calvin Lamphier of New York. After pleading with God to show him what he ought to do, he began a prayer meeting for businessmen in the city on 23 September 1857. The meeting was to last for one hour. The first half-hour he was alone, then one, then another and eventually five people joined him. The following week the numbers grew to twenty, and the following week to forty. This meeting was so good that they decided to have a daily prayer meeting. After a few weeks the numbers had grown to over a hundred, and by 23 October, Lamphier called upon the newspaper editors to take notice of what was happening in the city. After three months the numbers had reached four figures and after six months some twenty-five different prayer meetings were held throughout the city. It was the beginning of revival in America that saw some two million souls added to the church. It began by the prayer of intercession of one man.

Isaiah, who had known the disappointment of finding no intercessors in his day (Isa. 59:16), saw another day in which watchmen were posted on the walls to pray constantly for Jerusalem (Isa 62:6-7). But Ezekiel did not. In his day there was no one to stand in the gap.

Summary

A fire is said to sweep through the land from south to north. The fire becomes a sword in the hands of Nebuchadnezzar, King of Babylon. He has come to fight against Israel and the peoples related to her. The God who fights for his people promises a glorious future. The church continues to grow despite all that Satan has thrown in its path. But the end of the wicked is sure, too: it is destruction. There is no hope for those who remain God's enemies. Without reconciliation, the sword is even now hanging, like the sword of Damocles, above our heads!

12.
Oholah and Oholibah:
a tale of two cities

Please read Ezekiel 23:1-49

This chapter follows closely the theme of chapter 16. Both describe Israel's sinful ways in terms of marital unfaithfulness; both use similar language to convey God's sense of outrage. If, as we noted earlier, chapter 16 proved difficult for Spurgeon to read to his Victorian audience, chapter 23 is even more graphic in its language.

A tale of two cities

The story tells of two women, Oholah and Oholibah, **'daughters of the same mother'** (23:2). They are allegorical representations of two cities: Samaria, the capital of Israel in the north, and Jerusalem, the capital of Judah in the south. The nature of the offence, and the hurt that follows, is immediately apparent at the outset of the allegory: **'They became prostitutes'** (23:3) and **'They were mine'** (23:4). Both kingdoms had a common ancestry in Egypt, where the beginnings of their sinful ways can be discerned (23:3; cf. 20:5-21). The specific nature of the crime is that both Israel and Judah have sought refuge in alliances with Assyria and Babylon; rather than trusting in the Lord, they looked to political treaties and compromise to save them. They have sold themselves like fallen women in the streets of Samaria and Jerusalem. They have cheated their Husband and lusted for gratification wherever it could be found.

The two names given to these 'sisters', **'Oholah'** meaning 'tent' and **'Oholibah'** meaning 'my tent within her', are probably not terribly significant: both convey overtones of the tabernacle (a tent) where God met with his people. Both names, therefore, remind us of God's covenant dealings with Israel and Judah. Nevertheless, 'Both are ... typical sorts of Hebrew names, useful for the story.'[1]

Oholah's story (23:5-10)

Samaria's story is told first. She is described as being **'the older'** (23:4), even though technically she was far and away the younger. Jerusalem is some 3,000 years older than Samaria (which was founded by King Omri in the ninth century B.C.), but since Samaria 'died' first (it was ransacked by the Assyrians in 722 B.C. — Jerusalem was to fall to the Babylonians in 586 B.C.) it is treated as being the older.

Israel's propensity to be taken in by foreign alliances is tragically revealed in Hosea 7:8-13. Though Hosea uses the masculine name 'Ephraim' to describe Ezekiel's 'Oholah', the description is withering. Ephraim 'mixes with the nations' and is no better than a 'flat cake not turned over' (Hosea 7:8). The flat cake in question would be of dough baked either side on hot stones or pressed against the side of an oven. The fact that it is 'not turned over' implies that the cake is burnt on one side, and not cooked on the other — a fine illustration of a 'stormy marriage'.[2]

A few important lessons emerge.

1. God's judgement upon Oholah comes in verse 9, and it underlines a principle we have seen before in chapter 16: that *we get what we ask for; we reap what we sow*. Oholah wanted **'her lovers'** (23:9) and this is what she received. She had spent so much time with the Assyrians that God gave her over to them. Consequently, Oholah became a slave of the Assyrians. This illustrates an important truth: that those who serve sin become the slaves of sin. If we dally with temptation we soon find that it plants its roots in our hearts and becomes our master. Christians need to have a mind-set that is ruthlessly opposed to sin. Even though as Christians we are 'free from sin' (Rom. 6:18) in the sense that we are no longer its slaves, it soon becomes apparent that sin's presence has not yet been abolished. There is still sin in our hearts and minds. As Christians we are the battleground for the conflict between the flesh and the Spirit, and this underlines the need to mortify sin at all costs before it acquires a hold on our lives. 'Kill sin,' the Puritans would say, 'before it kills you.'

2. Israel's tendency to make alliances with Assyria is likened to a woman plying her lustful trade in the streets. But a warning is given: sin always reaps its reward. **'They stripped her naked, took away her sons and daughters and killed her with the sword. She became a byword among women...'** (23:10).

The lesson, for those who serve sin, seems to be that *sin always has the last word.* Those who give themselves to unlawful sexual gratification will find that, though the pleasure may be momentarily satisfying, the reward is invariably death: the death of disease, broken relationships and guilt. And lest any of us should think that this has nothing to say to us, we need only take note of how many have fallen at this very point. As Frederick Buechner has written, 'Lust is the ape that gibbers in our loins. Tame him as we will by day, he rages all the wilder in our dreams by night. Just when we think we're safe from him, he raises up his ugly head and smirks, and there's no river in the world flows cold and strong enough to strike him down.'[3]

3. Another lesson emerges: 'Therefore let him who thinks he stands take heed lest he fall' (1 Cor. 10:12, NKJV). In an age when holiness is a forgotten word, and that for which it stands a forgotten lifestyle, passages like these should make us tremble and cry out to God that we might be kept from stumbling. Too many evangelists and preachers have fallen at the altar of sexual deviance, only to be reinstated with undue haste. Such behaviour has created the impression that sin is trifling and pardon cheap. Men and women want power and success and will stop at nothing to achieve them. God wants holiness: a way of life that is separate from the world's idea of how things ought to be. It is costly and painful and is the explanation why, at the end of the twentieth century, the Christian church has ditched it. It should be our earnest prayer that God might spare us from becoming a 'byword' among the nations through moral lapses on our part (cf. 1 Kings 9:7; Ps. 44:14).

Oholibah's story (23:11-21)

Ezekiel's listeners, as Judeans, must have appreciated his denunciation of Israel, for ever since the death of Solomon a smouldering civil war had existed between the two nations. They perhaps nodded with solemn approval as the prophet told of God's anger with their northern neighbours. It is something that we do all the time when listening to a finely honed application during the course of a sermon. We can tell immediately for whom it is meant. We are always seeking to avoid the application of the Word of God to our own hearts. What a shock it must have been, then, when Ezekiel turned upon Judah and implied that they were not only as bad as the Judeans, but worse! **'In her lust and prostitution she was more depraved than her sister'** (23:11).

It was not only Israel who had made alliances with Assyria; Judah had done so too (23:12; see 2 Kings 18). And now she was attempting to do the same with Babylon (**'Chaldea'** 23:14), recalling, perhaps, the attempt of King Josiah to ally himself with Babylon and against Assyria in a skirmish with Egypt, a campaign in which good King Josiah lost his life (2 Kings 23:29-30).

Judah had made a **'bed of love'** with Babylon (23:17). She had lusted after the young men like a common prostitute. Whether or not there were actual paintings of Babylonian soldiers on buildings in Jerusalem is not known, but there may well have been, suggesting that Ezekiel meant his description of such paintings to be taken quite literally (23:14-16). It is not too far from the mark to suggest that the scourge of pornography blights our own age also. From the television to magazines, the allurement of illicit sexual pleasure is unabating. It is one reason why we need to be strong in the Lord and in the power of his might: to resist the powerful suggestions of Satan.

Even at the very end — and her fall is only months away — Jerusalem attempted to make alliances with Babylon and Egypt (23:19-21). By promising almost anything, Judah hoped to be free. Here we see the irony of all our lives: in serving sin, we hope to have our freedom; instead we become sin's slaves.

For Judah, dalliance with Babylon meant such things as paying taxes — money or produce — and supplying young men as so much fodder for their latest campaign. For us it might mean something quite different. The devil always exacts some price for his services.

'You have forgotten me...' (23:22-35)

There comes a point in God's dealings with the rebellious when he gives them over to their sinful inclinations. Oholibah (Jerusalem) lusted after her lovers, and lovers were what she got. But there is a twist to the tale: they were not the kind of lovers Oholibah had dreamed about. They were rapists and murderers! In graphic language Ezekiel warns Oholibah: **'They will deal with you in fury. They will cut off your noses and your ears, and those of you who are left will fall by the sword. They will take away your sons and your daughters, and those of you who are left will be consumed by fire. They will also strip you of your clothes and take your fine jewellery'** (23:25-26).

In trusting the Babylonians (made up of several nations, including **'Pekod', 'Shoa',** and **'Koa'** (23:23) — small nations east of the Tigris) Judah was turning her back upon God. She was now following in the footsteps that Israel had taken, 150 years earlier: **'You have gone the way of your sister; so I will put her cup in your hand'** (23:31). For Israel, it had been a path that had led to her destruction in 722 B.C. Judah is to understand that when Babylon comes with her chariots, wagons and war-horses (23:23-24), they will come as God's ambassadors of judgement. It is the Lord who has sent them. It is the Lord who 'delegates' to them the authority to deal severely with Judah: **'I will stir up your lovers against you... I will bring them against you from every side...'** (23:22). It is, perhaps, one of the most sobering truths of God's sovereignty that behind the most barbaric and malicious events of man lies the permissive will of God.

As in the previous chapter (22:12), the root cause of Judah's downfall is spelled out: **'You have forgotten me and thrust me behind your back'** (23:35). They must now **'bear the consequences'**.

The consequences (23:36-49)

The marks of ungodliness are further expanded upon in this section.

Unfaithfulness

Having used the words **'prostitute'** or **'prostitution'** fourteen times in this chapter to describe the sinfulness of Israel and Judah (23:3,5,7,8,11,14,18,19,27,29,35,43,44), in this section Ezekiel also brings in another element of their crime: **'adultery'** (five times, 23:37,43,45).

The prostitution of an unmarried girl was one thing, but prostitution by a married woman added another dimension to the offence, namely adultery. The punishment for adultery in the Old Testament was death by stoning, a sanction that is described for us in verse 47. The point of the tale is to remind Judah that she is God's bride. Ezekiel has described the marriage ceremony in 16:8. In her liaison with Babylon she had not only sold herself to the gratification of her allies, thereby demeaning herself; she had violated the terms of her marriage contract in which she pledged to be faithful.

When the Lord's people sin, they violate the covenant. That is why sin is such an abhorrent thing. This is Paul's great argument at the close of his letter to the Ephesians. He wants to underline the importance of godliness in the marriage relationship. He has some things to say to the husband and how he should love his wife. But it is important to see the basis upon which the apostle makes his advice: 'Husbands, love your wives, just as Christ loved the church and gave himself for her' (Eph. 5:25). And then he goes on a little later to make an even more crucial remark: 'For this reason a man will leave his father and mother and be united to his wife, and the two will become one flesh. This is a profound mystery — but I am talking about Christ and the church' (Eph. 5:31-32).

This is one of the most amazing truths in the Scriptures: that, as Christians, we share in the closest possible relationship with Jesus Christ. It is an intimacy analogous to the 'one flesh' relationship in a marriage. It is the highest expression of love and intimacy. It is a relationship bound by the most solemn obligations of fidelity and trust. To break this relationship is to violate the most precious thing we possess. It is a crime of the highest order. In the realm of marriage, adultery is the hardest sin to forgive. In the spiritual realm, its offence is of the greatest significance. If we imagine the pain brought upon an offended partner by the violation of marriage that adultery brings, we can begin to understand the reaction of God to the sins of his people. It is a violation of the covenant.

Idolatry

Israel and Judah brought shame upon themselves by introducing child-sacrifice into their worship — something which involved killing the infants and then 'passing them through the fire' as **'food'** for the gods (23:37; cf. 16:20; 20:26). In doing so, they **'defiled'**

God's sanctuary and **'desecrated'** the Sabbaths (23:38). In Jerusalem, Jeremiah was making much the same accusations: 'The people of Judah have done evil in my eyes, declares the Lord. They have set up their detestable idols in the house that bears my Name and have defiled it. They have built the high places of Topheth in the Valley of Ben Hinnom to burn their sons and daughters in the fire — something I did not command, nor did it enter my mind. So beware, the days are coming, declares the Lord, when people will no longer call it Topheth or the Valley of Ben Hinnom, but the Valley of Slaughter, for they will bury the dead in Topheth until there is no more room. Then the carcasses of this people will become food for the birds of the air and the beasts of the earth, and there will be no one to frighten them away' (Jer. 7:30-33).

The place where parents tried to buy their own salvation at their children's expense would become an open grave for their own remains! And its name, Topheth, would be a curse: firstly because it sounds like the word *bosheth*, meaning 'shame'; and secondly, because the Valley of the son of Hinnom where these rites took place would become Jerusalem's rubbish tip, whose shortened name Gehenna meets us as the New Testament word for hell! There could be no greater indication of Israel's and Judah's crime than that their sanctuary would become synonymous with hell. It is the same order of thought that prompted the Westminster Divines to suggest that some churches can become a 'synagogue of Satan'.[4]

Vulgarity

Israel's history is depicted in terms of a prostitute's attempts to make herself attractive: **'You bathed yourself for them, painted your eyes and put on your jewellery. You sat on an elegant couch, with a table spread before it on which you had placed the incense and oil that belonged to me'** (23:40-41). Although she is **'worn out'** (23:43) or 'old' she uses her husband's gifts of love and gaudily presents herself to her male admirers. Instead of remaining faithful to her husband she sells herself to **'Sabeans'** (a word that can be rendered 'drunkards from the wilderness'[5] and is meant to signify the depths to which Israel is prepared to sink to acquire her gratification).

Samaria and Jerusalem are guilty; they are both **'lewd women'** (23:44). Guilty of adultery and murder, crimes which incur the death penalty, they face a future of '**terror and plunder**' (23:46). Once again, God will bring upon them the curses of the covenant.

The tawdry behaviour of the Old Testament church is a reminder of how often the church has sought to make illicit alliances ever since. Today we face the spectacle of the contemporary church seeking union with those who deny the gospel. Ecumenical compromise, whereby the church sells herself for sake of union to the nearest admirer, is a replica of the church in Ezekiel's day looking to Babylon for salvation.

The chapter closes with no word of encouragement for Jerusalem. Ezekiel 'allows the curtain to drop without one gleam of hope as to the future. He sees that the hammer of the law in its strongest form is needed to break the hard and stony heart of the people. So urgent was the call for a work of conviction, and so great the danger of that not being effectually wrought, that he would not drop a word which might lighten the impression of guilt upon their minds, or afford the least excuse for delay. His message was, Now or never.'[6]

There are times when we need to feel the full force of God's anger with our sin without immediately receiving the comfort of his forgiveness. There are times in our presentation of the gospel when it is appropriate to allow the unconverted to feel the full effect of the law condemning them for their sins. There are times when it is inappropriate to immediately apply the gospel to those whose conviction of sin is only slight. This seems to have been the way Jesus dealt with the rich young man in Mark 10:17-31. Whereas many a modern evangelist would have urged him to believe on Jesus Christ and sign a pledge card, Jesus allowed him to go away under the full force of the law's condemnation of his covetous nature. That is the way Ezekiel conveyed God's wrath in this chapter.

A question arises from this chapter about the nature of God's dealings with his people — then and now. One the one hand, God speaks of the Israelites as being in covenant with him (16:8,60,62). The use of the word '**adultery**' (23:37,43) implies a marriage relationship. God has bound himself to these people (Israel and Judah) in a way that he has not done with other nations. They are his elect. On the other hand, the Israelites have broken the covenant (16:59; 17:18-19). They have '**forgotten**' their Husband (23:35), and must bear the '**consequences**' and suffer the '**penalty**' (23:35,49). God is about to 'divorce' his people for their unfaithfulness. A series of questions arises, therefore: Are true believers cast off? If God elects his people from eternity, how can they be cast away for their unfaithfulness? Do the elect persevere?

These questions are at the heart of the biblical presentation of the gospel. The answer to them lies in the understanding of the covenant between God and Israel. Although God remains firm as to his covenant, the Israelites evidently did not. There are those who in one sense at least are in the covenant, but who are cast away because of their unfaithfulness. There are others who, by their faithfulness, continue to prove God's favour and blessing. There are, within the covenant, those who are 'illegitimate children' who are eventually cast away.[7] There are also those who are the true children of God and receive all the blessings that issue from that covenant relationship (Readers are referred to the 'Focus on the nature of the covenant'). As Paul comments in his letter to the Romans, 'For not all who are descended from Israel are Israel' (Rom. 9:6).

Summary

The sinfulness of Israel and Judah, focused on their respective capital cities of Samaria and Jerusalem, has been portrayed in terms of an allegory of two fallen women: Oholah and Oholibah. The depth of the treachery, sinking into the mire of prostitution and adultery, is shocking. God's Old Testament church has committed the gravest of transgressions against the covenant. She has violated the bond of marriage.

13.
'Something's burning!'

Please read Ezekiel 24:1-27

Most households have experienced the time when a saucepan has been left on the cooker and its contents allowed to boil dry. The result is thick black smoke and a ruined saucepan. For a community that spent a great deal of time gathered around a fire, watching a pot gently warming the evening meal, an illustration of this kind was bound to have an immediate effect. Ezekiel uses it to make a homely and stinging truth about the current condition of Israel.

It is winter, possibly January 588 B.C. (24:1). It is an important date for it marks the beginning of the siege of Jerusalem, which was to last for two years. The prophecies of previous chapters have now begun to be fulfilled. Every word which Ezekiel now speaks takes on added weight and significance: doubters would only have to hear the latest news from Jerusalem to know that these were words to reckon with, and take to heart. God's warnings have a habit of being fulfilled. The scoffers need to be warned.

The cooking-pot (24:1-14)

Referring to a cooking-pot, Ezekiel now enlarges on an idea first mentioned in 11:3, where the people's oft-cited 'parable' stated that just as meat belongs in a cooking-pot, so they belonged in Jerusalem. God's response to their arrogant claim is to inform them that they will be hurled out of the pot (11:11). Once again, Jerusalem is the pot and its inhabitants the meat, but this time instead of hurling it away, God leaves the meat in the pot to boil until it is burnt. Instead of a tasty soup being produced, the pot is corroded, making the stew inedible. The cook, perceiving the concoction to be useless, pours out the liquid, leaving the pot on the fire. The dry remnants now burn due to the heat of the blaze, eventually scalding the contents and melting the pot itself. The scene, instead of one of domesticity, is one of destruction. They are to make no mistake about it: Jerusalem is going to be destroyed.

The error of the people of Judah in the sixth century is a common one. It is to infer that God's promise to the church is going to include them, no matter what the condition of the church's members may be. This is an error that mistakenly identifies all *professing* believers as the *true* people of God. The inhabitants of Jerusalem felt a natural confidence in their own powers since they had successfully withstood the Assyrian onslaught upon Judah over a century earlier (2 Kings 18:17-19:36). They had reasoned that since Jerusalem was the chosen city of God (Deut. 12:5,11) all its inhabitants were necessarily safe and secure; so long as the outward symbols of the faith were maintained, the people had every reason to believe that God would identify them as his own and preserve them. But they were wrong.

Theirs was an error of *presumption*. It was partly this error that Jesus had in mind when he warned the church to 'guard against the yeast of the Pharisees and Sadducees' (Matt. 16:6). The Pharisees took enormous pride in their descent from Abraham, and founded their entire security upon their natural lineage. It was a fatal error. 'Man,' Samuel was told by the Lord, 'looks at the outward appearance, but the Lord looks at the heart' (1 Sam. 16:7). Within the church, even among those who profess to be genuine Christians, there are those whose hearts are not made new. Commenting on Ezekiel 18:24 and the words, 'But if a righteous man turns from his righteousness', Calvin says, 'Many hypocrites make use of the name of God, and openly boast themselves pre-eminent in the Church, but inwardly they are wolves.'[1]

As we saw earlier, the difference between those who have no genuine faith and Christians who backslide is that in the latter case their 'inner seal' remains and they eventually are restored to repentance. Their fall is not permanent. '"The Lord knows those who are his"' (Num. 16:5; 2 Tim. 2:19).

We are to be 'eager to make [our] calling and election sure,' Peter says, by ensuring that the fruits of the Spirit — goodness, knowledge, self-control, perseverance and godliness — are manifested in

our lives (2 Peter 1:5-10). It is the error of countless numbers of
people that because they are in possession of the outward symbols
of Christianity, they supose they are therefore partakers of its
inward, spiritual reality. There can be no greater, or more costly
error. It is one that leads to eternal ruin.

It is also an error of *antinomianism*. The people of Judah had
convinced themselves of their security, no matter how they lived!
The promises belonged to them, no matter how disobedient they had
become to the law of God. This too is an error that is current in the
church today: the idea that since a person is saved by grace, apart
from the works of the law, no amount of ungodliness or ungodly
behaviour can rob someone of his or her eternal security once a
profession of faith in Jesus Christ has been made: 'Once saved,
always saved.' But this is seriously to misunderstand the nature of
God's saving activity. Those whom the Lord saves, he invariably
gives a spirit of holiness. Without it, a person cannot entertain the
assurance of salvation (Heb. 12:14). It is the repeated charge of the
prophet in these chapters that Judah (and Israel before them) had
broken God's covenant. They had failed to keep their side of the
promise. They had violated the terms of the treaty.

The prophet Malachi issued a similar warning to a generation of
Israelites who were divorcing their own wives and marrying
pagans, contrary to the laws of Moses, saying to them, 'But you have
turned from the way and by your teaching have caused many to
stumble; you have violated the covenant...' (Mal. 2:8). The Israelites throughout their generations were guilty of a false confidence
in the fact that they were descended from Abraham. They felt
themselves safe, no matter what evidence of godliness and separation was missing in their lives. It is not that the prophet is
suggesting that works play a part in man's salvation. They do not.
Salvation is of grace from beginning to end. But the evidence of
grace is a life that is devoted to the service of God. Even the works
which a Christian is obligated to demonstrate in his life are works
which God has 'prepared in advance for us to do' (Eph. 2:9-10).

Having witnessed too many 'converts' whose lives remained
unchanged, D. L. Moody exclaimed, 'It is a great deal better to live
a holy life than to talk about it. Lighthouses do not ring bells and fire
cannon to call attention to their shining — they just shine!'[2]

It is also an error of *wilfulness*. **'I tried to cleanse you but you
would not be cleansed...'** (24:13). They willed to sin and sinned

because they willed it. They continued in their sin because their will would not have it any other way! There is a point when all the entreaties and invitations, or even admonitions and threats, have no effect any more. Folk are determined to carry out what they have set their hearts upon to do. It is professing Christians whom the writer to the Hebrews warns: 'If we deliberately keep on sinning after we have received the knowledge of the truth, no sacrifice for sins is left, but only a fearful expectation of judgement and raging fire that will consume the enemies of God... How much more severely do you think a man deserves to be punished who has trampled the Son of God under foot, who has treated as an unholy thing the blood of the covenant that sanctified him, and insulted the Spirit of grace? For we know him who said, "It is mine to avenge; I will repay," and again, "The Lord will judge his people." It is a dreadful thing to fall into the hands of the living God' (Heb.10:26-31; cf.12:29). Only so long as we 'run with perseverance the race marked out for us' is there peace and assurance (Heb.12:1-3).

In a summary outburst, the Lord concludes his denunciation of Jerusalem's violations with a fourfold summary of his judgement in verse 14. It is *definite*: **'I the Lord have spoken.'** This is no idle threat! It is *imminent*: **'The time has come for me to act.'** *It is irrevocable*: **'I will not hold back; I will not have pity, nor will I relent.'** *It is unquestionably fair*: **'You will be judged according to your conduct and your actions.'**

It seems as though the threats of judgement issuing from God had no possible bearing upon them at all. They were not in need of any warnings. They were safe and secure. All this talk of judgement upon those who violate God's covenant was academic, even unnecessary. Many Christians feel this way when faced with a series of sermons on Ezekiel. Its harsh, unrelenting notes of warning and rebuke must surely be meant for someone else. Instead, God intended this word as a warning to the captives in Babylon. Ezekiel's voice, after all, could not be heard in Jerusalem!

Submitting a sorrowful heart (24:15-27)

In the midst of this chapter is an incident that must surely be one of the saddest and most difficult in Scripture. Ezekiel's wife dies and the prophet is asked to use her death, and his response to it, as an illustration to the exiles of the way they are to respond to what is going to take place in Jerusalem. He was to hide his grief and show no mourning.

It is one of the consummate features of the prophet that he has revealed so little of himself in this work. Many readers of Ezekiel have found this to be its weakness. But on the contrary, it is Ezekiel's strength that he so willingly complied with the Lord's request that he become nothing and that God be magnified. At no point does Ezekiel give way to his feelings as, say, Jeremiah does time and again. We can identify with Jeremiah's sense of frustration, but Ezekiel is different: he comes over as aloof and bland. Yet it is the greatness of Ezekiel's testimony that, in order for God's Word to be magnified, he himself hides behind it entirely. Nowhere is that seen more graphically than in this incident.

Ezekiel is told beforehand of his wife's imminent death (24:16). It is possible that she may have been ill for some time, but the passage seems to infer that the death was sudden: **'with one blow'**. It appears that she was fine in the morning and died that evening (24:18). Death can be sudden. It is a reminder that none of us knows what the next hour may bring. Without so much as a moment's notice we can find ourselves in eternity. It behoves us to be ready to die. 'Live each day,' urged Bishop Ken, 'as if thy last,' and he was right.

Interesting also is the insight into the prophet's love for his wife: **'the delight of your eyes'** (24:16). It adds to the difficulty of what Ezekiel is called upon to do for the Lord that his affection for her is highlighted in this way. The task which God calls his servant to perform is remarkably difficult. We cannot ever assume beforehand what God might ask us to do. Nevertheless, however difficult it may be, God assures us that he will provide the grace sufficient for its accomplishment: 'God is faithful; he will not let you be tempted beyond what you can bear. But when you are tempted, he will also provide a way out so that you can stand up under it' (1 Cor.10:13).

Ezekiel was not allowed to mourn in any way. Five typical ways are mentioned: groaning, removing his priestly turban, removing his sandals, covering his mouth and eating a funeral meal (cf. Jer 16:7). It was when people noticed his lack of mourning that they asked what this might signify (24:19). Just as Ezekiel did not mourn the loss of his wife, so the Israelites in captivity were not to mourn the destruction of Jerusalem (24:22-23). The reason for this may be, as Stuart suggests, that it was inappropriate to mourn in the case of capital punishment.[3] Others have suggested that no amount of mourning would be adequate to reflect the catastrophic loss Israel suffered at the hands of the Babylonians. In the destruction of Jerusalem and its temple, it effectively meant that God had abandoned Israel and that God's presence would be no longer among them. The event 'would be too great for resort to formal grief'.[4]

'The slings and arrows of outrageous fortune...'

A word seems appropriate here about suffering and the Christian life. Ezekiel is called upon to endure severe hardship in the course of duty, and to integrate the experience into his day-to-day walk with God.

Suffering has been described as 'getting what you do not want while wanting what you do not get'.[5] God does not shield any of his children from the trials of this world. Some come because Christians, living the way they do — for God and against the world (Eph. 5:8-14; Heb. 11:7) — actually foster the world's hatred and scorn; and behind it lies the hand of our greatest foe, Satan. Others come as part and parcel of living in a fallen world, under the curse that will, one day, lead it to its ruin. 'Crosses and losses', as the Puritans used to call these, are what we can expect when passing through a troubled environment. More trouble arises because of tensions with inner inclinations which, if left unchecked, lead us into ruination and remorse. Whatever the source, life in this world is punctuated with bad things and we had better get used to it. Ezekiel, holy man that he was, found it to be just so.

Two brief comments seem in order.

Firstly, the trials that Ezekiel faced produced in him, by God's grace, a godly, sanctified character. Pain educates, as the lives of countless saints testify. This is a point Scripture makes again and again (Rom 5:3-8; Heb. 12:7,10-11; James 1:2-4). To keep us from sleeping when we should be awake, God allows us to be prodded every now and then.

Secondly, in a roundabout sort of way, our suffering helps others. Paul put it like this: 'Praise be to the God and Father of our Lord Jesus Christ, the Father of compassion and the God of all comfort, who comforts us in all our troubles, so that we can comfort those in

any trouble with the comfort we ourselves have received from God
... if we are comforted, it is for your comfort, which produces in you
patient endurance of the same sufferings we suffer' (2 Cor. 1:3-6).
The way to handle suffering is to offer it to God (who has allowed
it into our lives) and ask him to make use of it — for the good of
others as well as, ultimately, of ourselves. Ezekiel's powerful and
effective ministry was the result of just such a submissive, unselfish
response to his trouble.

The section ends with a reminder that the fall of Jerusalem is not
far away. Ezekiel's ministry had begun in 593 B.C. (1:2) and it is
now six years later, with Jerusalem's destruction only a few months
away. The reference to Ezekiel mouth **'being opened'** on news of
the city's overthrow has led some to suggest that from the time of
the death of his wife (winter/spring 588 B.C.) until this news of
Jerusalem's fall (August 586 B.C.) the prophet was dumb.[6] More
likely, however, is the interpretation given by Stuart, that this refers
to the prohibition on Ezekiel's engaging in routine conversation
(3:26) — a prohibition that was lifted to allow him to speak to the
'fugitive' from Jerusalem (24:26).[7]

This change in the prophet's manner of speaking signals a
change in the emphasis of the entire book. We are halfway through
and so far the dominant note has been one of judgement and
destruction. From now on a new emphasis emerges — one of
enormous hope and encouragement. At this point, however, the
message is perhaps the worst in Israel's history: Jerusalem is falling
and there is none to lament her. It is one of the saddest moments in
the Bible.

Summary

Jerusalem has been likened to a cooking-pot that has burnt its
contents. Even the pot is melted and out of shape. It is good for
nothing. This is a picture of God's intense anger with those who
presumed they were 'safe in Zion', but whose every moment was
spent in violating the covenant. Covenant-breakers can expect the
curses of the covenant upon them. That is what happened to God's
Old Testament church. In a day of compromise by false ecumenism,

secularism and ritualistic formality, it is a lesson that the church needs to hear. It is not a popular one. Preachers who proclaim it will be despised as Old Testament prophets were. But they need to be faithful as Ezekiel was. His testimony, his willingness to subject his most sensitive feelings in submission to the Lord's overall purpose, is a singular mark of his discipleship. We need to pray for grace to follow in his steps.

Part V
Prophecies against the nations
(Ezek. 25-32)

14.
How the mighty are fallen!

Please read Ezekiel 25:1-28:26

Chapter 25 begins a new section of the prophecy of Ezekiel. The first twenty-four chapters have dealt largely with the future of Jerusalem and Judah. Now the focus of attention turns elsewhere — to the neighbouring nations. They include Ammon (25:1-7), Moab (25:8-11), Edom (25:12-14; 32:29), Philistia (25:15-17), Tyre (26:1 - 28:19); Sidon (28:20-24); Egypt (29:1 - 32:21; 32:31-32), Ethiopia or Cush (Nubia), Libya, Lydia, Arabia and Chub (30:4-9), Assyria (32:22-23), Elam (32:24-26), Meshech and Tubal (32:26-28).

One nation is, of course, missing: Babylon. All these nations would fall to the Babylonian expansionist policy of the seventh century B.C. and, for the time being at least, nothing is being said against this powerful nation. In effect, these chapters summarize the extent of the Neo-Babylonian empire (See Map 1, p.16).

Readers who are unfamiliar with the prophets will find these chapters strange, possibly dull. Their relevance to us is not always immediately apparent. We are reminded, however, that in every part of Scripture there is a doctrine or a lesson in godliness to be learned (2 Tim. 3:16-17).

The corrupting influences of godless neighbours

Commenting on the surrounding nations is something the prophets did continually (cf. Isa. 14:24 - 16:14; Amos 1:3 - 2:3). Nor did they confine their comments to merely spiritual matters. Every social and moral aspect of the behaviour of these nations came under the scrutiny of God's all-seeing eye. Just because they were not in possession of a Bible did not exempt them; their conscience was enough to condemn them. In one of Dryden's poems there is the line: 'Beware the anger of a patient man.'[1] Ezekiel would add the further thought: 'Beware the wrath of a patient God!'

Ammon (25:1-7)

Ezekiel has mentioned the Ammonites before (21:28-32). As we saw in our comments on that passage, Ammon and Moab (25:8-11) were Lot's two sons born of his incestuous relationship with his two daughters. Both were regarded as relatives of Israel, though both treated Israel with contempt.[2]

Ammon's crime was their delight in the downfall of God's kingdom (25:3,6). Not content to watch Judah fall in 586 B.C., Ammon relished it. They clapped and cheered at the desecration of the temple, the desolation of the land of Judah and the deportation of the Judeans to Babylon. It was the sin of glee in the face of another's downfall. 'You shouldn't mock the afflicted,' was a famous line of a late comedian. Behind the quip lies a solemn truth. We all too frequently find our amusement in the misfortunes of others. Ammon's heartless response to the fate of their neighbours was not only wrong, it was also blind; they too would fall (25:4).

The lesson is one of failure to appreciate that the fall of a neighbour is one that can befall us too, apart from the grace of God. Every time we see another fall into sin, even if he is our enemy, we should show no gleeful delight, but rather compassion and thankfulness: compassion, for we are to love even our enemies, and thankfulness that 'There go I, but for the grace of God.'

Moab (25:8-11)

The Moabites occupied land immediately to the south of the Ammonites, in the Transjordan. Like the Ammonites, they were a constant threat to the Israelites.[3] Moab, like Ammon, is depicted as gleeful over Judah's downfall, saying: **'Look, the house of Judah has become like all the other nations'** (25:8). A century earlier Isaiah had depicted Moab as arrogant:

'We have heard of Moab's pride—
  her overwhelming pride and conceit,
her pride and her insolence—
  but her boasts are empty'

(Isa. 16:6).

Moab has learnt few lessons, even from the consequences of the Assyrian invasion that followed Isaiah's warning. Now she boasts again that Judah's God was of no greater significance than any other god. This is the ultimate crime. The Moabites had failed to perceive that Judah's downfall was an act of judgement. Rather, they had depicted it as a sign of weakness. They had failed to reckon on the power of God. They had assumed that Judah's God was one they could safely ignore. Should he exist at all, he was of little significance to them. Countless numbers of people live in this way, in defiance of the reality of God. 'It is a dreadful thing to fall into the hands of the living God' (Heb. 10:31), warns one New Testament writer; but it falls on deaf ears. Moab's sin, that of pronouncing God as surplus to requirements, is one that has been repeated times without number.

It has to be said that one of the reasons why Moab saw Judah as 'like all the other nations' was Judah's own fault. Judah was suffering because she was experiencing the punishment of God due to her sin and waywardness. Her witness to the nations had been one of compromise and worldliness.

Edom (25:12-14)

'Edom' or 'Seir' (25:8) was where Jacob's twin brother Esau went (Gen. 32:3), and 'Edomites' is the Bible's name for Esau's descendants.[4] Following the siege of Jerusalem, Judah was powerless to prevent Edomite raids on southern towns and villages. It is to this 'revenge' that verse 12 refers. Obadiah adds that the Edomites even took advantage of Judeans who fled from the Babylonian armies (Obad. 14).

Ezekiel's prophecy warns that Edom's advantage is short-lived. There will come a day when Judah will not only recapture its lost lands, but conquer Edom also. This appears to be a reference to the subduing of the Edomites by Judas Maccabaeus (the so-called

'Maccabaean Revolt') in 164 B.C. and John Hyrcanus, c.120 B.C.[5] This was to be part of the Lord's **'vengeance'** (25:14). Vengeance is an important aspect of the covenant which the Bible is keen to stress (the word occurs five times in verses 14-17). Following the covenant renewal ceremonies on the plains of Moab, Israel was warned in clear terms: 'I will take vengeance on my adversaries and repay those who hate me' (Deut. 32:41). This truth was underlined later by Isaiah: 'For the Lord has a day of vengeance...' (Isa. 34:8; 61:2), and particularly by Jeremiah (Jer. 46:10; 50:28; 51:11). The 'vengeance of the covenant' is foretold in Leviticus 26:25 and expanded upon in verses 14-45, the broad truth being that God's saving work, the establishment of the covenant of grace, has two sides to it: God will save those who come to him through Jesus Christ; equally, to those who refuse to come, God will mete out the punishment that their sins deserve. It is something Paul is anxious to leave with God: we are not to take on this task ourselves (Rom. 12:19). Those within the covenant can expect to be chastised for disobedience. Those who remain unrepentant have no hope. They are a reminder to us of the need to persevere, yielding our lives as holy offerings to the Lord (cf. Heb. 12:1-14). God loves his people and will never forsake them, but he will chastise them when they fall into sinful ways. Those who abandon the Lord can expect only vengeance. It is a warning Jesus gave to an unbelieving Jerusalem (Luke 19:41-44). (A further prophecy against Edom is to be found in Ezekiel 35.)

Philistia (25:15-17)

The Philistines had been a thorn in Israel's side ever since she first entered Canaan.[6] It is interesting that the word **'hostility'** (25:15) — 'the old hatred' (NKJV) — is the same word ('enmity') used in Genesis 3:15 to describe the continual opposition of Satan to God and his purposes.[7]

The Philistine sin is described as **'vengeance'** (25:15), carried out with 'malice', or 'a spiteful heart'(NKJV). Vengeance, while proper in God as the reflex of his holy nature towards sin, is forbidden in man (Rom. 12:19). Philistine vengeance was nothing other than spite. Their malice would reap God's wrath. The **'Kerethites'** (25:16) will be **'cut off'** — the verb to 'cut off' and the word 'Kereth' (one of the Philistine tribes) sound the same in Hebrew.

The Scriptures encourage us to show forbearance and forgiveness to those whom we regard as our enemies (Eph. 4:2; Col. 3:13). The Philistines (and the Edomites) took every opportunity to get back at the Israelites for perceived wrongs committed in the past. The smallest revenge will poison the soul. The Philistines had become war-mongers; revenge and retaliation characterized the way they lived. The trouble spots of the world today, together with nations whose history is ingrained with hatred for past wrongs, need to take note that the Lord of the nations knows and sees all. He will not tolerate it for ever.

Tyre (26:1 - 28:19)

Does God care about scandals in the Stock Exchange, or Wall Street? Is he concerned at the exploitation by multi-national industries of the poor nations of the world? Does the Christian faith have anything to say about commercial fraud? The answer given by the Old Testament prophets is a resounding 'Yes!' Tyre was the commercial centre of the ancient Middle East, and in the next three chapters it comes under the scrutiny of the divine Accountant and Judge. If the previous chapter had dealt largely with the violence of the nations to the east of Judah, the next three chapters will focus on corruption in the commercial life of the nations to the north-west.

A time reference opens the chapter and informs us that the year is 587-586 B.C. — a few weeks after the fall of Jerusalem. As Ezekiel's companions were coming to terms with the collapse of their own city, they must have wondered at the justice of God in allowing the rich and prosperous people of Phoenicia to the north-west to do so well. Surely it was time for Tyre to fall, too![8]

'Tyre' (26:2) was the capital of Phoenicia,[9] which also included such independent states as 'Sidon' (28:21) and Byblos ('Gebal'[10] in the Old Testament, 27:9). These were all Mediterranean ports and, together with the Philistines, the Phoenicians were the great merchant traders of the ancient Near East, and hence: 'the gate to the nations' (26:2).

During the reigns of David and Solomon, Tyre established good relations with Israel; there is no record of any war between Israel and these Mediterranean coastal states. One moment of co-operation deserves to be mentioned: King Hiram I of Tyre provided wood and craftsmen for Solomon's temple (1 Kings 5:1-18) and sailors for his commercial fleet (1 Kings 9:27).[11]

If relations between Israel and Phoenicia had been generally good, there had been moments of tension over economic matters. As Stuart comments, 'The shipping industry in the Mediterranean had increased in influence to the point that shipping nations like Tyre and Sidon were economic cross-roads, reaping enormous profits from international sea trade, to the consternation of much poorer states such as Judah.'[12] It just so happens that as I write these lines, the headlines of the news bulletins have been relating an incident off the Devonshire coast where British Navy vessels have been called in to investigate accusations of French fishing trawlers having attacked English ships! Tensions between nations over commerce persist!

If the Edomites had taken advantage of Judah's battle with the Babylonians by plundering from the south-east (Obad. 13-14), the Phoenicians had been guilty of the same thing by incursions from the north-west. As Judah suffered at the hands of Babylon, they must have wondered at the relative ease of Phoenician lifestyle, particularly since it was they who profited from the Babylonian invasion of Judah by supplying these foreign armies with goods and services which they had plundered from Judah. If past relationships had been good, present ones were strained. It was time, so Ezekiel's contemporaries no doubt thought, for the folk of Tyre and Sidon to be taught a lesson. They must have listened with eager expectation as Ezekiel turned his focus on the 'fat cats' of the coastal plains.[13]

'A bare rock' (26:1-21)

As an example of engineering, the city of Tyre — built partly on the mainland and partly on an adjacent island (approximately one mile long and half a mile wide) and joined by a causeway — ranked alongside Hezekiah's famous tunnel through which water was supplied to the city of Jerusalem. The city of Tyre was noted for its trade and the sea-faring abilities of its inhabitants. Speaking of their eventual fall, Ezekiel says,

'How you are destroyed, O city of renown,
    peopled by men of the sea!
You were a power on the seas,
    you and your citizens;
you put your terror
    on all who lived there'

(26:17).

'Surrounded by the sea' (27:32), Tyre thought herself impregnable: 'I will prosper' she boasted, seeing Jerusalem's collapse (26:2). Using the fact that in Canaanite/Hebrew its name means 'rock', Ezekiel prophesies that Tyre will be returned to just that: 'a bare rock' strutting out of the sea (26:4). She too, despite her arrogant claims of self-confidence, will be defeated by 'many nations' (26:3), by an invader from the 'north' called 'Nebuchadnezzar' (26:7), i.e. Babylon. This was something Isaiah had foretold a century and a half earlier, saying that even if the people of Tyre crossed over to Cyprus they would find no resting-place (Isa. 23:11-12).

Several features of Tyre's godlessness are recorded.

1. Tyre's dependence on physical resources

Ezekiel provides us with a vivid description of the ensuing battle, including references to Babylon's military power which include 'horses', 'horsemen', 'chariots', 'wagons', 'battering rams', and 'weapons' (26:7-11). But Tyre had her military arsenal, too! Apart from her strategic location — the sea to the west, and the celebrated mountains and forests of Lebanon to the east, thus forming a natural defence — Tyre boasted of her 'towers' (26:4,9), 'walls' (26:9-10) and 'strong pillars' (26:11). But Tyre was no match for Babylon. Her confidence was misplaced. Instead of trusting in the Lord, she trusted in her own ingenuity. Better by far the confidence of the psalmist: 'Some trust in chariots and some in horses, but we trust in the name of the Lord our God' (Ps. 20:7).

2. Tyre put her trust in her leaders

In an astonishing display of humiliation, Tyre's leaders, 'princes of the coast', will wear the clothes of 'terror' instead of 'embroidered garments' (26:16). Twice the psalmist warns of misplaced confidence in rulers: 'It is better to take refuge in the Lord than to trust in princes' (Ps. 118:9), and 'Do not put your trust in princes, in mortal men who cannot save' (Ps. 146:3).

3. Tyre was materialistic

Ezekiel makes specific mention of Tyre's 'wealth', 'loot', 'merchandise', 'fine houses' and especially her 'timber' (26:12). Chapter 27 elaborates upon this aspect of Tyre's failure. It is a timely reminder of the danger of materialism. Isaiah had compared Tyre's commercial activity to prostitution (Isa. 23:15-17) and the figure seems apt: commercialism can easily assume the policy of the highest profit regardless of the means. The love of money *remains* the root of all kinds of evil (1 Tim. 6:10). It is this characteristic of ungodliness which is underlined in the book of Revelation:

'For all the nations have drunk
   the maddening wine of her adulteries.
The kings of the earth committed adultery with her,
   and the merchants of the earth grew rich from her
      excessive luxuries'

(Rev. 18:3).

We need to take heed of our Saviour's warning about the seductiveness of material things: 'Do not store up for yourselves treasures on earth, where moth and rust destroy, and where thieves break in and steal. But store up for yourselves treasures in heaven, where moth and rust do not destroy, and where thieves do not break in and steal' (Matt. 6:19-20).

4. Tyre was fond of the so-called 'good life'

Tyre's streets were filled with the sound of 'noisy songs' and 'music' (26:13). In that sense it is no different from a typical street in any modern city. It is a portrayal of a lifestyle given over to entertainment. It is essentially carefree and pagan. And God will not tolerate it for long.

The end of the wicked

Tyre's fall is complete. She is never to be rebuilt or heard of again (26:21). Her demise is likened to drowning — an apt choice for a seafaring nation (26:19). She will be brought **'down to the pit'** (26:20). This expression is used several times in Ezekiel (28:8; 31:14; 32:18,23,24,25,29,30) and is meant to convey roughly the same as the word 'Sheol' does: namely, the realm of the dead. It is associated with darkness and being lost. 'There is no hope of resurrection, simply a murky continuing existence alongside *the people of old* among the ruins of the past; a dreadful end indeed.'[14]

This prophecy is meant to signify Tyre's destruction, first at the hands of the Babylonians and later by Alexander the Great in a spectacular siege on the city in which he built a causeway out to the island in order to defeat it. Behind it, however, is a general warning to the wicked of what lies in store. There is life after death, no matter what, but the quality of that life depends upon what we have done with God's offer of forgiveness in this life. Those who die in their sins will be sent, as Jesus warned, 'into the darkness, where there will be weeping and gnashing of teeth' (Matt. 8:12).

A funeral dirge (27:1-36)

Chapter 27 is a lengthy lament on the decease of Tyre — something which has not yet happened, of course. Some might ponder as to the possible relevance of this to us today. Surely a chapter like this belongs in the archives, to be examined by specialists in ancient history. It cannot possibly have anything to say to me, today! This is where the principle of universality of application comes in.[15] Since God himself does not change (cf. Heb.13:8), his dealings with folk in a previous generation are a model of his dealings with us today. The self-aggrandizement shown by Tyre in these chapters (cf. **'I am perfect in beauty'**, 27:3), or Jerusalem in Isaiah 1-5 or Rome in Revelation 17-18 will always and everywhere evoke the same hostility. What we find in these Old Testament chapters are the universal principles of God's will and work. If we live like the inhabitants of Tyre, we can expect the same treatment as they received. Passages such as these serve as timely warnings to

Christians whose lives, though changed, are not what they should be, and to non-Christians whose lives need changing in a revolutionary way.

Since Tyre was a seafaring nation, it is apt that a metaphor associated with the sea is used. Tyre is likened to a great ship, built partly of wood from **'Senir'** (Mt Hermon), **'Lebanon'**, **'Bashan'** and **'Cyprus'** (27:5-6). Its sails are made from **'fine embroidered linen from Egypt'**, with deck awnings made from dyed fabrics **'from the coasts of Elishah'** — the non-Phoenician part of Cyprus (27:7). Men of Sidon, **'Arvad'** (an island off the north coast of Phoenicia), and **'Gebal'** (Byblos: another coastal city) are its **'oarsmen'**, **'seamen'** and **'sailors'** (27:8-9).

Changing the picture somewhat, Tyre's land-based army is now described. It consists of mercenaries from **'Persia'**, **'Lydia'**, **'Lybia'**, **'Arvad'**, **'Helech'** and **'Gammad'** (27:10-11).

Moving on to a description of Tyre's commercial life, trade was carried on with almost every conceivable nation east and west of this central coastal region. The list (27:12-23) includes places in what is today Sardinia (**'Tarshish'**), **'Greece'**, Turkey (**'Tubal'** and **'Meshech'**), Armenia (**'Beth Togarmah'**), **'Rhodes'**, Syria (**'Aram'**), the Arabian peninsula: modern Saudi Arabia and Kuwait (**'Dedan'**, **'Kedar'**, **'Sheba'** and **'Raamah'**) and Iraq (**'Haran, Canneh and Eden'**). The list also includes the trade of Judah and Israel (23:17).

As for the merchandise that passed through Tyre's ports, it includes an impressive array of raw materials and finished products, including: **'silver, iron, tin and lead'**, **'bronze'**, **'ivory tusks'** and **'ebony'**, **'turquoise, purple fabric, embroidered work, fine linen, coral and rubies'**, **'wheat'**, **'honey, oil and balm'**, **'wine'**, **'wool'**, **'blankets'**, **'lambs, rams and goats'**, **'spices and precious stones, and gold'**, and **'rugs'**. One need only go to a modern port where ships come and go from the nations of the world, carrying every conceivable kind of merchandise, to imagine how prestigious, and wealthy, Tyre was. Truly, Tyre was the centre of the commercial universe.

This section highlights the danger of pride and the sense of invulnerability that comes with it. Tyre boasted: **'I am perfect in beauty'** (27:3). This is the claim of conceit and arrogance. Scripture warns that it was pride that led to the downfall of both Uzziah and Hezekiah (2 Chron. 26:16; 32:26). It is pride that prevents sinners from seeking after God (Ps. 10:4). God says of it, 'I hate pride' (Prov. 8:13). It is the precursor to destruction (Prov. 16:18), as the next section of this chapter relates.

Pride followed by destruction (27:25-36)

Having likened Tyre to a great ship (27:3-9), Ezekiel portrays Tyre's destruction in terms of a **'shipwreck'** (27:27) caused by **'the east wind'** (27:26), that is, Babylon. Sailors and oarsmen find themselves at the mercy of the sea, drowning in its depths. Others, standing on the shore, look on with grief and shock (27:28-30). They raise a lament of pitiful and sombre tones. It includes much weeping and mourning (27:31).

Two responses to Tyre's demise are noted. First, there are those who are shaken by it:

> **'All who live in the coastlands**
> **are appalled at you;**
> **their kings shudder with horror**
> **and their faces are distorted with fear'**

(27:35).

This is the reaction of fear. It is the sudden realization on the part of the surrounding nations that what has happened to Tyre can happen to them too. It is a reminder to them of their vulnerability. No defence is a match for the anger of God when it is kindled. Their dependence on worldly means to save them in the hour of trouble will prove to be their undoing. This is a lesson that we need to learn.

Second, there are those who gloat at Tyre's downfall. Rather than learn the lesson, they **'hiss'** at Tyre's humiliation (27:36). This is, in fact, the treatment that Tyre had itself meted out to Jerusalem in her undoing (26:2). Our sins have a habit of 'coming home to roost'. 'Do to others what you would have them do to you' (Matt. 7:12).

Tyre's great might has waned. When we survey what has happened in the history of the twentieth century — its two world wars, the rise and collapse of Communism, the emergence of tyrants and the like — we are to perceive the hand of God at work among the nations. The sins of the nations have not altogether been dealt with yet; indeed, for some their iniquity is only now coming perilously close to the brim. But soon, God will arise and destroy the proud and arrogant, those who base their confidence on the material things of this world. They have no ultimate future. A day will come when the arrogant cry, 'I am perfect in beauty,' will be heard no more. Instead, there will be the noise of wailing and weeping. This is a solemn truth.

Falling from fame and fortune (28:1-19)

Democracy is not the saviour of the world, but it has the merit of at least some choice in as far as our leaders are concerned. In the ancient world, the removal of a despotic king was difficult. To be brutally honest, there was only one choice: assassination! This was the way several kings in Judah and Israel had met their end. Ittobal II, Tyre's king, was to be spared death at the hands of his people; instead, he was to be removed by a divine hand.

That pride was the cause of Tyre's downfall is something that finds confirmation in the claim Ittobal II made of himself: firstly, that he was wiser than a legendary figure of the ancient Near East called **'Daniel'** (28:3,6 — not the Daniel of Scripture); secondly, in his abilities as a leader which meant that in terms of wealth, Tyre had never had it so good (28:4-5); and thirdly, in the ultimate claim of all: **'I am a god'** (28:2,6). The judgement is swift and decisive: **'foreigners'** will come upon him (the king in particular, but the whole of Tyre that he represents is meant) and he will be brought **'down to the pit'** (28:8).[16] As the king dies, he will hardly then be in a position to boast that he is God Almighty! (28:9).

His death will be the death of one outside the covenant, the **'death of the uncircumcised'** (28:10; cf. 31:18; 32:19-32). Circumcision was the sign and seal of the covenant God made with Abraham and his posterity. It had a national as well as a spiritual significance. It served to introduce people into the externally organized community of Israel as well as representing a God-ward relationship that was the essence of the covenant. Repeatedly, the Philistines, for example, are designated as 'uncircumcised'. Goliath is the 'uncircumcised Philistine' (1 Sam. 17:26,36). Saul would rather die than fall into the hands of the uncircumcised (1 Sam. 31:4). The prophets became even more explicit, insisting that the Judeans circumcise the 'foreskins of [their] hearts' (Jer. 4:4, NKJV). They were already Israelites and in possession of the physical sign of identity. What was missing was the true essence of circumcision: their relationship with the Lord. To die 'the death of the uncircumcised' was to die the death of an unbeliever.

This is a sorry tale of one who once held such honour and power, who lived in such luxury and wealth, who dies in shame and descends 'into the pit'. Ittobal II was not the first to go this way; nor was he the last. Jesus spoke of another 'rich man' who died and went to hell. His pleas for mercy went unheeded because it is an irreversible condition (Luke 16:19-31).

Behind the description of the fall of the King of Tyre lies the shadow of Satan. Many commentators have believed that behind this passage and a similar one of the fall of the King of Babylon in Isaiah 14:12-14 lies a traditional account of the fall of Satan, whose image these arrogant monarchs bore. This theory cannot be proved,[17] but both kings were types of Satan, who is anti-Christ (Dan. 11:36; 2 Thess. 2:4).

In order to establish the relevance of the story to his readers, Ezekiel compares the King of Tyre to a primeval man in the Garden of Eden, **'full of wisdom and perfect in beauty'** (28:12). What Ezekiel is portraying in these poetic and difficult lines is the idea of a great fall from a 'perfect' existence. The king seemed to have everything: he is bedecked with the finest jewellery — and falls. Adam had everything — and fell! And with Adam, we too fell! Behind the Eden story lies the figure of Satan, who also had everything — and fell. Changing the figure, Ezekiel then compares him to a **'guardian cherub'** on the **'holy mount of God'** (28:14). This expression was a common way of alluding to the 'place' where God was thought to dwell. Thus the King of Tyre, who claimed to be a god, resides in the 'mountain of God', but falls: **'wickedness'** is found in him (28:15). And the cause of wickedness? Greed, self-aggrandizement, summed up in a simple, self-condemning sentence: **'Your heart became proud'** (28:17). These were the elements which Adam found so alluring. Augustine was insistent that pride was the essence of Adam's sin in Eden, and is the essence of sin in general. The King of Tyre's fall, spectacular and shocking as it was, is a symbol of what sin can expect, no matter where it is found. If he was banished from Eden, the fault lay entirely within himself. It is a salutary warning to shady business practice, something of which Tyre was guilty, that its end is destruction. Many a tycoon has found it to be just so.

Epilogue: Sidon and Israel (28:20-26)

'Sidon' (28:21) was the second largest city of ancient Phoenicia after Tyre and about twenty-five miles to the north on the Mediterranean coast; by New Testament times they were often joined together (cf. Matt. 11:21-22; 15:21). No immediate reason is given for Sidon's judgement, but we may assume that the city had sided with Tyre, perhaps contributing to Judah's downfall to the Babylonians.

When the prophet Habakkuk, who preached just slightly before Ezekiel and may well have still been alive when Ezekiel ministered, allowed himself to think about the way God was going to use the Babylonians in his devices, he seems to have had many problems. He tells us in his opening chapter how he cried to the Lord about it. He was a puzzled prophet, unable to account for what was happening and why it was happening in the way it was. God's answer to him was to take refuge in his covenant. It was true that he was going to use the Babylonians, but reminding Habakkuk of his promise to Abraham, he told the prophet, 'The righteous will live by his faith' (Hab. 2:4; cf. Gen. 15:6). The righteous, that is, those who are reckoned to be righteous by faith, will live. The promise will never fail. It is the same reassurance that God now gives to Ezekiel's audience. As Calvin comments on an earlier verse relating to the same promise, 'If the exile had been perpetual, that promise might seem vain.'[18] After four chapters of judgement upon the nations, and when Israel (Judah) has already felt the force of that judgement at the hands of the Babylonians, God's people must have wondered if this was all God had to say. Was there any hope for the people of God? In a message of unsurpassed comfort, Ezekiel sings eloquently of Israel's restoration from exile. There will come a time when **'They will live in their own land... They will live there in safety and will build houses and plant vineyards; they will live in safety when I inflict punishment on all their neighbours who maligned them. Then they will know that I am the Lord their God'** (28:25-26).

The charge that Ezekiel is 'full of judgement' is imbalanced. The prophecy certainly does contain some of the strongest notes of God's anger towards sin found anywhere in the Scriptures. In that sense it is not an 'easy' book to read. But it is also suffused with statements of God's grace. The sentiment in verses 25-26 is yet another of many such in Ezekiel (cf. 11:17; 20:34,41-42; 29:13; 34:13; 36:24; 37:21; 38:8; 39:27). Though God is justly angry with Judah, his anger lasts only for a while, and once the lesson has been learnt he will restore them to their land again. That this is true is something the books of Nehemiah and Ezra relate.

Summary

The Old Testament story focuses largely upon Israel as God's chosen people, but it is equally anxious to stress that God is Lord of the nations. The whole world belongs to God and he is anxious to exercise his lordship over it all. God judges others. There is a measure of comfort in the knowledge that when we witness the brutality of the present world — violence, murder, rape, the abuse of children, etc. — God is not indifferent to it. Sometimes we are tempted to ask, 'What is God doing?' The answer is that he is being patient (cf. 2 Peter 3:15). He gives people a certain amount of rope, but he will not be patient for ever. Though none of these nations possessed a Bible and they were not recipients of special revelation, they were still without excuse. God judged them as sinners who had broken his laws. It is a salutary lesson that people do not need a Bible to be held accountable to God for their actions. This is something Paul makes very clear (Rom. 1:18-20; 2:14-15). In the judgements pronounced on Ammon, Moab, Edom and Philistia, God has reminded the nations of the world that, one day, they will be called to account for their actions.

These chapters, Ezekiel 26-28, have dealt principally with the seafaring state of Phoenicia, or Tyre, as it is collectively known here. Proud and greedy as it had become, its end will be swift and devastating. This once great prosperous state, renowned throughout the world for its commercial success, was to be brought to a heap of rubble. What looked so important in Ezekiel's time now lies buried beneath the debris accumulated over the centuries. Nations, empires, moguls — these come and go. It is only the sovereign purposes of God that endure.

15.
Egypt

Please read Ezekiel 29:1 - 32:32

When Ezekiel penned these words, Egypt's wonderful sights were already old. Undoubtedly, some 900 years earlier some of Ezekiel's ancestors had helped build the Sphinx, Karnak and the great pyramids. Now, once more, Egypt's power was rising. She seemed to many onlookers and interpreters of history to be the only possible threat to Babylonian intentions in the world. Consequently, many of the smaller countries sought ways to flatter Egypt's powers, thus hoping that in the day of reckoning Egypt would spring to their defence.[1]

It had been, of course, Zedekiah's disastrous policy to listen to the pro-Egyptian faction in Jerusalem in the hope of thwarting Babylonian aggression (Ezek. 17:15-16; Jer. 37:5). Egypt's defence proved short-lived and ultimately worthless. After all, Egypt had been Israel's enemy from the beginning. Even in Israel's recent history, Egypt had sought to attain control of her land. Any trust in Egyptian help had to be suspect.

In the light of the glorious promise made at the close of the previous chapter (28:24-26), which included the words, 'No longer will the people of Israel have malicious neighbours...' (28:24), the power of Egypt would obviously have to be seriously curtailed. It is the decline of Egypt's power, suggesting that she would be a threat to Judah no longer, that the next four chapters are concerned to point out. Egypt's future is now portrayed in terms of seven separate prophecies.

'I am against you...' (29:1-16)

It is January 587 B.C. (29:1)[2] and Jerusalem has been under siege for some time. The situation is hopeless and the wise believe the prophet's word from the Lord about Jerusalem's ultimate downfall. It must have come as some relief to the exiles along the banks of the River Kebar to know that even mighty Egypt was to suffer the same fate as little Judah. In a poem, Ezekiel likens the Pharaoh of Egypt to a fish of the Nile that has been thrown onto the land as food for the animals (29:3-7).

There can be no more terrifying words than these: **'This is what the Sovereign Lord says: "I am against you..."'** (29:3). When the psalmist sought for the ultimate expression of his assurance he put it in these terms: 'God is for me' (Ps. 56:9). Paul was to pick up the words and draw the obvious conclusion: 'If God is for us, who can be against us? ... I am convinced that neither death nor life, neither angels nor demons, neither the present nor the future, nor any powers, neither height nor depth, nor anything else in all creation, will be able to separate us from the love of God that is in Christ Jesus our Lord' (Rom. 8:31,38-39). This is the ultimate truth: God is either *for* us or *against* us.

Egypt had a remarkably unvaried geography. Its low-lying valleys through which the Nile flowed were one of its most dominant features. All of Egypt's great cities — Thebes, Hermopolis, Heliopolis, Memphis, Sais and Tanis — were situated on the edge of the great river. It is Pharaoh's bombastic claim to have created the Nile that receives severe criticism from the prophet (29:3). The pharaoh is compared to **'a great monster'**. The word may also mean 'crocodile', a creature many Egyptians would have feared. Crocodiles were caught by means of hooks in their jaws and then pulled on to dry land where they were slaughtered. The figure is apt, for just as Pharaoh was thought to be divine, so was the crocodile. Sebek, as the crocodile god was known, was considered to be Egypt's protector. The point is to underline the fact that when God judged Egypt, he also humbled her 'gods' (Exod. 12:12; Num. 33:4). Scripture, more than once, uses the figure of slaying a dragon to describe this event (cf. Isa. 51:9).[3]

Thus the Egyptian Pharaoh, Hophra (Apries), is portrayed as arrogant and untouchable. In claiming that no god could dislodge him, he was dangerously mistaken. During his reign he sent an expedition to Cyprus, besieged and took Gaza (Jer. 47:1) and claimed victory over Phoenicia. History records of him that he was not given a royal burial in the Valley of the Kings, thereby fulfilling Ezekiel's prophecy.

As for Egypt's promise of support, which Zedekiah had hoped would be the salvation of Judah in her hour of need, Egypt's strength is like a staff of reeds that breaks as soon as Judah leans on it (29:6-7). The prophetic denunciation is withering: Egypt's 'help is utterly useless. Therefore I call her Rahab the Do-Nothing' (Isa. 30:7). 'Pharaoh king of Egypt is only a loud noise; he has missed his opportunity' (Jer. 46:17). **'You have been a staff of reed for the house of Israel. When they grasped you with their hands, you splintered and you tore open their shoulders; when they leaned on you, you broke and their backs were wrenched'** (29:6-7).

In contrast to the arrogant deception of Egypt's claims, God will make her **'a ruin and a desolate waste from Migdol to Aswan'**, that is, from north to south (29:10). Following their captivity, which was to last for **'forty years'** (29:11) — though the Hebrew word is capable of a general translation along the lines of the English 'dozens', in the sense of a long time (29:11) — the Egyptians were not to receive the blessing that Judah had been promised at the close of the previous chapter (28:25-26). Instead, Egypt will remain **'a lowly kingdom ... and will never again exalt itself above the nations'** (29:14). Egypt's decline as a world power was to serve as a constant reminder of the sin Israel had committed in placing her trust in her instead of God (29:15). God will have his people look to no one else but himself for help. He is jealous to guard his right to be his people's sovereign Protector. Misplaced trust in the arm of flesh to save us from our troubles is evidence of an unbelieving heart. That was the shameful discovery Judah was to make about herself.

The Lord of history (29:17-21)

This section begins with yet another date (29:17), but this time sixteen years have passed since the prophecy of 29:1-16! In the spring of 571 B.C. Ezekiel was still serving faithfully as a prophet many years after the fall of Jerusalem and twenty-six years after the start of Ezekiel's own exile. For over a quarter of century, Ezekiel had served as a faithful prophet. Learning to serve the Lord throughout the whole of our lives is a lesson we need to learn. Too often Christian work is begun and then left when the excitement has worn away and the difficulty of the labour has become evident.

The Babylonian invasion of Egypt came in 568/567 B.C., still some three years away at the time of this prophecy. Ezekiel describes the rich plunder the Babylonian soldiers will take from them. It came after the thirteen-year siege of Tyre (from 586-571 B.C.) which proved of little benefit as far as booty was concerned (29:18; cf. 26:7-14). The Tyrian siege had been so difficult that the heads and shoulders of the soldiers had been made raw by the chaffing of their armour (29:18). But Egypt was to prove quite different. Soldiers were poorly paid, but could become instantly rich by finding booty which was granted to them to keep. God seems to have been concerned about these Babylonian troops. Why? Because they **'did it for me'** (29:20). The success of the Assyrian king, Sennacherib, in Isaiah's day had been possible only because God had allowed it: Sennacherib was simply carrying out the eternal purpose of God (Isa. 37:26; cf. Acts 4:28). Assyria had been a 'club' in God's hand to chastise his people (Isa. 10:5-19). It is the same with Nebuchadnezzar's conquests in Ezekiel's time.

Trouble in North Africa (30:1-19)

For the first time in Ezekiel we come across the phrase, **'the day of the Lord'** (30:3; cf. 'The day is near', 7:7). While the 'day of the Lord' can sometimes refer to an event which is in the near future, it usually describes the consummation, the end of all time, when God will come to judge the world. Here the idea is of an event in the not too distant future, the ransacking of North Africa by the Babylonians, but it has to be understood that all of these passages are foretastes of the judgement that will come upon the world at the end of time.

For centuries, Israel had entertained the thought that the 'day of the Lord' would bring nothing but blessing for them. But this was a naïve view. Isaiah had warned Israel before its collapse to the Assyrians that

'The Lord Almighty has a day in store
   for all the proud and lofty,
   for all that is exalted
(and they will be humbled)...
The arrogance of man will be brought low
   and the pride of men humbled;
the Lord alone will be exalted in that day'

                                         (Isa. 2:12,17).

Ezekiel, like Amos, warns that the 'day of the Lord' will be 'dark' (30:18; Amos 5:18,20; cf. 8:9). And Zephaniah spoke of it as:

'... a day of wrath,
   a day of distress and anguish,
a day of trouble and ruin,
   a day of darkness and gloom,
   a day of clouds and blackness'

                                  (Zeph. 1:14-15). [4]

The focus of attention in this passage, however, falls not on Israel but on the North African states. Mentioned are such states as **'Egypt'**, **'Cush'** (Ethiopia), **'Put'** (Libya), and **'Lydia'**.

Four particular features of the 'the day of the Lord' are worth noting.

1. It is a day of darkness

It will be **'a day of clouds'** (30:3; cf. Zeph. 1:15). **'Dark will be the day'** (30:18). A storm is gathering; it is the anger of the Lord against his enemies that is about to be unleashed.

2. The 'day' is imminent

'The day is near' (30:3). While the primary reference here is to an event which was only a few years away, all of these judgements were precursors of the 'the Day of Judgement'. From the perspective of Bible-writers, not only were such events as the Babylonian invasion near, but so also was the end of time itself. We may look back with the benefit of hindsight and suggest that they were mistaken. This has been what liberal theologians have done with many of the references in the New Testament, for example. But the Bible itself gives us the answer to this problem when it tells us that God measures time in a different way: 'With the Lord a day is like a thousand years, and a thousand years are like a day. The Lord is not slow in keeping his promise, as some understand slowness' (2 Peter 3:8).

3. It is a day of judgement

Ezekiel calls it **'a time of doom...'** and says, **'Wail'** (30:2), for **'Anguish will come'** upon them (30:4). As Malachi makes plain at the end of the Old Testament period of revelation, the purpose of this 'day of judgement' is to administer God's covenant retribution upon his enemies (Mal. 3:1-5). Egypt's cities will soon **'lie among ruined cities'** (30:7,13-19). Egypt's **'doom'**, we are told, **'is sure to come'** (30:9).

One important point to note in Egypt's judgement is its *theological* nature. God is jealous to safeguard his honour; he will share it with no one else. Thus, the Egyptian god, Sebek ('the crocodile god', 29:3-4) is to be destroyed. Here again, God says, **'I will destroy the idols and put an end to the images'** (30:13). Man's religions have been his greatest crimes.

4. No one can escape the effects of this day

In a widely sweeping arc, God's judgement of Egypt scans the entire land from Memphis and back again (note the repetition of **'Memphis'** in verses 13 and 16). The effect of this was to convey an impression of inescapability. God's anger will sweep across the entire land. It is a precursor of 'the end' when 'He will judge the world with justice by the man he has appointed' (Acts 17:31).

Pharaoh's broken arm (30:20-26)

This is the fourth prophecy about Egypt and is dated in the eleventh year of the exile, that is, 587 B.C., the very time that the Babylonians were besieging Jerusalem. No doubt some of Ezekiel's compatriots anticipated, as did their relations in Jerusalem, a deliverance from Egypt. In the previous year news had filtered to the banks of the

Kebar River that Pharaoh's armies had distracted the Babylonian siege for a while, but the entire escapade was short-lived (Jer. 37:5-11). Pharaoh's arm is broken: **'It has not been bound up for healing or put in a splint so as to become strong enough to hold a sword'** (30:21).

Any hope now of another such attack is quickly put down by saying that Pharaoh's other arm is to be broken also (30:22). Why is this? Because, **'I am against Pharaoh king of Egypt'** (30:22). Pharaoh Hophra was defeated in war and finally assassinated by his own people, just as Jeremiah predicted (Jer. 44:30). The would-be conquerors became the conquered, suffering the same fate as Judah — defeat and exile (30: 23-26). The Lord of history reveals himself in charge of these momentous international matters.

In a day when Christians are apt to confine God to purely personal issues, we need to regain the cosmic perspective of the prophets as they speak of the Lord of the universe intimately involved in the international issues of the day. There is not an item of news that the Lord is not involved in.

A falling tree (31:1-18)

In the Sequoia National Park in America stands the so-called 'General Sherman Tree', 270 feet high, thirty-six feet in diameter and reputed to be 3,500 years old — it was there long before Ezekiel came into the world! This is, arguably, the greatest tree in the world. The fifth prophecy against Egypt, which is dated fifty-three days after the preceding one (31:1), is in the style of a funeral dirge for Egypt's past glories, and takes the form of a poem likening Egypt to a **'a cedar in Lebanon'** (31:3)⁵ Only, in this case, the tree is felled. Just as Assyria had fallen a century earlier at the battle of Carchemish, so too, Egypt's power will be destroyed.

The poem describes the greatness of the tree (31:3-7), even extolling it above any tree to be found in Eden (31:8). This, of course, is Egypt's own self-appraisal. Like Assyria before her, and the would-be conquering nations since, the pride of nationhood in which Egypt revelled knows no bounds. The lesson is immediately forthcoming: pride leads to a fall. Babylon, **'the ruler of the nations'**, will cut her down to size (31:11). The cause of Egypt's downfall is her **'wickedness'** (31:11). In a sombre passage, Egypt is depicted as in Sheol (**'the grave'** 31:15), lying alongside other trees (that is, 'other nations' who have 'died' because of their opposition to God). The point of the allegory is a comparative one: if Egypt was to fall, what chance had the tiny nations that depended on her for their survival?

The doom of those who live in habitual wickedness is to **'lie among the uncircumcised'** (31:18; cf.28:10). Uncircumcision is a word used in the prophets to depict uncleanness, defilement and unworthiness (cf. Jer. 9:25,26).This is a theme that Ezekiel will take up at length in the next chapter (32:19-32).

Weeping and wailing (32:1-32)

The sixth (32:1-16) and seventh (32:17-32) prophecies are both in the form of laments for Pharaoh and Egypt respectively (cf. **'lament'** in verses 2,16). The sixth prophecy is almost identical to the first one (29:1-16). It is dated in the early spring of 585 B.C., shortly after Ezekiel's compatriots have received news of Jerusalem's downfall. The allegory is once again a **'monster'** (32:2; cf. 29:3), probably a 'crocodile', as before in chapter 29. The monster is caught in a net and left bleeding to death on the banks of the river (32:3-6). Once more the coming judgement is spoken of in terms of a **'day'** of God's visitation (32:10; cf. 30:3,18).

The seventh and final prophecy occurs in the year 586 B.C., two weeks after the sixth prophecy. It is a most reassuring way to end these chapters of oracles against the foreign nations. No matter how sorry for themselves Ezekiel's compatriots might have felt at their lot in Babylon, the fate of Egypt and her associate nations was worse. There is coming a day when their pride will be broken and, instead of occupying the glory and limelight that they now enjoy, they will inhabit the pits of 'hell'. Using the Old Testament figure of Sheol (**'the grave'** in NIV, 32:21,27), Ezekiel depicts the nations being brought to the realm of the dead, being greeted by the various chiefs of antiquity and then being sent to a remote corner of this dark existence. Various nations, including **'Assyria'**, **'Elam'** (a nation to the east of the Tigris river), **'Meshech and Tubal'** (nations occupying a region south-east of the Black Sea), **'Edom'** (though technically a 'brother' nation, Edom is routinely considered as a 'foreign' nation in Scripture), and the various city states of

Phoenicia (e.g. **'Sidonians'**), are imagined buried together in groups, some evidently in more difficult situations than others.

Mention of Sheol reminds us of the Old Testament way of depicting 'hell'. The word itself means 'the depths' or 'the unseen state'. It occurs some sixty-five times in the Old Testament and is more or less equivalent to the Greek word 'Hades'. Sometimes the word 'Sheol' denotes the state of death into which both believers and unbelievers are brought (1 Sam. 2:6; Job 14:13,14; 17:13-16). Sometimes the word means 'the grave', as in Job 7:9. But it has to be said that there are occasions when the word quite clearly means 'hell'.[6] What is depicted in these chapters in Ezekiel is the condition of certain individuals and groups of people *after* death. Though much of the language is poetic, it is reasonable to conclude even from these verses that some kind of existence in which men are conscious of their shame (32:24) is in view. This is not annihilation!

Jonathan Edwards once wrote that 'God hath had it on His heart to show to angels and men, both how excellent His love is, and also how terrible His wrath is.'[7] Here we are meant to be horrified at the end of the wicked and weep for them (**'Wail'**, 32:18). During his first furlough, Hudson Taylor addressed a large missionary conference in Scotland. Beginning his talk by relating a tearful story of a Chinese man who fell into a river and was allowed to drown by indifferent onlookers, he turned to his shocked audience and said, 'You are very upset by their refusal to rescue a drowning man from physical death, but what of your indifference to the spiritual death and hopelessness of thousands and thousands who die each year in China without ever hearing of the Lord Jesus?'[8] After reading these chapters we are to ask ourselves, 'When did I last weep for the lost?'

Summary

Several important truths emerge from these chapters.

The first concerns *the scope of God's work*. For many Christians the Bible's message is confined to that concerning man's personal relationship with God. This is, of course, one of the Bible's main and greatest themes, but it is a mistake to think that this is *all* the Bible has to say. Ultimately the message of Scripture concerns the condition of the entire world and its destiny. When we look at the world today and note what is happening we are not to despair, as though things were in some way out of control.

This leads to a second thought: *every event in the course of history is under the control of God.* He orders not only his own people, but the course of history itself. Every nation on earth is under the hand of God, for there is no power in this world that is not ultimately controlled by him.

Then again, the Bible makes it clear that *God's main interest is not the world, but his own church.* Patrick Fairbairn rightly summarizes the content of these chapters in Ezekiel by saying that 'All other dominions are destined to pass away, that alone of Israel becomes permanent and universal.'⁹

But it is vital to see that even though for a season God allows the heathen nations of the world some perceived liberty to act out their policies of self-aggrandizement, their ultimate powers are soon curtailed. The key to the understanding of history is the kingdom of God. The story of these foreign nations is only relevant in so far as it bears on what God is doing with his kingdom, Judah. What really matters in the world today is God's church. That is where media reports on current world affairs are so sadly imbalanced, for all their attempts at being fair and unbiassed. It is not Egypt, nor even Babylon, that will inherit the earth, but God's own people. Consequently, he promises to **'make a horn grow for the house of Israel'** (29:21). 'Horn' in the Old Testament is often a symbol for strength and power. It is a promise of Judah's importance as God's kingdom that is being underlined here. When strange things are happening all around us in the world, we should be reassuring ourselves that the infinite Lord of history is working all things together for the good of his people (cf. Rom. 8:28-39).

Part VI
The fall of Jerusalem
(Ezek. 33-37)

16.
Watchmen and shepherds

Please read Ezekiel 33:1 - 3 4:31

The previous eight chapters (25-32) have been concerned with the judgement of the nations. The next five chapters (33-37) return to the theme which occupied the opening chapters (1-24): the fall of Judah and Jerusalem to the Babylonians. There is, however, a difference in perspective: rather than being judgemental, these chapters are full of comfort and promises of renewal and restoration. After the surgical knife has been applied, it is time to close the wound. Chapter 33 returns us to a theme we have already come across in chapter 18: we are each one of us responsible for our actions and their consequences. There is no point in blaming God for the mess in which we find ourselves.

The watchman

Ancient cities were vulnerable to attack at almost any moment. Consequently, one of the most important civic offices was that of a 'watchman' (33:2). Occupying a suitable vantage-point from which he could survey the surrounding countryside, he would blow a trumpet so as to give warning of any approaching parties, whether friendly or not. The amount of time a city would have to get its inhabitants safely within its city walls and ready for defensive action against marauders depended largely on the swift actions of its watchman. The lives of the people were dependent upon his vigilance.

The watchman in view here is a spiritual one (33:2-5). The focus, however, falls not so much on the watchman himself, but on the response of the people. Having blown his trumpet and given adequate warning, the watchman could not be held to account if the people chose to ignore his warning. The watchman had a responsibility: to warn of approaching danger. But the people were likewise responsible — to react accordingly. If they failed to run into the city, they had only themselves to blame if they fell under the sword of the invading army.

Ezekiel has been Israel's watchman. He has sounded the notes of warning of God's judgement against them because of their sins. They should be in no doubt about the coming of the Babylonians. This was Ezekiel's commission. It is the responsibility of every Christian in a sense to give due warning to those who are not Christians of the consequences of their rebellion. We are to imagine ourselves as the Lord's representatives, as Paul did: 'We are therefore Christ's ambassadors, as though God were making his appeal through us. We implore you on Christ's behalf: Be reconciled to God' (2 Cor. 5:20). We are held accountable for the witness we bear to the lost. Failure to warn a sinner of the consequences of sin renders us **'accountable for his blood'** (33:8). Christians can expect to be judged for their failures in evangelism when an opportunity for witness has been given.

Likewise the sinner is responsible to respond in an appropriate manner. Assuming an adequate testimony has been given, failure to respond will be blamed on the sinner in question: **'He will die for his sin, but you will be saved yourself'** (33:9). It is not the fault of God that sinners end up in hell.

Ezekiel 33:11 repeats the longing of God for the salvation of sinners that we examined earlier in chapter 18:23,32. God is genuinely grieved when human beings destroy themselves: **'As surely as I live, declares the Sovereign Lord, I take no pleasure in the death of the wicked, but rather that they turn from their ways and live. Turn! Turn from your evil ways! Why will you die, O house of Israel?'**[1] This is God's universal desire for all sinners.[2]

Elsewhere in Ezekiel the God with whom sinners have to do is portrayed in terms of his sovereign, awesome character. But the belief that God is sovereign in grace and judgement in no way abrogates the responsibility of the individual sinner. God never treats us as mere pawns. The person who rejects God's warning, whether directly given or mediated through one of his watchmen, thereby becomes the cause of his own condemnation. Unbelief and rebellion are never excused in Scripture on the grounds of God's sovereignty. The cause of Judah's exile was her own rebellion against the warnings of God's prophets. She had violated the terms of God's covenant and was now to be held responsible. The Bible never says that sinners miss heaven because they are not elect, but rather because they 'ignore such a great salvation' (Heb. 2:3).

Two things emerge at this point.

1. A person is not saved by his works of righteousness

At first glance, the ways of God appear unfair. This is the twice-repeated complaint made in these verses: **'The way of the Lord is not just'** (33:17,20). A man who is basically upright (**'righteous'**, 33:12) commits a transgression and is rendered guilty; his righteousness will not save him. A man who has lived his entire life in sin repents and is acquitted. Where is the justice in it all? Why should a righteous man be rendered guilty? The problem with this analysis of fairness is that the premise is wrong: there is no one who can claim to be righteous (cf. Rom. 3:9-20). We have all sinned and fallen short of God's glory. There is no one who *deserves* to be saved as of right. If God were to deal with us according to the strict demands of justice, we should all be lost. Salvation is a matter of *grace* and not of merit. Those who depend upon their own righteousness to save them can expect to be lost (33:13).

2. The genuineness of a person's salvation is judged by his repentance

Grace is not contradicted by the need for repentance to be evident. A man who gives genuine evidence of his repentance — fulfils his vows, repays his debts, and offers restitution for that which he has stolen — is not in some way *earning* his way into God's favour. For, as Scripture makes clear elsewhere, the repentance is the *evidence* of faith — a faith that is given by God (Eph. 2:8). Wisely did Martin Luther nail to the Wittenburg church door as his first of Ninety-Five Theses: 'Our Lord and Master Jesus Christ, in saying "Repent ye" etc., intended that the whole of the life of believers should be repentance.'

This is the emphasis of Ezekiel in this chapter. As chapter 18 made abundantly clear, the salvation that God offers is a salvation evidenced by repentance. And how were folk to prove the genuineness of their repentance? By their rejection of ungodliness and return to the ways of the covenant (33:12,14,19; cf. 18:21,23,27).

When we tolerate a bare outward routine and external performance as the evidence of our faith, we are in a state of decline. In Isaiah's time, God rounded on the people for their empty formality in worship:

> '"The multitude of your sacrifices—
>   what are they to me?" says the Lord.
> "I have more than enough of burnt offerings,
>   of rams and the fat of fattened animals;
> I have no pleasure
>   in the blood of bulls and lambs and goats.
> When you come to appear before me,
>   who has asked this of you,
>   this trampling of my courts?
> Stop bringing meaningless offerings!
>   Your incense is detestable to me.
> New Moons, Sabbaths and convocations—
>   I cannot bear your evil assemblies.
> Your New Moon festivals and your appointed feasts
>   my soul hates.
> They have become a burden to me;
>   I am weary of bearing them'
>
>   (Isa. 1:11-14).

In Christ's day it was even worse, as Jesus accused the Pharisees of rank hypocrisy (Matt. 23:23-28).

It is a principle of Scripture, often repeated, that the acceptability of our worship is dependent upon the sincerity with which it emerges from our hearts. The deepest and best Christians are those who strive after depth. Superficiality is the curse of much of our religion.

The fall of Jerusalem (33:21-33)

References to Ezekiel's imposed dumbness go back to 3:26. In chapter 24, following the death of Ezekiel's wife, the prophet had been reminded once again of his condition (possibly, as was suggested in our comments on that chapter, a prohibition from routine conversation only) as a symbolic gesture of Jerusalem's imminent collapse. In fact, at the close of chapter 24 we find the prophet anticipating the return of his voice following the arrival of a messenger who would inform him of Jerusalem's demise (24:26,27). (Chapters 25-32 are a chronological diversion and the sequence is picked up again in 33:1.) Here in chapter 33 (the date is winter of 586/587 B.C — six months after the fall of Jerusalem, 33:21) the messenger finally arrives with the news that **'The city has fallen!'** (33:21). The news brings to an end Ezekiel's period of dumbness (33:22). The delay of six months is hardly surprising. It took Ezra four months to make the reverse journey in a time of peace (Ezra 7:9). For a messenger to do so in a time of war, avoiding being captured, is quite another story.

Slogans were as popular in Ezekiel's time as they are today. We have come across several already, including the one: 'This city is a cooking pot, and we are the meat' (11:3) — an arrogant claim by Jerusalem's inhabitants as to their inviolability. Another is that found in the first half of this chapter: 'The way of the Lord is not just' (33:17,20). Yet another now confronts us: **'Abraham was only one man, yet he possessed the land. But we are many; surely the land has been given to us as our possession'** (33:24).

The greed and heartlessness that lie behind this statement are breathtaking. Yet here we have an example of something that we have seen taking place time and again. Those inhabitants of Jerusalem who were not taken captive now saw houses and lands vacated in Jerusalem by those forced into exile. Greed always finds a way to justify its gratification and thus they reasoned that by possessing these lands and dwellings they were, in fact, merely fulfilling the covenant promise of land that God had given to Abraham! In the war in Bosnia, formerly part of Yugoslavia, homes and lands have been occupied as the policy of 'ethnic cleansing' takes place. Times have not changed!

The problem with this slogan is that the people who cited it were unfit to dwell in Jerusalem. They claimed allegiance to Abraham, but failed to comply with the ethical demands of Abraham's faith. They transgressed Israel's ceremonial and moral laws (33:25-26). The collapse of Jerusalem to the Babylonians had taught these people nothing at all. Ezekiel has nothing but a solemn word of judgement for them (33:27-29). Greed and exploitation, those hallmarks of an unregenerate, arrogant heart, can expect no mercy from God. The conditions that those who were left in Judah following the collapse of Jerusalem were to face would be grim indeed.

How long had Ezekiel been warning of Jerusalem's collapse? The answer seems to be at least seven years: his call as a prophet came in 596 B.C. (see 1:2). Throughout that period the prophet had experienced the vilification and hostility of some, the scepticism of others and the indifference of the majority. How many responded to his words in faith is unclear, but we get the impression that it was only a few. Now, however, things were different. After all, his words had been vindicated. Jerusalem had collapsed, just as he had said it would. Everyone was talking about him (33:30).

But with popularity comes a danger of compromise. The interest among those people who now apparently flocked to hear his sermons was superficial. They sit and listen to Ezekiel's words, but they **'do not put them into practice'** (33:31). In a withering description of their condition, God says of them, **'With their mouths they express devotion, but their hearts are greedy for unjust gain'** (33:31). Apparently, folk would have sat and listened to a singer of love songs, only to leave unaffected by what they had heard. It was the same with Ezekiel's sermons. Sermons need a discipline of delivery, to be sure, but they need just as surely a discipline of listening — a listening with a view to obedience. It is noteworthy that in Hebrew the word 'listen' is the same as the word 'obey': there is no gap between what we hear and what we are to do. It must surely underline the shame of these listeners that they looked for **'gain'** in what they heard. Like Simon Magus they continually asked, 'What is there in this for me?' (Acts 8:18).

Summary of chapter 33

Chapter 33 has given us two pictures: that of a watchman calling out words of warning and danger to a city under siege, and that of the city, fallen and destroyed. In both pictures the people have responded with astonishing arrogance. This is superficiality at its worst. Times of great crisis are meant to soften our hearts, but history reveals that they often have the opposite effect. The situation facing Ezekiel's compatriots could hardly have been worse. Their country has been invaded, their city overrun and they themselves are taken as prisoners of war. Yet despite all that Ezekiel has said to them, they are still reluctant to believe that God could be angry with them. Those in Jerusalem saw an opportunity to steal in the name of Abraham, and those in exile found a fleeting, but hollow interest in the prophet's preaching.

But however clear their blindness appears to us, we need to ask ourselves how we have responded in times when God's judgement has fallen on us. Have we also not been guilty of superficiality in our religion? Have we not listened to sermons, casting aside the words of rebuke as applicable to someone else, seeking only what brings us immediate profit? Before we castigate those of Ezekiel's day, we had better make sure that we have not committed the very same error.

Shepherds (34:1-31)

It would be understandable for the first-time reader of Scripture to conclude that there was no future for God's people following their exile into Babylon. This was their darkest hour. We, of course, know how the story proceeds, but it would be an error of judgement to think that it was equally evident to the godly who pondered what the future might hold for them. From the days of Solomon, the history of Israel was a story of increasing apostasy and judgement: of forty-three kings, only David, Hezekiah and Josiah were consistently loyal to God, and possibly half a dozen others had a mixed reputation. Yet the Lord did not forsake his people, but sent prophets to them who warned them of the consequences of their sin, urging them to return to the Lord. But they did not listen. Judgement had come and now some, no doubt, cried themselves to sleep at night wondering whether or not God had utterly forsaken them. He had every right to do so.

But this is not the way of God. His **'covenant of peace'** (34:25) was inviolable. God had promised to save a people for himself and throughout the history of the Old Testament we find him determined to do just that. Even now, when Israel's candle is almost entirely extinguished, God has a faithful remnant (cf. 9:8; 11:13). But if the scattered people of God are to be gathered into one, they need a shepherd to gather them together. Israel's shepherds have proved to be a dismal failure, concerned for themselves and not for God's sheep. God himself must be that saving Shepherd! That is the theme of this chapter.[3]

The failure of the shepherds (34:1-10)

The rulers of the ancient Near East were often designated as 'shepherds' (Isa. 44:28; Jer. 2:8; 10:21; 23:1-6; 25:34-38) as were Israel's greatest leaders, Moses and David (Isa. 63:11; Psa. 78:70-72). To rule was to ensure the protection and well-being of the people — the main function of a shepherd. It is here in Ezekiel 34 that we discover the most comprehensive analysis of the true nature of the shepherd's responsibilities. Three features of the false shepherds are roundly condemned, thus signalling what was expected of the true shepherds of Israel.

1. Their self-interest

They **'only take care of themselves'** (34:2).

2. Their love of ease.

'You eat the curds, clothe yourselves with the wool and slaughter the choice animals, but you do not take care of the flock' (34:3).

3. Their heartlessness

'You have not strengthened the weak or healed the sick or bound up the injured. You have not brought back the strays or searched for the lost. You have ruled them harshly and brutally' (34:4). As a consequence, the sheep were **'scattered'**[4] and **'wandered over all the mountains and on every high hill'** (34:5-6). The false shepherds are called to account and promptly dismissed them from their posts (34:7-10).

This 'parable' has been a reflection of what has happened to Israel. We hear God's analysis of their condition as false shepherds when he pronounces yet again: **'I am against the shepherds'** (34:10; cf. 13:8; 21:3; 26:3; 28:22; 29:3,10; 35:3; 38:3; 39:1).

The Good Shepherd (34:11-16)

Who, then, can rescue the sheep from destruction, if not the shepherds of Israel? The answer given in this chapter is that God himself will rescue them (34:11). Over a dozen times the passage (34:11-16) uses the first person to identify the singular authority of God at work: he alone is the Good Shepherd. He alone is able to save the sheep. We have here the most beautiful and reassuring passage in Ezekiel so far: **'For this is what the Sovereign Lord says: I myself will search for my sheep and look after them. As a shepherd looks after his scattered flock when he is with them, so will I look after my sheep. I will rescue them from all the places where they were scattered on a day of clouds and darkness. I will bring them out from the nations and gather them from the countries, and I will bring them into their own land. I will pasture them on the mountains of Israel, in the ravines and in all the settlements of the land. I will tend them in a good pasture, and the mountain heights of Israel will be their grazing land. There they will lie down in good grazing land, and there they will feed in a rich pasture on the mountains of Israel. I myself will tend my sheep and make them lie down, declares the Sovereign Lord. I will search for the lost and bring back the strays. I will bind up the injured and strengthen the weak, but the sleek and the strong I will destroy. I will shepherd the flock with justice'** (34:11-16).

Included within the description of a true shepherd are the qualities of *love*, in taking care of sheep who appeared ungrateful for the self-sacrifice of the shepherd, *patience* in diligently seeking after the lost sheep, *strength* in delivering the sheep from their enemies, and in particular, *courage*, since the long dry summers would demand that a shepherd frequently look for new pastures. It was a dangerous and unsettled life, open at any moment to attack. Even in the tranquil meditations of Psalm 23, we are reminded that the shepherd carries a 'rod' to fend off attacks from would-be assassins (Ps. 23:4). In a parallel passage in Zechariah the good shepherd is first of all rejected (11:7-11), pierced (12:10) and then struck (13:7). The shepherd had to be prepared to pay the ultimate price in caring for his sheep.

Israel's shepherd promises to be their nurse (he will **'bind up'** their wounds, 34:16), rescuer (34:11,12), protector (they will **'lie** down' in safety, 34:15), provider (34:13,14), guide (their exile had been because of their desire to stray from God's path, 34:11,16).[5]

Bad sheep within the flock (34:17-22)

With a change of metaphor, the false shepherds of Israel are called **'fat sheep'** (34:20). They are selfish in the extreme; not content to feed themselves, they even destroy what is left and thus deprive others of the benefit (34:17-19). God will judge between them, promising that those who **'shove with flank and shoulder, butting all the weak sheep with [their] horns'** will be driven away (34:21).

The Messianic Shepherd (34:23-24)

Having declared that he will be their Shepherd (34:11-16), God now suggests that his **'servant David'** will **'be their shepherd'** (34:23,24). There is no contradiction, for the passage speaks of the coming of Christ, who is God, of course! Jeremiah was currently giving a similar prophecy in Jerusalem at about this time (Jer. 23:5-6). And before that, one of the psalmists gave expression to similar ideas in Psalm 89 (especially, vv. 3-4,20,29). This passage is a glimpse of the one who called himself 'the good shepherd' (John 10:11,14), and elsewhere is referred to as 'the Chief Shepherd' (1 Peter 5:4), 'that great Shepherd of the sheep' (Heb. 13:20) and 'the Shepherd and Overseer of your souls' (1 Peter 2:25).

This passage is not to be taken as a promise that David himself will return (resurrected) to rule over Israel. Ezekiel is speaking of the return of one like David. 'David was the man whom God chose and in whom He delighted; the king who triumphed against all his foes and who extended his kingdom in all directions; the man of Judah under whose genius the whole nation was for a time united.'[6] It is this idealized David, Jesus Christ, that is in view here.

What was to become of those faithful believers in Jerusalem, and others now in exile, who looked for a deliverer to save them from their plight? And what of the lost and perishing whose hearts groaned under the weight of their sin — who would show them the way of peace? What Israel needed was someone like Jesus of Nazareth who, when he had sought for a quiet place to talk with his disciples, discovered as they came ashore a great crowd of people rushing towards the little boat — a sight which looked to all intents and purposes like a flock of sheep lacking in order, discipline, guidance and leadership (Mark 6:30-44). Their shepherds, the priests and teachers of the law, and especially Herod the king, had failed to nourish them. These false shepherds had looked after their own needs. Jesus proved that day that he was indeed the Good Shepherd in a miracle of feeding that fed five thousand. Quite deliberately he gave expression to the thought that had crossed his mind when he had first viewed them as shepherdless sheep; he would shepherd them. God will not abandon his promise to save a people for himself.

It is important to note that the promise in this covenant was not an entirely new matter. It is **'my servant David'** that he promises to set over them, thus linking the New Testament fulfilment with the Old Testament promise (34:23).[7] David was a type of the Messiah to come. This was a promise which prophets had celebrated *before* the exile (Amos 9:11; Micah. 5:1-5), on the *eve* of the exile (Jer. 23:5-6; 30:9), *during* the exile (as here in Ezek 34:23-24 and 37:21-25), and *after* the exile (Zech. 12:8). Moreover, it was a promise which David himself had been pleased to recite (Ps. 110).

When Jesus spoke of himself in terms of 'the good shepherd' (John 10:11,14) he was quite deliberately identifying himself with the Shepherd of the Old Testament: God himself. That is why the Jews immediately charged him with blasphemy (John 10:33). They understood full well that the claim to be the Good Shepherd carried with it immediate implications of deity. It was one of the clearest claims to divine identification that Jesus made! As Douglas Macmillan once put it, 'Don't listen to the preachers who will tell you today that Jesus never claimed to be divine; of course he did! Just read John 10, and you will find that not only did he make the claim, but he was understood to make it. He made it unmistakably: "I am the good shepherd."'[8]

The covenant of peace (34:25-31)

Ezekiel, as prophets often did, having spoken of the coming of an idealized David, the Messiah, now looks even further into the future and sees an idealized existence for God's people, one characterized by peace. It is an age when wild animals are banished and the people are enabled to live in safety and productivity. It is spoken of in terms of a **'covenant of peace'** (34:25; 37:26; cf. Num. 25:12; Isa. 54:10). What is in view here is the eternal kingdom of peace which will characterize the new heavens and the new earth. This is what we have to look forward to![9]

The effects of God's promised dealings are staggering: not only the presence of the Shepherd himself (34:24), but security (**'they may live ... in safety'**, 34:25), **'showers of blessing'** (34:26), fruitfulness (34:27), deliverance (34:28), peace and prosperity (34:29) and the reassurance of the presence and fellowship of God (34:30-31). These are features which emerge in the New Testament era but only find their complete fulfilment in heaven itself. As members by faith of the Israel of God (cf. Gal. 6:16), we may look forward to our restoration to the land that God has promised: the new heavens, the new earth and the new Jerusalem are to be our eternal habitation. And, unlike the present condition of Jerusalem as Ezekiel spoke these words, the future of the city includes a promise of blessing. The desert will bloom and every man will reside in peace under his own vine and his own fig tree (Isa. 35:1; Zech. 3:10). This is a theme that Ezekiel takes up again in the vision of the valley of dry bones in chapter 37: the blessings of restoration that God is even now planning for his people who love him.

There is an interesting contrast introduced at the conclusion of this chapter. Over twenty times the prophet has warned of a day when men would 'know that he is the Lord' (6:10,13,14; 7:27; 12:15,16; 24:27, etc.). These were occasions when Israel or the foreign nations would feel the wrath of God and thus be forced to recognize his sovereignty. Here it is different. The Lord speaks to his people and says, **'Then they will know that I, the Lord their God, am with them and that they, the house of Israel, are my people.'** This is the language of promise: the true Israel will know that God is with them. They are his people and he is their God. Over a century earlier, Isaiah had preached in the streets of Jerusalem that a day would arrive when this covenant promise would find its fulfilment in the coming of Immanuel (meaning 'God with us'), Jesus Christ: 'Therefore the Lord himself will give you a sign: The virgin will be with child and will give birth to a son, and will call him Immanuel' (Isa. 7:14; cf. Matt.1:23).

The character of the Good Shepherd

Several points seem to emerge as a reflection of the Shepherd's character.

1. The Shepherd knows his sheep

He calls them **'my sheep'**. He seems to be acquainted with their identity. This is something Jesus noted expressly: 'I know my sheep' (John 10:3,14-15). Unlike modern Western sheep that are kept only for a short duration for their meat, Palestinian sheep were kept for their wool over the period of their life-span. Relationships developed between pastor and sheep of an intimate and loving nature. Nathanael was astonished at the fact that Jesus *knew* him (John 1:47-48).

2. The Good Shepherd serves his sheep

God's chief complaint about Israel's leaders was this: **'Woe to the shepherds of Israel who only take care of themselves! Should not shepherds take care of the flock?'** (34:2). Anyone who has been raised on a farm, as I have been, will know that sheep are not the woolly, cuddly creatures that are depicted in children's picture books! They have no concern for their personal cleanliness whatsoever, and are subject to the most awful diseases and pests. Some of my clearest memories of childhood are of days when the sheep were 'dipped' into pools of foul-smelling chemicals to destroy all manner of nasty infections. Ezekiel was right when he referred to shepherding as involving strengthening the weak, healing the sick, binding up the injured and retrieving the strays (34:4). Jesus gave the ultimate sacrifice on behalf of his sheep by laying down his own life for them (John 10:15).

3. The Good Shepherd leads his sheep

Oriental shepherds did not use dogs to retrieve their sheep; they simply called and the sheep followed. Though it is only hinted at in this chapter, Ezekiel does portray the shepherd as **'search[ing]'**, and **'bring[ing] them out'** (34:11, 13). God had led Israel 'like a flock'

(Ps. 80:1). The sheep were to recognize God's voice and follow him (Ps. 23:1-2).

4. The Good Shepherd feeds his sheep

He **'pastures'** them (34:13-15). Jesus was to add: 'I am the gate; whoever enters through me will be saved. He will come in and go out, and find pasture' (John 10:9).

5. The Good Shepherd rules his sheep

As we saw earlier, the term 'shepherd' was synonymous with 'ruler' or 'king' (it is used this way in 34:2). Instead of the false rule of Israel's kings, God's people are to governed by God himself. In the grand design of things, the chapter ends with a picture of the kingdom as it will be at the end. The sheep are gathered together with God as the ruler: **'You my sheep, the sheep of my pasture, are people, and I am your God, declares the Sovereign Lord'** (34:31).

6. The Good Shepherd protects his sheep

He will keep them from every danger: **'They will no longer be plundered'** (34:22). Sheep were harassed by wolves. When hunting in packs the wolf was an animal to be feared. Thus hired hands would run away and leave the sheep to be killed, but the true shepherd would risk his life for them (John 10:12-13). The shepherds of Israel (34:2) had been 'false prophets', wolves in 'sheep's clothing' (cf. Matt. 7:15; Acts 20:29-30).

7. The Good Shepherd seeks his sheep

'I myself will search for my sheep' (34:11). 'I have other sheep', Jesus said, 'that are not of this sheep pen. I must bring them also. They too will listen to my voice, and there shall be one flock and one shepherd' (John 10:16). Jesus is determined to find his sheep, wherever they are!

This is a model both of Jesus' ministry and that of his 'under-shepherds'. Christian ministers are to fashion their ministry on the standards set by the Chief Shepherd. They, too, are to give their lives in service, recalling that God's flock has been purchased by Christ's blood (Acts 20:28). They, too, are to lead their flock by the example of their own godliness and devotion (1 Peter 5:2-3). They, too, as Jesus exhorted Peter, are to feed their flock with the finest of the wheat (John 21:17). They, too, are to rule over their flock; the sheep are to 'submit to their authority' (Heb. 13:17). They, too, are to protect their flock from danger, refuting those who oppose sound doctrine (Titus 1:9). And they, too, are to seek the lost, remembering the indictment made against Israel's false shepherds that **'My sheep ... were scattered over the whole earth, and no one searched or looked for them'** (34:6). God's 'under-shepherds' are to be evangelists (2 Tim. 4:5).

Summary

In contrast to the cruel oppression meted out to the Israelite believers, first by their own people, and then by the Babylonians, God promises to shepherd them himself, by sending 'his servant David' to save, nourish, protect and guide them. The coming of Jesus, God's own Son, will ensure that God's promise to save a people for himself will not fail. His coming will be the assurance that ultimately his people will be gathered to him in safety, to dwell in a kingdom of peace and prosperity for ever. It is the gospel according to Ezekiel that those who put their trust in God's promise are assured of everlasting life and peace with God.

Focus

The land of promise

Jeremiah is the only prophet to use the phrase 'new covenant' (Jer. 31:31-34), but Ezekiel develops the same idea (16:60-63; 34: 1-31; 36:24-38; 37:24-28). One of the elements in this new covenant is the promise given to God's exiled people that they will return to the land: 'For I will take you out of the nations; I will gather you from all the countries and bring you back into your own land' (36:24; cf. 34:13). While this promise includes the immediate promise of return from Babylon — something which began with Cyrus' decree in 539 B.C. and is recounted in the books of Ezra and Nehemiah — there are indications that something far bigger is in store (cf. 34:25-31; 36:33-38). The land is to be a reflection of Eden (36:35).

Exile was a condition which spoke of God's disfavour; it was a reversal of the covenant blessings of the Old Testament. The promise that God's original promise to Abraham was now to be realized must have sounded like music in their ears. But what does this promise mean to us today? Some say that it means that every Christian can expect a portion of Palestine some day in the future. It is a bizarre notion to think that every Christian who has lived over the centuries will occupy tiny Palestine!

A better solution is to imagine the promise that God gave to Abraham (Gen. 12:7; 17:8) as a picture of the paradise God originally made for Adam and Eve: 'This land ... has become like the garden of Eden' (36:35). Canaan was, after all, a land which flowed with milk and honey (Exod. 3:8,17; 13:5; 33:3; Lev. 20:24; Num. 13:27 etc.). The promise of Palestine was in effect a promise of paradise!

This view is confirmed by what John tells us in the last book of the Bible. The New Jerusalem is said to measure 1,500 miles in length, width and height (Rev. 21:16) — a problem for those who see it as a reference to literal Palestine! It is paradise, the new heavens and the new earth, that Christians (Old and New Testament ones) can look forward to. When Jesus pronounced in the Sermon on the Mount: 'Blessed are the meek, for they will inherit the earth' (Matt. 5:5), it is of this paradise that he speaks.

This paradise is pictured in terms of fruitfulness and prosperity (34:25-31) — summarized beautifully by Isaiah when he prophesied that the desert will blossom as a crocus (Isa. 35:1). It is dramatically portrayed in Ezekiel's vision of the dry bones in which the bones come alive (Ezek. 37). The point of the vision is clear: 'I am going to open your grave... I will bring you back to the land of Israel' (37:12). That this is an anticipation of the final consummation is confirmed by Paul when he says that together with the whole creation, which has been groaning as in the pains of childbirth, we too 'wait eagerly for ... the redemption of our bodies' (Rom. 8:22,23).

Three fundamental errors are made when interpreting Old Testament prophecy relating to Israel.

1. I is a mistake to think that God has an entirely different purpose for Israel from the one he has for the church. Our understanding of unfulfilled promises made to Israel in the Old Testament must be governed by such New Testament passages as Paul's interpretative comment in Galatians 6:16, where he refers to the New Testament church as 'the Israel of God'; or Galatians 3:39, where he refers to Christians as 'the children of Abraham'; or when Peter describes the church, in peculiarly Old Testament language, as 'a chosen people, a royal priesthood, a holy nation, a people belonging to God' (1 Peter 2:9).

2. It is a further mistake to think that the Old Testament expects a future earthly millennial kingdom. The New Scofield Bible introduces chapters 40 to 48 of Ezekiel with such headings as: 'The Millennial Temple and its Worship' (40:1 - 47:12) and 'The Division of the Land during the Millennial Age' (47:13 - 48:35). There is an immediate difficulty with a future kingdom which includes animal sacrifices (a problem which the Scofield Bible readily concedes by suggesting that these passages are not to be taken literally!).[1] As we shall see, this is to misunderstand the nature

of these prophecies. Ezekiel is describing in chapters 40 through 48 the glorious future of the people of God in the age to come in terms that Jewish readers in Ezekiel's day would readily understand.

3. It is a mistake to think that these passages teach a restoration of the Jews to their land that goes beyond what happened during the days of Ezra and Nehemiah. Passages such Ezekiel 34:12-13 are often cited to prove this: 'As a shepherd looks after his scattered flock when he is with them, so will I look after my sheep. I will rescue them from all the places where they were scattered on a day of clouds and darkness. I will bring them out from the nations and gather them from the countries, and I will bring them into their own land. I will pasture them on the mountains of Israel, in the ravines and in all the settlements in the land.' The New Scofield Bible applies this section to the restoration of Israel to its land during the millennium. But this would mean little to Ezekiel's immediate listeners. A more natural interpretation is to see it as referring to the immediate return of the Jews, beginning in 538 B.C., and what elements of it are yet unfulfilled must surely apply to the church as a whole — something that awaits all the people of God on the new earth!

Ultimately, what we have in these passages in Ezekiel are glimpses of heaven!

17.
Mountains

Please read Ezekiel 35:1 - 36:38

One of the most remarkable instances of revival occurred on 21 June 1630, when John Livingstone preached in the churchyard at Shotts in Lanarkshire, Scotland, on Ezekiel 36:25-26. It is estimated that 500 people were converted as a result of that single sermon![1] This section of Ezekiel is one God has richly blessed in the past.

When nations found themselves in difficult situations, their enemies would take advantage. Following the collapse of Jerusalem (to Babylon in the north and east), Judah was in no position to fight its enemies to the south. Indeed, the description of things given by Jeremiah is of a land in the grip of internal violence (Jer. 41:1-15). Edom, one such long-standing enemy to the south-east, saw it as a golden opportunity to wage war. Ezekiel has already delivered a prophecy against Edom (25:12-14) in which he has warned of God's vengeance on them for their treachery towards Judah in her time of weakness. Now he expands on the theme once more.

Why the repetition, particularly since the previous chapter has taken us to the heights of restoration and glory? The answer seems to lie in the fact that these chapters were delivered soon after the news of Jerusalem's collapse had come to Ezekiel, and therefore at the very time when what was prophesied in chapter 25 was now actually coming to pass. But more pertinently, chapters 35 and 36 belong together. It will be noticed that the word 'Edom' does not occur at all, but rather **'Mount Seir'** (35:2) — the mountainous region east of the Arabah, the rift valley running south from the Dead Sea, in which lived the Edomites. Today, this area is to be found in Jordan. Chapters 35 and 36 comprise a contrast between Mount Seir (the Edomites) and **'the mountains of Israel'** (36:1).

Though they were linked by ancestry (Esau) and geography (a mountainous terrain), their futures were to be entirely different. God has a plan for our future; what it is depends on whether we are his friends or his enemies.

One of the saddest psalms in the Bible is Psalm137. It is a description of the sorrow felt by the Israelites when they found themselves in exile in Babylon. Mocked by their captors and told to sing, the psalmist describes how they could not sing: 'How can we sing the songs of the Lord while in a foreign land?' (Ps. 137:4). In addition, the psalm mentions the Edomites. The remembrance of what the Edomites have done is still fresh in their memory:

'Remember, O Lord, what the Edomites did
    on the day Jerusalem fell.
"Tear it down," they cried,
    "tear it down to its foundations!"'

(Ps. 137:7).

The Edomites are found guilty on three counts.

1. Their treachery

The Edomites struck Judah **'at the time of their calamity'** (35:5). Some of the inhabitants of Jerusalem managed to escape the lengthy Babylonian siege (one which resulted in such awful atrocities as cannibalism caused by starvation), only to be caught and slaughtered by the Edomites (Obad. 10,14). The Edomites had **'harboured an ancient hostility'** which went back over a thousand years (35:5). It is the memory of past wrongs that is the cause of conflict today in Northern Ireland, former Yugoslavia and Southern Africa, to name but three areas of the world. Times have not changed and once again the relevance of these chapters in Ezekiel comes to the surface.

2. Their expansionist policies

The Edomites had eyes for both Judah and Israel (35:10). They coveted that which was not theirs. It is the drive for more that is the cause of the world's ills. It was, after all, the disastrous policy of King Ahab that despite his enormous wealth he desired the vegetable garden of his neighbour Naboth. The latter's failure to comply with the sovereign's wishes cost him his life (1 Kings 21). In our own economy-dependent society, policy-makers need to re-evaluate the role of covetousness in 'market forces'. Covetousness, it can be argued, lies behind economic recession and the instability of the world's currencies, and unemployment.

It is the same ill as befell King David when sexual greed overcame him as he looked across the rooftops of the city at Bathsheba (2 Sam. 11). Covetousness can sting the best of men as well as the worst of men. This is why we should pray,

> 'Give me neither poverty nor riches,
>   but give me only my daily bread.
> Otherwise, I may have too much and disown you
>   and say, "Who is the Lord?"
> Or I may become poor and steal,
>   and so dishonour the name of my God'
>
> (Prov. 30:8-9).

3. Their blasphemous boasting

The Edomites gloated in the downfall of Israel. But Israel belonged to God and thus their boasting was an insult against God himself: **'You boasted against me and spoke against me without restraint, and I heard it'** (35:13). Their boasting constituted blasphemy against God. Several things come to the surface here.

The first is *irreverence*. To speak or think of God in a way that insults him is a violation of the third commandment, in which we are urged not to 'misuse the name of the Lord' (Exod. 20:7).

The second is *bad language*. The Edomites referred to God euphemistically, not mentioning him by name, but speaking in derogatory terms of 'the mountains of Israel' (35:12; 36:1-2). But in doing so they might as well have used God's name, for their insults meant the same thing in the end. Words that are uttered in times of rage can be blasphemous, even though God's name has not been used. Scripture exhorts us that even the frustrations of life are ordered for our sanctification (Heb. 12:5-11) and we are to be careful what we think and say under pressure.

The third matter is, no doubt, a most humbling discovery: whatever it was the Edomites actually said, God heard it! Nothing can be hidden from him. He knows the secrets of our hearts (cf. Ps. 44:21).

A fourth conclusion emerges: *man's arrogance is short-lived.* God is **'against'** Edom (35:3; cf. 35:2). The land will be ruined (35:3-4) as a result of bloodshed (35:6). It will become **'desolate for ever'** (35:9)[2] It is difficult to be sympathetic when you learn of the downfall of those who have claimed invincibility, particularly when they have mocked your own afflictions. It is understandable why the entire world rejoiced in Edom's demise (35:14). Arrogance is short-lived. This is a word to chill the hearts of the perpetual war-mongers in the world today. God sees and hears and is coming to judge!

The mountains of Israel (36:1-15)

The hearts of many of the Israelites were hardened. A **'heart of stone'** is the root of their trouble. 'A hard heart,' wrote Thomas Watson, 'is the worst heart. It is called a heart of stone (Ezek. 36:26). If it were iron it might be mollified in the furnace, but a stone put in the fire will not melt; it will sooner fly in your face... A hard heart is the anvil on which the hammer of God's justice will be striking to all eternity.'[3]

Does God have a word for those who had experienced the destruction of Judah at the hands of the Babylonians? Israel was **'ravaged and hounded [on] every side'** (36:3). It had **'suffered the scorn of the nations'** (36:6). What does God have to say to those in Jerusalem and southern Judah whose future looked so appallingly gloomy? The news was awful: Babylonian atrocities in Jerusalem and Edomite cruelty in the south. It must have been hard to entertain any faith at all in times like these. And what about Ezekiel's companions in Babylon? What could they look forward to?

Joni Eareckson Tada testifies that 'Early on in my disability there were times when I felt He was asking too much of me: to trust and obey Him in spite of severe paralysis and a life sentence in a wheelchair. I felt like a martyr. That martyr complex, I've come to realize, was fostered by concentrating too much on what God asked of me — and not enough on what God had *given* me.'[4] This is a lesson God is about to teach his suffering people. He has a **'word'** to deliver to them (36:4).

A link is made immediately with the previous chapter by referring again to Edom, Israel's **'enemy'**, and their arrogant claim:
'Aha! The ancient heights have become our possession' (36:2).
He has already spoken of Edom's doom, as well as that of the rest
of the nations (36:5).

Another link is made with an earlier prophecy delivered to the
'mountains of Israel' in chapter 6:1-14. In contrast to the prophecy
of ruin and destruction in chapter 6 — something which Israel has
already experienced — chapter 36 is a prophecy of prosperity and
renewal.

Five main themes are highlighted.[5]

1. God's people are to experience his favour

Israel is to come home again **'soon'** (36:8). In the year 538 B.C. —
some fifty years in the future — King Cyrus of Persia, having
overthrown the Babylonians, issued a decree to send the exiles home
again (though it took over a century to complete the return). Israel
is to be blessed with great prosperity (36:8-12) because God is
'concerned for' them (36:9). When God is 'for' us, no one can be
against us (Rom. 8:31).

2. God is going to vindicate his own name

Currently, Israel was in bad shape. Their inhabitants were scattered
to the four winds. Few of the Israelites who had suffered exile under
the Assyrians had returned. Now, in addition, there was further
displacement by the Babylonians — some as far as North Africa
(Jer. 41:17), others to eastern Iran (Neh. 1:1) and still others to
Europe (Joel 3:6). Cities were ruined and in the southern regions of
Judah the Edomites were causing further havoc. The cause is once
again highlighted: it is Israel's sin. Murder and bloodshed are
singled out (36:18). He compares their condition to that of the
impurity of a woman during her monthly period (36:17).[6] But, one
day, things will be different. God is no longer going to suffer the
ignominy of folk saying that his people have nowhere to live! He
will bring them back **'for the sake of my holy name'** (36:22;
cf.36:21).

This is a theme that runs throughout Ezekiel. God is anxious to
vindicate his own honour. The mountains of Israel will once more

be inhabited by Israelites (36:12). The spies who had scouted
Canaan in Moses' time had concluded that the land 'devours those
living in it' (Num. 13:32). Even in Ezekiel's time folk were still of
the same opinion, often repeating a familiar saying: **'You devour
men'** (36:13). Now that the Babylonians had conquered the land,
they repeated the saying with even greater conviction.

But times are going to change; no longer are the mountains of
Israel to prove so inhospitable (36:15). Days of blessing for God's
church are on the way. One thinks of Pentecost in the first century,
the Reformation in the sixteenth century, the Great Awakening in
the seventeenth century and the missionary expansion of the eight-
eenth and nineteenth centuries as pointers towhat these verses refer
to.

3. God is going to establish a new covenant

How can God bring back from captivity a people whom he has sent
there as just punishment for their sin? One thing is sure: he cannot
do so without a change of heart on the part of Israel! To offer them
forgiveness without a repentant heart on their part would be in
violation of his holy nature. It is a question that can be put more
generally: 'How can a man dead in trespasses and sins, and at enmity
with God, answer a call to the fellowship of the Father and the Son?
How can a mind darkened and depraved have any understanding or
appreciation of the treasures of divine grace? How can his will
incline to the overtures of God's grace in the gospel?'[7]

John Murray, who asks these questions, gives the moving reply:
'The only possible answer is that there must be a change that man
himself cannot initiate, a change that cannot take its origin from
resources resident in human nature, a change radical and all-
pervasive. The only outlet is that man's subjective disposition and
habitus be renewed, that an all-pervasive moral transformation,
changing the whole man in heart, disposition, inclination, desire,
motive, interest, ambition and purpose, be effected.

'The glory of the gospel in this connection is that the divine
remedy ... descends to the lowest depths of man's need, and meets
all the exigencies of man's moral and spiritual conditions. What is
impossible with man is possible with God, for he calls the things that
are not as though they were. We have to reckon with the revelation
and exercise of God's re-creative power and grace. In promise and

fulfilment the message of the gospel is: "A new heart also will I give you, and a new spirit will I put within you: and I will take away the stony heart out of your flesh, and I will give you an heart of flesh"(Ezek. 36:26; cf. 11:19)'.[8]

The precise mechanics of Israel's deliverance highlight several important issues.

First, *God is going to renew the hearts of his people*. God speaks of giving a **'new heart'** and putting in them a **'new spirit'** (36:26). It involves having their hearts 'circumcised' (Deut. 30:6; Jer. 31:31-34). This is what Paul means by suggesting that a Christian is a 'new creation' (2 Cor. 5:17). B. B. Warfield speaks of this change as 'a radical and complete transformation wrought in the soul (Rom. 12:2; Eph. 4:23) by God the Holy Spirit (Titus 3:5; Eph. 4:24), by virtue of which we become "new men" (Eph. 4:24; Col. 3:10), no longer conformed to this world (Rom. 12:2; Eph 4:22; Col. 3:9), but in knowledge and holiness of the truth created after the image of God (Eph. 4:24; Col. 3:10; Rom. 12:2)'.[9]

Second, *it is a cleansing process*. The allusion to sprinkling **'clean water'** (36:25) was a reminder of how important cleansing rituals were for acceptable worship in Israel (cf. Num. 19). Scripture views sin not only as guilt needing to be forgiven, but also as filth needing to be cleansed. Isaiah looks for a day when 'the Lord will wash away the *filth* of the women of Zion ... by a spirit of judgement and a spirit of fire' (Isa. 4:4). And Jeremiah called upon Jerusalem to 'Wash the evil from your heart' (Jer. 4:14). Malachi warns that God 'will be like a refiner's fire or a launderer's soap. He will sit as a refiner and purifier of silver; he will *purify* the Levites and *refine* them like gold and silver' (Mal. 3:2-3). So, too, does Ezekiel report God as saying, **'I will sprinkle clean water upon you, and you will be *clean from all your impurities* and I will *cleanse* you from all your idols'** (36:25). Sinful behaviour makes us dirty and just as we are repelled by dirt, so is God.

Cleansing from sin and sin's effects lies behind the use of water in baptism as a symbol of what spiritual conversion is all about: a washing and a cleansing from sin (John 13:10; 15:3; Acts 22:16; 1 Cor. 6:11; Eph. 5:25-27; Heb. 9:13-14; 10:22; 1 John 1:7-9). Nicodemus was chided for not picking up the reference to Ezekiel 36:25-27 in Jesus' words to him about the need to be born again by 'water and the spirit'.[10] As a teacher in Israel, he should have known better! Forgiveness is effected by washing — not the symbol of

baptism, but the reality of Jesus' blood applied by the Holy Spirit
(1 John 1:7). 'You were washed,' Paul assured the Corinthian
believers (1 Cor. 6:11). 'Unless I wash you,' Jesus warned Peter,
'you have no part with me' (John 13:8). Indeed, the entire Christian
life can be described in terms of cleansing of oneself from whatever
makes one dirty in God's eyes (2 Cor. 7:1; Eph. 5:3-5; 2 Tim. 2:20-
22; 1 John 3:3).

Third, *it is a change that results in the indwelling of the Holy
Spirit.* **'I will put my Spirit in you,'** God says (36:27). Every
believer 'receives' the Holy Spirit (Acts 2:38; Gal. 3:2) as a 'seal'
of God's ownership (2 Cor.1:22; Eph. 1:13). The Holy Spirit's
presence in the hearts of believers serves as a transforming agent:
cleansing, protecting, encouraging and assuring. This is what is
meant by Ezekiel's words in verse 26: **'I will give you a new heart
and put a new spirit in you; I will remove from you your heart
of stone and give you a heart of flesh.'** Though it must be insisted
upon that Old Testament believers participated in this ministry of
the Holy Spirit, too — take, for example, David's fear in Psalm 51
that his adultery might result in the withdrawal of the Holy Spirit
(Ps. 51:11) — the prophets foretold the dawning of a new age in
which this ministry would be heightened dramatically (cf. Isa. 42:1;
44:3; 59:21; Joel 2:28-32).[11]

Fourth, as a consequence of the Spirit's indwelling, *God's
people will be characterized by a desire for holiness.* **'And I will put
my Spirit in you and move you to follow my decrees and be
careful to keep my laws'** (36:27). Christians are to 'walk in the
Spirit' (Gal. 5:16), saying 'No!' to the 'desires of the flesh' (cf. the
loathing of past sins signalled in verse 31: **'You will loathe
yourselves for your sins and detestable practices'**) and, instead,
allowing the Spirit to bring forth nine 'fruits' of Christlikeness: love,
joy, peace, patience, kindness, goodness, faithfulness, gentleness
and self-control (Gal. 5:22-23). As a preface to his commentary on
the New Testament, Matthew Henry wrote, 'All the grace contained
in this book is owing to Jesus Christ as our Lord and Saviour and
unless we consent to take him as our Lord we cannot expect any
benefit from him as our Saviour.'

Fifth, and in summary, *God is going to establish a new covenant.*
The restoration of which Ezekiel speaks in these verses is one which
anticipates the renewal of the blessing which was at the heart of
every divine covenant: **'You will be my people, and I will be your**

God' (36:28). From the start, God had been revealing his single purpose of establishing a relationship of fellowship and trust between himself and his elect people. Time and again he had repeated it as his aim: pledging himself to men, to bless them; they, in turn, pledging themselves to him, to serve him. 'I will be your God, and you shall be my people,' had been the commitment to a relationship repeated throughout the Old Testament and into the New (Gen. 17:7-14; Exod. 19:4-6; Lev. 26:12; Deut. 7:6; 14:2; Jer. 11:3-4 30:22; 31:33; Ezek. 11:20; 36:28; Zech. 8:8; 2 Cor. 6:16; Rev. 21:3). Luther once said that the very essence of Christianity was these personal pronouns: 'my' and 'your'.

Sixth, *the new covenant era is portrayed in terms of the restoration of Eden.* The language used here is that of rebuilding and restoring the land so as resemble the pristine condition of Eden in its beauty and productivity: **'They will say, "This land that was laid waste has become like the garden of Eden"'** (36:35). John Milton was right to refer to the work of God in salvation as *Paradise Regained.*

Ezekiel is only reflecting what his fellow-prophet in Jerusalem a century earlier had said: 'He will make deserts like Eden' (Isa. 51:3). Earlier in his prophecy, Isaiah had spoken of the wilderness becoming a fruitful field (32:15), the desert blossoming as the crocus (35:1), the dry places turning into springs of water (35:7). If the Messiah is the second David (34:23; 37:24), he is also the second Adam reigning in a restored Eden. This is the idea that lies behind all the passages which speak of the natural beauty of the Messianic kingdom. Amos depicts it in terms which are equally graphic: there will not be sufficient time to gather in either the corn crops or the vintage. In each case the sower of seed for the next crop will find the reaper of the last crop still at work. The abundance will be such that the mountains will ooze with 'sweet wine' (Amos 9:11-15). The curse is gone! Here we see fulfilled the very blessing that the covenant made with Moses had promised (Deut 30:1-3). It is what John glimpses as he speaks of the new kingdom in terms of 'a tree of life' and a 'paradise' to be gained (Rev. 2:7).

Seventh, *the new covenant era is portrayed in terms of an ingathering of a vast number of people.* **'I will make their people as numerous as sheep, as numerous as the flocks for offerings at Jerusalem during her appointed feasts. So will the ruined cities be filled with flocks of people'** (36:37-38). On the three great feast days (Passover, Pentecost and Tabernacles) the streets of Jerusalem were filled with worshippers from all parts of the land. Of even greater interest would have been the sheep and goats mingling with the pilgrims in the narrow streets of the city. The animals had been brought for sacrifice. This must have been a sight that Ezekiel's listeners wondered whether they would ever see again. But a day will dawn when God's blessing will ensure that multitudes will throng the city again. This is not a promise to literal Jerusalem as such, but to the purposes of God as regards his church. The number of the redeemed will not be trifling.[12]

Eighth, this is a blessing for which *God's people are to pray.* **'Once again I will yield to the plea of the house of Israel and do this for them'** (36:37). Jonathan Edwards once wrote, 'When God has something very great to accomplish for his church, it is his will that there should precede it, the extraordinary prayers of his people ... and it is revealed that, when God is about to accomplish great things for his church, he will begin by remarkably pouring out the spirit of grace and supplication (Zech. 12:10).[13] God has resolved to bring back his captive people according to the good pleasure of his will. He announces his grand design without qualification or contingency. Yet this revealed purpose will be worked out through the prayers of his people. God has planned to use our prayers in accomplishment of his redemptive purposes.[14]

It was this belief in the effectiveness of human prayer as well as the sovereignty of God that encouraged Daniel, upon discovering God's promise of deliverance in Jeremiah 25:11-12, to pray for it! (Dan. 9). This is a vision we need to catch. Whatever we do, wherever we are, all through life, God has his plan for our daily lives. One of the ways this plan is realized is by the prayers of God's people. As Spurgeon once wrote, 'It is well said that "Asking is the rule of the kingdom." It is a rule that will never be altered in anybody's case. If the royal and divine Son of God cannot be exempted from the rule of asking that he may have, you and I cannot expect to have the rule relaxed in our favour.

'God will bless Elijah and send rain on Israel, but Elijah must pray for it. If the chosen nation is to prosper, Samuel must plead for it. If the Jews are to be delivered, Daniel must intercede. God will bless Paul, and the nations shall be converted through him, but Paul must pray. Pray he did, without ceasing; his epistles show that he expected nothing except by asking for it.'[15]

Summary

Chapters 35 and 36 have been a study in contrasts: the treacherous Edomites are going to be judged; the people of God are going to be restored and blessed abundantly. These chapters contain one of the greatest statements of God's intention to gather his people to himself so far in this book. What has emerged clearly at the close of the chapter is a principle God's people are to be careful to note: that blessing comes in answer to prayer. When God's people are under threat, they must turn to God and claim his promises of deliverance and protection. In 1588, when the Catholic forces of the Spanish Aramada set out to conquer England and establish Catholic rule over England, various skirmishes took place in the English Channel. Then, just as suddenly as they had arrived, a storm blew the Spanish ships off course and they were driven home again. Why? Because the people of God in congregations all over England had gone to their knees to pray for deliverance. Prayer changed the course of history. It can do it again!

18.
The valley of dry bones

Please read Ezekiel 37:1-28

This is a chapter which features the work of God's Spirit. The word 'spirit', in both Hebrew and Greek, is a picture word. It pictures breath breathed, or panted out, as when you blow out candles on a birthday cake or puff and blow as you run. Spirit, as J. I. Packer delightfully illustrates, 'was what the big bad wolf was threatening the little pigs with when he told them, "I'll huff, and I'll puff, and I'll blow your house down!" The picture is of air made to move vigorously, even violently, and the thought that the picture expresses is of energy let loose, executive force invading, power in exercise, life demonstrated by activity.'[1] When 'Spirit' is used of the Holy Spirit, it is meant to convey the powerful effect of his work.

Here, in Ezekiel 37, the word 'spirit' refers to breath, wind and the Holy Spirit in quick succession. It is meant to signal (as it evidently did to Hebrew readers) that the work of the Holy Spirit is both powerful and visible.

Not since chapter 11 have we been told that Ezekiel was taken somewhere by the **'hand of the Lord'** (37:1). The prophet is taken to a **'valley'** to observe a gruesome sight: the unburied, skeletal remains of a fallen army. It is a depiction of Jerusalem after its fall to the Babylonians, and it comes at what must have been one of the lowest points in the recorded history of Israel. At such a point, God comes with a word of great encouragement to cheer the hearts of his despondent people. It is a vision in which the bones come to life by the intervention of his sovereign power. When things are at their lowest ebb, God intervenes with promises of hope, blessing and revival.

Upon inspection, Ezekiel finds that the bones are 'very dry'

(37:2). The Israelites had been in exile for over ten years and the vision is meant to signify that what hope they had once possessed is now gone. They were, just as these bones, 'very dry'. It is a picture of deadness and desolation. The question is asked: **'Can these bones live?'** (37:3). The answer is, of course, negative as far as any inherent power in the bones themselves is concerned. They are utterly dead and lifeless. Any possibility of life must come by the intervention of an outside force or agency, one who alone has power to bestow life: that is, God himself.

How do these bones live again? God uses three means to accomplish it.

1. The preaching of the Word

Ezekiel is told to **'prophesy'** (37:4; literally: 'preach God's Word'), and does as he is told (37:7).

2. The prayer of God's servant

God urges Ezekiel to call upon the **'breath'** to come and breathe into the slain (37:9). As we have already seen, the passage uses the words 'wind,' 'breath' and 'spirit' interchangeably. Even though God may have promised something, he invariably links the promise with the prayers of his people.

3. The power of the Holy Spirit

'This is what the Sovereign Lord says to these bones: I will make breath enter you, and you will come to life' (37:5; for 'breath' we can read 'Spirit').

These are the ingredients of any work of revival by God. It is the explanation of what occurred at Pentecost, when 3,000 people came to faith as the result of preaching (Acts 2:14-39), prayer (Acts 1:14) and the powerful work of the Holy Spirit (cf. Acts 2:18,38).

It must have been difficult for the Israelites to imagine themselves as a nation again. Other nations had gone into oblivion before them, and the faithless no doubt reasoned that the same fate awaited Israel now. But they were wrong. God had a purpose to establish with this nation, not least the birth of his own Son as the Redeemer of sinners. Consequently, they are to return to the land: **'I will put my Spirit in you and you will live, and I will settle you in your own land'** (37:14). Changing the picture slightly — this only highlights the fact that this was a vision — the bones, instead of lying on the surface depicting a battlefield, are now described as buried in **'graves'** (37:13). In any case, the graves are to be opened to give up their dead. The dead, lifeless army is to come to life again!

It is probably a mistake to think that this passage is meant to signify a belief in the resurrection of the body. The Old Testament for sure does teach it (Dan. 12:2), but the point of Ezekiel 37 is quite different. Its purpose, first of all, is to give a vivid demonstration to a dejected people that a return of the exiles to their land again was going to take place. In their present condition, it would be like life from the dead. But it was also a way of signalling that God has a greater purpose to accomplish with his people than they might have imagined. Persia, Babylon's eventual conqueror, was hardly observable at this point in history, and even if it had been possible to predict its rise to power, the chances were that the Persians would prove no less amenable to the Jews than the Babylonians had been. Resettlement and favour of the order predicted in Ezekiel 37 (and the preceding chapters) looked like so much 'pie in the sky'. But their reasoning was the reasoning of unbelief. They had not reckoned on the power of God.

When Elisha's servant saw the Syrian forces camped on the hills surrounding the prophet's tent, he cried out in despair: 'Oh, my lord, what shall we do?' (2 Kings 6:15). It was a cry of despair. But Elisha was not afraid of the Syrian king nor his intimidating army. His eyes, unlike those of his servant, were wide open. In words of supreme confidence he was able to say, 'Don't be afraid. Those who are with us are more than those who are with them' (2 Kings 6:16).

'Honour the Holy Spirit' was the cry of Evan Roberts during the Welsh revival of 1904 and it would appear to be the very theme of Ezekiel 37. Initially, it is about the restoration of the exiles from Babylon. But this chapter provides us with principles which apply in every age, for the truth at the heart of this passage is that the unregenerate man is 'dead'. He has no more power to effect a change of heart than does a skeleton. It means, as Paul applies with rigorous logic, that the natural man is dead in sin, unable to respond to the gospel or exercise faith, and the only solution to his predicament is sovereign grace (see Eph. 2:1-10).

And if this is true of individuals, it is also true when considered

collectively. The conversion of large numbers of people all at once
— in effect, what this chapter foresees — is something that can be
brought about only by the Spirit's efficacious power. Thus, revival
— something that the Bible describes as God 'awakening', 'aris-
ing,' or 'drawing near' (see Ps. 44:23-26; 69:18; 80:14) is a work of
the Holy Spirit's power. If we desire revival in our day, then we must
honour the Holy Spirit!

Nehemiah describes the revival that took place at the return of the
exiles. He tells of a six-hour service in which the people fasted, read
the Scriptures, wept, repented of past sins and committed themselves to renewed service (Neh. 8-10). Revival comes when God
turns away his wrath, revitalizes the church by stirring the hearts of
his people and gathers in a great number of the lost. It is a work of
sovereign grace. 'The only organizer of revival is God the Holy
Spirit.'[2] As Ezekiel insists, it is something for which we should pray
(36:37).

The symbolism of the two sticks (37:15-28)

One of the more obvious indications in Israel of God's disfavour,
even before the exile, was that of her disunity. Since the time of
Jeroboam in the tenth century B.C. the land had been divided into
two: Israel to the north and Judah to the south. Skirmishes had taken
place between the two nations at periodic intervals. Israel collapsed
in 722 B.C., annexed by the Assyrians, and Judah was left to face
the Babylonians alone. Now that Judah had fallen too, 'The idea of
a reunified Israel of the sort that David and Solomon had ruled over
in the ninth century would have seemed ludicrous to any observer
of international events in Ezekiel's day.'[3] As I write these lines,
Germany has been reunited following almost fifty years of division
as a consequence of the Second World War. Ten years ago, it would
have been thought impossible that East Germans, who were frequently shot for attempting to cross over to West Berlin, should now
live with West Germans in a united country. Nothing is impossible
to God.

Since the passage speaks of a reunification, many readers of
Ezekiel have wanted to see its fulfilment in quite literal terms.
Further, since political reunification never did take place after the
exile — Israel was gradually submerged under the influence of the
great empires that followed (Persian, Greek, Seleucid, Roman etc.)

— there is still in many quarters a desire to see this reunification and many have seen its fulfilment in the formation of the state of Israel in 1947. This is a mistake.[4]

To demonstrate his prophecy, Ezekiel is once again required to use a practical illustration by taking two sticks, upon which were written, **'Judah and the Israelites associated with him,'** and **'Ephraim's stick, belonging to Joseph and all the house of Israel associated with him'** (36:16). The northern kingdom is referred to as 'Joseph' and 'Ephraim' because, as we have noticed already, Ezekiel has used the term 'Israel' to denote Judah (as all the prophets did at this time) since the northern kingdom had long since disappeared.[5]

The addition of 'all the house of Israel associated with him' in both cases is meant to indicate that the prophecy thus concerns the whole nation descended from Jacob. In joining the two sticks as **'one'** in his hand (37:17), the prophet thus symbolized 'Israel's' return from exile (37:21) and complete reunification (37:22). The reunited Israel is to be ruled over by one king: **'There will be one king over all of them and they will never again be two nations or be divided into two kingdoms'** (37:22). This is something he has said before (34:24).

The heart of the promise is breathtaking in its scope: **'My servant David will be king over them, and they will all have one shepherd. They will follow my laws and be careful to keep my decrees. They will live in the land I gave to my servant Jacob, the land where your fathers lived. They and their children and their children's children will live there for ever, and David my servant will be their prince for ever. I will make a covenant of peace with them; it will be an everlasting covenant. I will establish them and increase their numbers, and I will put my sanctuary among them for ever. My dwelling-place will be with them; I will be their God, and they will be my people. Then the nations will know that I the Lord make Israel holy, when my sanctuary is among them for ever'** (37:24-28).

Several features are highlighted and repeated.

1. The renewal of the covenant

God is going to renew his covenant relationship with his people, underlining the essential feature of it as *union and communion with himself*: **'They will be my people, and I will be their God'** (37:23, 27; cf. 11:20; 14:11; Gen. 17:8; Jer. 24:7; 31:33; 32:38; 2 Cor. 6:16; Heb. 8:10).

2. Continuity with the old

In speaking of what God will do *in the future,* Ezekiel combines allusions to what God *had already promised* by way of a covenant to Abraham (they are to live in the promised land), Moses (they are to keep all of God's commandments) and David (a prince, king and shepherd is to rule over them). The essential features of the covenant in both the Old Testament and the New are one and the same. They are in a sense an anticipation of the final relationship that God will have with his people in the age to come and referred to as the *covenant of peace.* Just as we would expect the **'covenant of peace'** (37:26) to be described as **'everlasting'**, so, too, we find that previous anticipations of it been so described; so, for example, the covenant made with Abraham (Gen. 17:7; Ps 105:10), and that with Moses (Exod. 40:15; Lev. 16:34; 24:8; Isa. 24:5) and with David (2 Sam. 7:13,16; Ps. 89:3,4; 132:11,12). But 'God's previous covenants may be regarded as "everlasting" only insofar as they find their realization in the new covenant.'[6] And eventually the new covenant gives way to its final expression in the 'covenant of peace', where 'all the promises of God find their consummation'.[7]

3. The people are to be restored to the 'land'

The covenant of peace promises the regathering of Israel to their own land (37:21,26; cf. 34:13). Jeremiah, writing about the same time, put it in similar terms: 'I will bring my people Israel and Judah back from captivity and restore them to the land I gave their forefathers to possess' (Jer 30:3; cf. 32:37; 50:5). This, as we have seen, is a reference to the return of the Jews to Palestine following the decree of Cyrus in 538 B.C. But this prophecy also anticipates the blessing God's people will receive at the coming of Christ and the future kingdom of glory. This is the new heavens and the new earth promised as a dwelling-place for God's people.[8]

As Calvin comments on Jeremiah 32, where a similar promise is given, 'When Christians explain this passage and the like, they leave out the liberation of the people from Babylonish exile, as though these prophecies did not belong at all to the time; in this they are mistaken. And the Jews, who reject Christ, stop in that earthly deliverance. But the prophets, as I have said, begin with the return of the people, but they set Christ also in the middle, that the faithful might know that the return was but a slight taste of the full grace, which was alone to be expected from Christ; for it was then, indeed, that God really planted his people.'[9]

4. Christ is the focus of the covenant

The theme, 'I shall be your God and you will be my people' (cf. 37:23,27), reaches its climax in Jesus Christ. It has been something that Isaiah has already made plain in speaking of the coming Saviour as 'a covenant for the people' (Isa. 42:6). When Jesus arrives, it will not be the 'blood of the covenant' that he will administer as Moses had done, but his *own* blood: 'This is *my* blood of the covenant...' (Matt. 26:28). The anticipated Messiah-king (37:24) finds his fulfilment in Jesus of Nazareth. The title 'Christ' was not just a label, like an English surname, but a title of royalty: 'Jesus Christ' corresponds to '*Prince* Philip' not 'Philip *Mountbatten*'. The title marked him out as God's Messiah, the anointed son of David (cf. 37:24).

5. The work of the Holy Spirit

An important feature of the new covenant involves the work of the Holy Spirit. The Holy Spirit is going to dwell in the hearts of God's people to a degree that he did not do during the Old Testament administration. The effect will be a cleansing from sin (37:23), a writing of the law upon the hearts (37:24; cf. Jer. 31:33) and a unity among God's people (37:15-17).

Summary

When Israel first entered the land under Joshua they remembered the blessings of the covenant they were to expect for their obedience to God's ways (Deut. 27-29). It is the most remarkable testimony to God's faithfulness that these blessings were to be kept, despite Israel's profligate ways. To be sure, their apostasy brought upon them God's judgement of exile. But Israel is to return to the land and be blessed in a way they could hardly imagine. God is going to gather his people again and circumcise their hearts (Deut. 30:6). But the blessing God has in store is not for ethnic Israel. God has a far greater purpose in store. Even here in Ezekiel, 'Israel' begins to take on an entirely different meaning. Glimpses of God's grand design had been given already: the famine that Elijah brought down on Israel was to result in the blessing of a Gentile widow (1 Kings 17:8-24; Luke 4:26). Naaman, a Syrian general raised up as a scourge on Israel, was healed by Elisha in order to continue his vengeance on Israel. Jonah is commanded to preach the Word of God to a Gentile city, a task that he finds quite offensive (Jonah 1:2). God is going to gather his people from every tribe and tongue and nation. The apostasy of Israel is blessing for the Gentile nations of the world.

When God's judgement came, the tree was felled leaving only a stump (Isa. 10-11); only the gleanings were left in the corner of the field, only a few olives left unpicked at the top of the tree (Isa. 17:6). Despite the severity of the judgement, a remnant remains. From this remnant will arise God's people.

God is going to save his people; it is a task that he alone can accomplish. In answer to the question, 'Son of man, can these bones live?' (37:3), God revealed the coming power of the Holy Spirit in drawing lost humanity to himself. It is this very image, of a valley of dry, lifeless bones, that Paul must surely have had in mind as he recounted to the Ephesians the nature of the natural man as dead in trespasses and sins (Eph. 2:1). If sinners are to be saved, God must do a mighty work. This he promises to do. He will not only deliver them; he will take away their hearts of stone (36:26-27). He will establish a new covenant (Jer. 31:31-34) in which peace with God and with one another will be the characteristic feature. This is the reason why Ezekiel refers to this covenant as a covenant of peace (37:26).

From the start, Israel had been characterized by disunity and disobedience. From the time of Jeroboam onwards, the decline had been obvious. Israel's history had been a parable on the nature of man himself: twisted, perverse, unreformable. What Israel needed was a new beginning. From Elijah to John the Baptist, all the prophets were preparing for the one who was to come. Indeed, even Moses had foretold his coming (Deut 18:18). Prophets like Ezekiel spoke and wrote painful messages of Israel's apostasy, judgement and doom. But they were more than just prophets of doom. They were watchmen on the walls of Jerusalem anticipating the coming of God's Saviour and the people's salvation (cf. Ezek. 33; Isa. 62:6-7).

Part VII
Times of tribulation ahead
(Ezek. 38-39)

19.
Gog

Please read Ezekiel 38:1 - 39:29

The promises in the previous chapters of a return to the land might have sounded fine if Babylon was all there was to contend with. After all, the Babylonian empire was already beginning to wane. But, as Paul put it, 'Our struggle is not against flesh and blood, but against the rulers, against the authorities, against the powers of this dark world and against the spiritual forces of evil in the heavenly realms' (Eph. 6:12). The devil is a force to be reckoned with, and we should make no mistake in thinking otherwise. To do so would be his victory and our loss.

There are chapters in Ezekiel which are difficult and these are two of them! We should not be put off by this. Peter admits to us that he found certain passages in Paul's letters more than a little baffling (2 Peter 3:16). When the Holy Spirit inspired the Word of God, he did not always use the simplest language to convey the message. He asks us to think and study, and thus get to grips with Scripture's message.

Bible students have fallen into the trap of misinterpreting these chapters again and again. So, for example, with an eye to the fact that a figure called 'Gog' comes 'out of the north' the range of interpretations knows no limit. For the past half-century, Russia has been the hot favourite as the evil Gog from the north.[1] The collapse of the Soviet Union will, perhaps, prove to be the undoing of this interpretation!

Israel was well aware that she had enemies. When Ezekiel singled out, in earlier chapters, such countries as Ammon, Moab, Edom, Philistia, Tyre, Egypt etc., it proved no great surprise to his listeners. They were, after all, Israel's enemies. But there were countries about which Israel knew nothing, states which were at that time either too far away, or of too little importance, to be a threat to her existence. If God's promise of complete victory is going to mean anything, these potential enemies must also be dealt with.

The identification of **'Gog'** and **'Magog'** (38:2) must take into consideration the fact that they are mentioned again, at the close of the book of Revelation (Rev. 20:8). The issue is complicated further by the differing views held with regard to the nature of the Second Coming of Christ and the issues which accompany it. Before we consider a definite interpretation, we need to examine what is said by way of a description of Gog and his intended opposition against the people of God.

1. His name and origin

Ezekiel is told to set his face against **'Gog, of the land of Magog, the chief prince of Meshech and Tubal'** (38:2; cf. 39:1-2). Meshech and Tubal have been mentioned before in Ezekiel: both traded with Tyre (27:13), and both suffer the same terrible end as the Egyptians (32:26). The people of Meshech, we know, were of Indo-European descent and lived in an area south-east of the Black Sea where they allied themselves with the people of Tubal, who lived in the same region. Magog is mentioned twice before in the Old Testament (Gen. 10:2; 1 Chron.1:5), but has proved unidentifiable. All we know for certain is that it was in the far north (cf. 38:6,15; 39:2). As Stuart puts it, 'We know nothing of this place, and Ezekiel's original audience probably didn't either, thinking of it as a distant, obscure land having the same sort of connotation that "Timbuktu" has in our ears.'[2] Ezekiel is to set his face against a distant, warlike nation of unidentifiable origin. Already we get the hint that 'Gog' and 'Magog' are being used as symbols of an enemy to come — whoever it might be, and from whatever region.

2. His warlike nature

Gog and his coalition of forces (28:5-6 mentions **'Persia'**, **'Cush'**, **'Put'**, **'Gomer**, and **'Beth Togarmah'**)[3] is bent on making war. The picture is vivid: **'your horses, your horsemen fully armed, and a great horde with large and small shields, all of them brandishing their swords'** (38:4; cf. 5-6). It is immediately apparent that these forces form a circle of opposition originating from the furthermost regions of the then known world. Their approach is likened to a coming storm cloud (38:9,16). Already, however, we are told of the limitations of the enemies' powers. Though Gog and his allies are a force to be reckoned with — the destruction caused will be breathtaking — God imposes limits. He places boundaries upon Gog's powers. Mention is made of controlling Gog's power in the same way as a fisherman might control a fish by using **'hooks'** in its jaws (38:4).

3. The time of the battle

Gog and his allies are told to prepare for a battle (38:7), a battle that is to take place **'after many days ... in future years'** (38:8). The timing is vague and imprecise, just as the identity of Gog and Magog has been. Once again Ezekiel seems to be preparing them for a battle 'some time in the future'. With an eye on Revelation 20, we can already see that Ezekiel is speaking, if not exclusively, then partially of an event at the end of time.[4]

4. The extent of the battle

Everything Israel has worked for is to be plundered (38:10-12). The Israelites have no real protection: it is **'a land of unwalled villages ... peaceful and unsuspecting ... living without walls and without gates and bars'** (38:11). Other nations, unwilling to instigate the attack, join in the plundering and profit from the sale of goods (38:13).

5. The size of the invading army

In the description of the massacre of Gog's forces, Ezekiel tells us that it would take seven months to bury the corpses (39:12). The burial ground is referred to as **'the Valley of Hamon Gog'**, meaning 'Gog's Multitude' (39:11). Their wooden shields, bows and arrows would provide enough firewood for seven years! (39:9).

6. God's intervention on behalf of his people

Gog will suffer for his crimes. God will not stand helplessly by as he watches his people being persecuted. The 'weapons' to be used against him are listed, including **'a great earthquake'** (38:19), **'a**

sword' (38:21), **'plague and bloodshed ... torrents of rain, hailstones and burning sulphur'** (38:22). In the confusion, Gog's forces will kill each other (38:21).

Chapter 39 focuses on this deliverance in even greater detail. When God arises, his enemies are powerless: **'Then I will strike your bow from your left hand and make your arrows drop from your right hand'** (39:3). In summary, Gog's army falls and their bodies are left scattered on the mountains of Israel as a prey to wild beasts, and their remains will take seven months to bury. Their weapons will also provide the people of Israel with sufficient firewood for seven years to come (39:4-20). Even those who were not part of the invading force, but allied themselves with it, will be destroyed by fire (39:6). The figure seven, once again, is meant to convey the symbolic nature of the picture Ezekiel is drawing. In a scene of total destruction, Israel now plunders. Gog's defeated army is so much carrion for birds and wild animals (39:17-20).

7. The vindication of God's name

Israel was to learn three fundamental lessons from this episode.

First and foremost, they were to appreciate that *the Babylonian captivity was not to be the final source of difficulty in their future history*. Having encouraged them with promises of a return to blessing (chapters 32-37) Ezekiel now wishes them to know that there will be trouble in the earth right up to the very end.

Secondly, their afflictions, both present and future, *would be due to their sin* (39:23-24). It had been so in Egypt, Assyria and Babylon. It will be the same with Gog's forces.

Thirdly, they are equally to appreciate that *God has not abandoned them entirely*. Just at the point of their final overthrow, God will intervene to save them. It will teach them that though he must punish, he will not forsake. In all of this his purpose is to glorify his own name: **'I will display my glory among the nations...'** (39:21).

Having mentioned the **'exile'** in verse 23, Ezekiel has brought matters right back to his own day. The ending (39:25-29) is a summary of what he said before. Having received her just deserts (39:26), Israel will once again be a praise to God (39:27). The exile will be temporary; soon they will return to their homeland. And once again God will vindicate his reputation: **'I will be zealous for**

my holy name' (39:25).This is the lesson that Scripture is most anxious to get across: that God is working out his purpose for his people in every circumstance of their lives (cf. Rom. 8:28). They will know 'trouble ... hardship ... persecution ... famine ... danger ... sword' (Rom. 8:35). But the purpose is, as Daniel was to say concerning another difficult time in the church's future, 'so that they may be refined, purified and made spotless' (Dan. 11:35).

What is the significance of all of this for us today?

1. God is in control

God both instigates (38:14-16) and controls (38:4) what Gog does. God uses the unregenerate to accomplish his overall plan and purpose. This is a truth which Isaiah had made clear when talking about the Assyrian invasion (Isa. 10:5-34). God has used Egypt in Israel's past history to similar effect. The same lesson is taught in the death of Christ. Peter insists that though wicked men put him to death — an act for which they are held responsible — it was, nevertheless, according to the 'set purpose and foreknowledge' of God (Acts 2:23).

Whatever happens in the history of this world, the events cannot be evaluated properly without taking into consideration the fact that God intervenes. Historians study events and attempt, if they can, to trace the sequences of cause and effect. But, more often than not, they do not reckon on divine intervention. As Abraham Kuyper once wrote, 'If once the curtain were pulled back, and the spiritual world behind it came to view, it would expose to our spiritual vision a struggle so intense, so convulsive, sweeping everything within its range, that the fiercest battle ever fought on earth would seem, by comparison, a mere game. Not here, but up there — that is where the real conflict is waged.'[5]

This is a message which ultimately proved to be a source of encouragement to God's beleaguered people. Ezekiel's vision describes wave upon wave of Gog's coming attacks. The aim is clear: he is set on Israel's complete destruction. But the kingdom of darkness never learns the lesson: 'Man proposes, God disposes.'[6] Gog, like the Pharaoh of Egypt, or Nebuchadnezzar of Babylon, or Antiochus Epiphanes of Syria, or the Antichrist of New Testament revelation, will never consider for one moment that he is doomed to destruction.

2. A period of tribulation foretold

The passage indicates that we are to expect a period of tribulation at the end of history.[7] It becomes clear that the battle in view here is one which other prophets have spoken about (38:17). To be sure, Gog has not been mentioned anywhere else among the prophets, but many had predicted danger coming from the north. Among them is Joel, who spoke of a 'northern army' sent against Israel but destroyed in the last battle (Joel 2:1-11). Another passage which Ezekiel may be thinking of here is Deuteronomy 28:49: 'The Lord will bring a nation against you from far away, from the ends of the earth, like an eagle swooping down, a nation whose language you will not understand.' The 'nation' in view here is not specified, but represents Assyria (Isa. 5:26; Hosea 8:1), and Babylon (Jer. 5:15; 48:40; Hab. 1:8).[8]

The non-specific nature of this prophecy is meant to convey a threat that the church can expect at any time, right up to and including the 'Battle of Armageddon' as represented in Revelation 16 and 19. And in Revelation 20, following a description of the binding of Satan for a thousand years (understood to be the period of the New Testament right up until the advent of Christ), Satan is said to be 'set free for a short time' (Rev. 20:3).

Both Old and New Testaments expect a period of tribulation to characterize the period prior to the end. Jeremiah speaks of a 'time of trouble', adding concerning the day, 'None will be like it' (Jer. 30:7). Daniel speaks of a 'time of distress such as has not happened from the beginning' (Dan. 12:1).[9] And in the Olivet Discourse (Matt. 24:3-51), Jesus not only tells of the immediate destruction of Jerusalem in A.D. 70 (Matt. 24:2), and further admits that the entire history of the church is to know tribulation (Matt 24:9-10), but also warns that the church can expect a final tribulation — one which is anticipated by the destruction of Jerusalem: 'For then there will be great distress, unequalled from the beginning of the world until now — and never to be equalled again...' (Matt. 24:21).[10] In addition there are the signs of apostasy that mark the period before Christ's coming (2 Thess. 2:1-3) and the appearance of Antichrist (Dan. 11:36-45; 2 Thess. 2:4).

3. God will be glorified

God is going to be glorified, no matter what he does. The picture of judgement given us in Ezekiel 39:17-24 is an extremely graphic one. God invites birds and wild beasts to feast upon the remains of fallen warriors as though they were participating in a huge sacrificial meal. This picture is repeated in Revelation 19:17-21. It is a horrifying description and the reality it depicts must surely be even worse. But though we may shy away from these powerful descriptions of God's holy nature (Ezekiel did not!) we must remember that God is going to be glorified, even in the destruction of the wicked. When the holy God asserts himself in righteous judgement then he is 'sanctified': 'But the Lord Almighty will be exalted by his justice' (Isa. 5:16). It is precisely this theme which God is anxious to get across in these chapters: **'And so I will show my greatness and my holiness, and I will make myself known in the sight of many nations. Then they will know that I am the Lord'** (38:23). God is going to make himself known, even in judgement, and get honour to himself. God is *jealous* of his name (39:25, 'zealous' NIV). **'I will make known my holy name among my people Israel. I will no longer let my name be profaned, and the nations will know that I the Lord am the Holy One in Israel'** (39:7).

If God is zealous to maintain his honour, then so should we be. 'A zealous man in religion,' wrote J. C. Ryle, 'is pre-eminently *a man of one thing*. It is not enough to say that he is earnest, hearty, uncompromising, thorough-going, whole-hearted, fervent in spirit. He only sees one thing, he cares for one thing, he lives for one thing, he is swallowed up in one thing; and that one thing is to please God.'[11]

4. *The scale of opposition is huge* (39:9-12)

Gog and his allies have represented the formidable challenge that the church will face before the end of time. It is a challenge which will prove unsuccessful; the forces of opposition will be massacred. On the Day of the Lord, his enemies will be unable to fight (39:3). Behind this opposition lies the anger of Satan, whose intended scheme is to destroy Christ and all that belongs to him (Rev. 12: 1-17). Paul's remedy for Christians caught up in this struggle is clear: 'Finally, be strong in the Lord and in his mighty power. Put on the full armour of God so that you can take your stand against the devil's schemes. For our struggle is not against flesh and blood, but against the rulers, against the authorities, against the powers of this dark world and against the spiritual forces of evil in the heavenly realms.

Therefore put on the full armour of God, so that when the day of evil comes, you may be able to stand your ground, and after you have done everything, to stand... And pray in the Spirit on all occasions with all kinds of prayers and requests. With this in mind, be alert and always keep on praying for all the saints' (Eph. 6:10-13,18).

Summary

Fantastic, yet real, forces of evil are at work in our midst, seeking to destroy everything that God has made. The church, God's supreme creation (Eph. 2:10), is currently under attack by the forces of darkness.

Satan, now bound by a chain, is to be loosed 'after many days' (for a season, Rev. 20:7-10). He is going to deceive the nations and gather them for battle. Compare Revelation 16:14, where the 'kings of the whole world' are gathered 'for the battle on the great day of God Almighty' — the so-called 'Battle of Armageddon'; or Revelation 17:14, with its description of the ten horn-kings in battle against the Lamb who is King of kings; or Revelation 19:19-21, where the 'beast' gathers 'the kings of the earth and their armies' to fight against the rider on the white horse. Ezekiel and John are depicting the same battle and it becomes clear that the language forbids us thinking of 'Gog, from the land of Magog' as any one nation or people. John's description in Revelation 20 is on an epic scale: 'the nations in the four corners of the earth... In number they are like the sand on the seashore' (vv. 7-8). It seems as though the true identity of Gog covers all 'those who do not know God and do not obey the gospel of our Lord Jesus' who will 'be punished with everlasting destruction and shut out from the presence of the Lord and from the majesty of his power' (2 Thess. 1:8-9).

We are led to expect from certain biblical passages that this battle is billed for the end of time. Satan will have one last attempt to overthrow Christ and his kingdom. The outcome, however, is certain. Jesus' death 'disarmed the powers and authorities...' (Col. 2:15). His resurrection and ascension were the proof of his victory. The end is sure: Satan and his minions are to be destroyed. Jesus will be Conqueror! Hallelujah!

Part VIII
The plans for the New Jerusalem
(Ezek. 40-48)

Focus

Ezekiel 40-48

The book of Ezekiel consists of two themes: the threat of judgement and the restoration of God's people. Following a lengthy and detailed exposition of judgement in the first half of the book, whose climax comes as the Lord leaves the temple (8:1 - 11:25), chapters 40-48 speak of restoration. Ezekiel is carried to a high mountain overlooking the new Jerusalem (40:1,2) where he sees the return of God to dwell in the temple (43:1-12).

A guided tour of the new city is depicted in extraordinary detail, but with one aim: to shame the people for their previous treatment of God's house (43:10). At the end of the section, Ezekiel depicts a stream of water running from beneath the temple to the Dead Sea, providing a source of blessing, refreshment and productivity to the land (47:1-12). The vision ends with a glorious pronouncement of God's new name for the city of Jerusalem: 'The Lord is There' (48:35).

What is it meant to convey? Some have wanted to interpret these chapters quite literally. They think that Ezekiel was anticipating such a temple being built after the return of the exiles to Jerusalem following the decree issued by Cyrus. This view, however, requires us to believe that Ezekiel and the Holy Spirit who inspired him were mistaken, since no such temple was ever built.

Others look forward to a future millennial age, following the so-called 'rapture' at the return of Christ, when a temple will be built, and sacrifices offered in Jerusalem. This has serious difficulties. As we shall see in examining the relevant section (45:15-17), to expect blood-sacrifices to be offered at some future point seriously violates a principle underlined in Hebrews that such blood-letting sacrifices are now forbidden (Heb. 10:8-10).

One thing is sure: the dimensions of Ezekiel's temple do not fit anything we know about Solomon's temple or that of Herod. And no river has ever flowed from the site of either temple. A key to understanding these chapters lies in an examination of the river that flows from beneath the temple (47:1-12). As we shall see in more detail when we come to consider chapter 47, Jesus identifies *himself* as the fulfilment of Ezekiel's prophecy. Ezekiel's vision is 'a type of the Christian believer'[1] as well as of believers considered collectively, i.e. the church.

This interpretation provides us with a useful key to understanding the entire section. Ezekiel's temple is the New Testament church — to be considered sometimes in terms of one of its members, and more especially as the collective community of God's people.

What we have, therefore, is an impressionistic painting. Ezekiel 40-48 is in the style of apocalyptic writing, conveying truths by means of abstract and exaggerated details. It can be compared to the music of Claude Debussy, or the paintings of Renoir.

This is not as fanciful as might at first be suspected.[2] The New Testament temple is Christ's church (Eph. 2:21; 1 Peter 2:5; Heb. 3:6). This explains why E. J. Young's title for this section is : 'The vision of the Church of God upon earth symbolized by the description of the Temple.'[3]

The time of fulfilment

A word needs to be said about the time period referred to in chapters 40-48. If, as has been suggested, the battle of Gog and Magog refers to a period just prior to the return of Christ, it necessarily follows that chapters 40-48 refer to the church following this period of tribulation, that is, the eternal state. This is indeed the primary focus of these chapters.

However, as we noted in our discussion of chapters 38 and 39, while the ultimate fulfilment of the prophecy of Gog and Magog seems to be in the future, other partial fulfilments of it are seen in history (thus, Antiochus Epiphanes in 169 B.C. and Emperor Titus in A.D. 70 are both candidates for this prophecy). In the same way that the destruction of Jerusalem in A. D. 70. serves as a precursor to the tribulation at the end of time in Jesus' Olivet sermon (Matt. 24; Mark 13; Luke 21), so too, Gog and Magog represent, in one sense, times of severe tribulation that may come upon the church throughout the last days, but ultimately find their fulfilment in a short-lived period of tribulation prior to Christ's return.

In a similar fashion, it is appropriate to see the depiction of the church in terms of the temple in chapters 40-48 as a description of the church throughout the last days, but ultimately its fulfilment is that of the glorious church in heaven. In so far as the church already conforms to that model, applications of these chapters to the present age are appropriate. Thus in our examination of the chapters that follow we shall have cause to speak of the church in terms of its present-day condition. The constant aim of these chapters, though, is to guide our eyes heavenward and to a condition that currently the church can only anticipate. It is vital that the 'multiple fulfilment' of these prophecies be grasped.

20.
The Lord's return to Jerusalem

Please read Ezekiel 40:1 - 43:27

In some ways, everything that Ezekiel has said up to this point has been a preparation for these last nine chapters of his prophecy. Readers who have formed an opinion that Ezekiel's message is unremittingly depressing (despite the wonderful things said in chapters 36 and 37) need to persevere through these final chapters. At the advent of colour cinematography, promotional clips used to advertise their films made 'in glorious technicolour'. Ezekiel 40 - 48 is in 'glorious technicolour', too.

Life in Babylon — for those who refused to yield to Babylonian ways — must have been depressing. Jerusalem had been razed to the ground; Solomon's temple ('the delight of your eyes', 24:21) was destroyed. From Ezra 3 we understand that even the very foundations of the temple had to be rebuilt. We catch a glimpse of their melancholy in the opening verses of Psalm 137. They had no heart for singing. In response to Babylonian taunts, they hung their harps on the branches of willow trees. What they needed was a word of encouragement, and these final chapters in Ezekiel are designed to cultivate it. God has a wonderful plan for his people, a plan which is described in terms of Jerusalem, its temple and the land of promise.

The previous two chapters (38-39) have warned of a time to come when massive forces of evil will be arrayed against the church. And following the conquest of these evil forces, Ezekiel describes for us the new heaven in a new paradise setting (40-48). It is a foretaste, a glimpse of evil's power and its final destruction as depicted in the closing chapters of the Bible (Rev. 20:10; cf. v.2). John follows his depiction of the conquest of the dragon with a picture of the new heaven and new earth described in distinctly architectural terms (Rev. 21). The comparison is more than a superficial one. Ezekiel 40-48 is an Old Testament reflection of Revelation 20-21.

Students of Scripture unfamiliar with Ezekiel's final chapters may be shocked, even put off, by the tedious and uninteresting attention to detail in these chapters. Even making sense of it is going to prove difficult! Readers should bear in mind that the temple (Solomon's, that is) and its structure were very familiar and precious to Ezekiel's listeners — and to Ezekiel himself as a priest! Every month I purchase a specialist magazine which contains over a hundred reviews of classical music recordings from Bach to Wagner. I read it, usually in bed, from cover to cover and often more than once. I used to keep back issues going back over twenty-five years! My wife never reads a single issue! And as far as I know, neither do any of the members of the congregation in which I minister. For me, the magazine provides a welcome break from routine and an interest which I endeavour to keep in check. My life would be tolerable without it, but very much duller. Perhaps you can sense my enthusiasm, even if you cannot quite share in it! Detailed descriptions of the temple fascinated Ezekiel and we can sense his enthusiasm, even though we find it hard to get quite so excited over the size of various rooms and porticoes!

At the end of this section (43:10-11), Ezekiel reveals to us the overall purpose behind the lengthy, detailed sketch of the temple. Solomon's temple had been destroyed because of the sins of Israel (43:6-9). The new temple which God is going to build is one characterized by holiness and love for his law. Ezekiel's listeners are to consider the plan in all its detail and be ashamed of what they allowed to happen to Solomon's temple. They are to repent and turn to God with new hearts, upon which God's law has been written.

A visit from an angel (40:1-4)

Time has moved on. It is now fourteen years after the exile (573 B.C., 40:1). Ezekiel is transported, in a vision (cf. 8:3), to a high mountain near to Jerusalem (probably Mount Zion). The fact that the mountain is **'very high'** (40:2) signifies that this is not the Jerusalem Ezekiel and his friends knew, for the holy city of the Old

Testament was built on a relatively low mountain. Already, we are meant to infer that this is a *new* Jerusalem. Ezekiel sees an angel, described as **'like bronze'** (40:3; cf. Dan. 10:6; Rev. 1:15), who bids Ezekiel note everything that is shown to him and relate it accurately to **'the house of Israel'** (40:4). The angel has two measuring devices: **'a linen cord'** of unknown length and a **'measuring rod'** (40:3) of **'six cubits'** length, i.e. just over ten feet (40:5).

The outer court's three gates (40:5-16; 20-27)

The temple — not so much a building as an enclosure — consisted of a covered area, into which only the priests entered, and two courtyards: an inner courtyard which surrounded this covered area and an outer courtyard which surrounded the inner courtyard. The outer courtyard was itself surrounded by a wall with three entrances, or 'gates' (located in the east, north and south). It was in these courtyards that people gathered for worship. The three gates are complicated in their design and are described in succession: the east gate (40:6-16), the north gate (40:20-23) and the south gate (40:24-27). The descriptions of the north and south gates do not differ significantly from that of the east gate, which we shall now describe in detail. In order to follow this description, it is best to consult the sketch below.

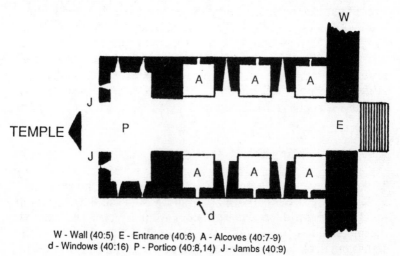

W - Wall (40:5) E - Entrance (40:6) A - Alcoves (40:7-9)
d - Windows (40:16) P - Portico (40:8,14) J - Jambs (40:9)

In Ezekiel's vision the outer courtyard (and thus the entire
'temple area', 40:5) was surrounded by a wall **'one measuring rod
thick and one rod high'**, i.e. approximately ten feet by ten feet
(40:5). The entrance at the east gateway is also measured and found
to be the same width (40:6). Leading through this gateway and
protruding into the outer courtyard was a three-chambered structure
having three alcoves on each side (each alcove measuring ten feet
by ten feet), which from above made it look like a letter 'E' with its
mirror image (40:7-9). In these alcoves were stationed temple
guards (40:10). Windows were also found in these alcoves through
which those approaching could be seen (40:16). At the end of each
gateway was a **'portico'** (porch, or vestibule, 40:8,14) consisting of
'jambs' (side posts for doorways) three feet thick (40:9).

The outer courtyard (40:17-19)

The outer courtyard consisted of a covered pavement running along
the outer wall, divided up into thirty rooms (ten along each of the
eastern, southern and northern walls; i.e. five on either side of each
gate). These rooms provided space for worshippers to eat. The
distance from this pavement to the inner courtyard was **'a hundred
cubits'** (about 175 feet, 40:19). It is estimated that this outer
courtyard (shaped like a 'U' surrounding the inner courtyard) was
about four and a half acres, thus providing sufficient space for
thousands of worshippers.[1]

Glancing at the sketch of this elaborate structure (see p.270) we
might begin to wonder what possible significance this could have
for us today. Is Ezekiel 40 meant only for Christian architects to get
excited over? What specific doctrine, rebuke, correction, or instruc-
tion in righteousness do we find in this passage? Why was worship
made so difficult? Why the guards? Why is there such a great
distance from the gate to the inner courtyard? Why was there a ten-
foot thick wall surrounding the temple in the first place? The entire
description speaks of inaccessibility. It is more a description of a
fortress than a church. The point being made is that not everyone is
entitled to come within the walls of the temple. And even those who
are allowed will have to pass through various rites before they can
approach God. It is a symbolic representation of what sin has done
to us. In Old Testament times God took pains, by means of various

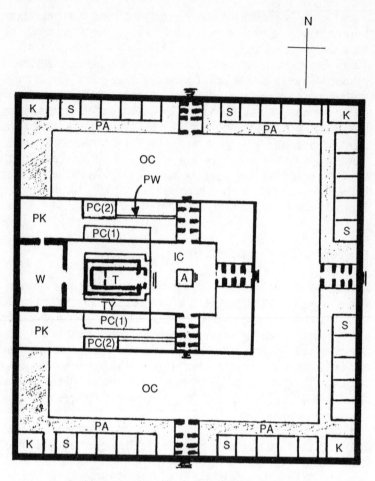

S - Side Rooms (40:17) PK - Priests' Kitchens (46:19-20)
PA - Paved Area (40:17; 41:8) A - Altar (43:13-17)
TY - Temple Yard PC(1) - Priests' Chambers (40:45-46: 42:13-14)
PC(2) - Priests' Chambers (42:3) IC - Inner Court (40:28-37)
K - Kitchens (46:21-22) W - West Building (41:12)
OC - Outer Court (40:17) Pw - Passageway (42:9) T - Temple (40:48-41:12)

The temple courts

taboos and purity regulations in matters of food and hygiene to teach the lesson that sinners are in a state of defilement. They are not able to approach God unless their sins have been dealt with. They must be kept away from him, at a distance. The vision of Ezekiel's temple is meant to reinforce this lesson. Many longed to be back in Jerusalem and pined for the glory of Solomon's temple. But they needed to realize just how holy God is. The fact of their judgement in exile should have reinforced the point. Returning to him was not as simple a matter as some may have thought.

The inner court (40:28-49)

In many ways, the inner court was just like the outer court, only smaller! (40:28-37). It, too, had gateways; it, too, was 'U' shaped. But in some essential ways, it was entirely different.

No wall is mentioned surrounding the inner courtyard, but since there were three gateways (north, south and east), then a wall must be assumed. These gateways were situated directly opposite their counterparts on the outer wall and were on a higher level, eight steps leading from the outer courtyard into the inner courtyard (40:37). One immediate difference was that the gateways into the inner courtyard seem to have been mirror images of their counterparts into the outer courtyard. This meant that the porticoes (vestibules) came first and not last in the inner gateways (40:31).

Much of the Old Testament temple resembled an abattoir. Priests regularly slaughtered animals, dissecting them for their meat. It is doubtful if many of us would have the stomach to visit the areas of the temple where animals were regularly butchered, flesh was burnt, offal discarded and blood poured, or sprinkled in generous amounts. Ezekiel's temple is no different. An elaborate set of rooms, furniture and equipment was necessary for this to take place efficiently (40:38-43).

Around the edge of the inner court (**'outside the inner gate'**, 40:44), on the north and south sides, were chambers for the priests to rest and get dressed in. These chambers were divided into two groups (40:45-46): the ones facing south were for those in **'charge of the temple'**, i.e. the day-to-day running of the temple, while those facing north were for those priests in charge **'of the altar'**, that is, the Zadokites (who are further described in 44:15-21). The inner court is said to cover an area of three quarters of an acre (40:47).

The temple (40:48-41:26)

A flight of stairs ascended into the temple area itself (40:49). The temple consisted of three sections: a **'portico'**, or vestibule area (40:48-49), an **'outer sanctuary'**, or holy place (41:1), and an **'inner sanctuary'**, or holy of holies (41:3). The outer entranceway, some twenty-four and a half feet wide (40:48), leading into the portico, had no doors. Worshippers from the outer courtyard were allowed into this area for sacrifice. The entranceway from the vestibule to the holy place, some seventeen and a half feet wide, had doors. Only priests were allowed into this area. The doors into the holy of holies were ten and a half feet wide (41:3), and only the high priest was allowed to pass through these doors, once a year on the Day of Atonement (Heb. 9:7) — though no Day of Atonement is mentioned in these chapters. Not even Ezekiel, who was only a priest (1:3), was allowed through these doors.

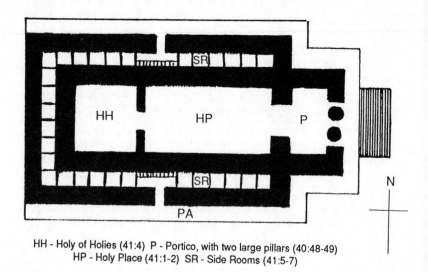

HH - Holy of Holies (41:4) P - Portico, with two large pillars (40:48-49)
HP - Holy Place (41:1-2) SR - Side Rooms (41:5-7)

The temple was used for storing all kinds of treasures, including money (offerings), cups, bowls, silverware, candlesticks and incense burners. These needed storage areas, and so, as in Solomon's temple (1 Kings 6:5-10), Ezekiel's temple provides for chambers (**'side rooms'**, 41:6) on all three sides of the temple.

Some features of the temple are worth noting.

1. Its perfection

It is no coincidence that the temple area and its courtyards measured a hundred cubits square (41:13-14). The dimensions of the entire temple area including the outer courtyard is said to have been five hundred cubits square (roughly, eighteen acres, 42:16). Everything about God's plan for the future worship of his people is perfection itself. The meticulous care over the design of this structure, given in a way that Ezekiel's listeners would readily appreciate, was meant to convey how carefully he plans every detail.

2. Its purpose

The entire function of this elaborate building was to facilitate the worship of God. As such it provided a place where God was to come and make his abode. It had been David's longing to provide a place for God to dwell in that would prove to be a house of prayer for his sons and the whole of Israel (1 Kings 8:27-53; 2 Chron. 7:15-16). This sentiment was echoed in one of the Ascent Psalms:

'I will not enter my house
    or go to my bed—
I will allow no sleep to my eyes,
    no slumber to my eyelids,
till I find a place for the Lord,
    a dwelling for the Mighty One of Jacob'

(Ps. 132:3-5).

3. Its beauty

The interior of the temple was wood-panelled (41:16), and many surfaces were adorned with intricate carvings of **'cherubim'** — no doubt reminding those who saw them of divine things (cf. the cherubim in Ezekiel's opening vision of chapters 1 and 10), and **'palm trees'** — perhaps reminding them of a cool, refreshing oasis, something particularly appropriate in the hot climate of the Middle East (40:18). More importantly, the trees were symbols of Eden (in Ezekiel 47 the sanctuary is said to contain the river and trees of life).

4. Its symbolism

The main event of temple worship consisted in the sacrifice of **'burnt offerings, sin offerings, and guilt offerings'** (40:39).[3] Every detail of its architecture was intended to reinforce the point that this building was designed to take away sin and present the sinner with a way to approach 'the Holy One of Israel'. The writer to the Hebrews makes it clear that both the sanctuary and the temple were meant to be 'copies' of heavenly realities (Heb. 8:5; 9:23-25). Ezekiel is describing the glorious future of the people of God in terms which the Jews of that day would understand. Since their worship previous to their captivity had centred around the Jerusalem temple, it is understandable why Ezekiel chooses to picture a temple as a way of describing future blessedness.

Priests' rooms in the outer courtyard (42:1-14)

Moving outside once more, Ezekiel describes further **'rooms'** (42:1) at either end of the 'U'-shaped outer courtyard. Here were situated large rooms for priestly use in the wall which made up the inner courtyard (but presumably accessible only from the outer courtyard). These faced similar, but smaller, chambers in the perimeter wall of the outer courtyard. The description given here is intensely complicated but appears to suggest that each room was divided in two: one section (the smaller of the two) was a three-storey affair facing directly onto the outer courtyard (42:3) and not accessible from the outer courtyard, but rather from the east, via a passageway ten cubits wide (42:4), presumably from the north and south gateways (42:9). The other, and larger, part of the room led directly to the temple yard of the inner courtyard. It is in this room that the priests stored offerings given to them, ate and changed their priestly garments (42:13-14).[4]

This section ends with a statement of the perfect symmetry of the overall temple structure: some five hundred cubits square (42:16).

The return of God's glory (43:1-12)

One of the saddest moments in Israel's history occurred when the ark of the temple was taken into Philistine hands and Israel was left bereft of God's help. When Eli heard of the consequent death of his two sons, he fell backwards and broke his neck. His daughter-in-law, in the shock of all the events, gave premature birth, dying in the process. Before she died she gasped out that the child should be called Ichabod, meaning 'The glory has departed' (1 Sam. 4).

Israel's current condition in exile was a similar low point. The collapse of Jerusalem and the destruction of Solomon's temple underlined the fact that God had departed from his holy city. Ezekiel had been taken to Jerusalem in a vision in chapter 10 to see God depart! That was in 592 B.C. Almost twenty years have passed since that awful day. Nothing could be worse than that. If the new temple in Ezekiel's vision is to be of any significance other than for architects, the essential nature of its glory has to be underlined. This involves the return of God to dwell in his temple again. This is what these verses now describe.

Ezekiel is brought to the east gate of the temple complex (43:1); this gate led directly to the temple area. It was from this gate that God's glory had departed in 10:18-19. What we have in chapter 43 is the reverse of chapter 10: God is going to come back through the same gate by which he left. What Ezekiel sees, he tells us, is a reminder of the glory of God that he first encountered in the opening chapters: a vision of glory in chapter 1 and a vision of God coming to destroy the city in chapter 9 (43:3). Ezekiel for the third time in this book has come face to face with the living God.

If sin had driven the Lord from the temple, then it will be the holiness of his people that will keep him there. It is a word about holiness that Ezekiel now hears as God speaks to him (43:6-9). Solomon's temple had been defiled by **'their prostitution and the lifeless idols of their kings at their high places'** (43:7). This seems to be a reference to the practice of burying kings near the temple — fourteen such burials are mentioned (cf. 2 Kings 14:20; 21:18,26; 23:30; 2 Chron. 21:20). Solomon's temple did not have an outer wall as depicted in Ezekiel's temple, and thus did not have an outer courtyard in the strict sense. Solomon surrounded the temple with many of his own private buildings, including the palace (1 Kings 7:1-12). The wealthy and powerful have too often manipulated

religion to suit their own ends.⁵ That had been the reason why God
had destroyed Solomon's temple (43:8). Ezekiel's listeners, as we
noted at the beginning of this chapter, are to examine the detailed
nature of Ezekiel's temple plans, repent of what they allowed to
happen to Solomon's temple, and turn to the Lord in repentance and
faith (43:1-12).

The altar (43:13-27)

Ezekiel now returns to the temple itself and examines some of the
regulations concerning its use. After what he has just said about
God's return to the temple, this appears to be somewhat of an
anticlimax. But this is to misunderstand the flow of ideas as the
chapter develops. So far, what Ezekiel has described for us is a
building. Now he wants us to see the central altar: the main purpose
for the entire building.

Standing more than twelve feet high, the altar itself was simple.
Made of stone, it comprised three blocks: the central hearth supported by two pedestal blocks. Each block was slightly smaller than
the one below it, so as to give a pyramid effect. The entire altar stood
on a horizontal base. At each corner of the topmost hearth were the
'horns' of the altar (43:13-16).

This visionary altar (it did not exist in reality) has to be conse-
crated before it can be used and for one week the priests **'of the
family of Zadok'**⁶ (43:19) are to offer special sacrifices upon the
altar. The blood of a bull has to be sprinkled on the altar in liberal
quantities (43:18-20). This is followed by **'burnt offerings'** (43:18)
where the flesh of the sacrificed animal is to be burnt entirely upon
the altar. On the following six days (43:25), similar sacrificial rituals
are to be carried out using a **'male goat'** (43:22,25), another **'young
bull'** together with a **'ram'** (43:22,25) — both of which to be
'without defect'. When this has been accomplished, the altar is
ready to be used for the routine sacrifices of **'burnt offerings'** and
'fellowship offerings' (43:27).⁷

Several features of the altar are worthy of comment.

1. The steps

Steps were necessary for the priests to reach the hearth of the altar
(some twelve feet high), and these were situated at the **'east'** end

(43:17). This meant that whenever the priest ascended or descended these steps he was always 'facing the Lord', symbolically directly ahead of him in the sanctuary. Two things are meant: it would be improper for the priest to turn his back on the sanctuary, for in effect it would be symbolically a sign of irreverence to the Lord; but, principally, it is a reminder that the sacrificial offerings are offered to God. It is the Lord's wrath that needs to be appeased.

2. The sprinkling of blood

The liberal application of blood on the horns and sides of the altar (43:18-20) is to symbolize an important truth: that without the shedding of blood there can be no forgiveness of sins (Heb. 9:22). Blood is the Bible's symbol for life itself: 'For the life of a creature is in the blood' (Lev. 17:11). Blood-shedding was a way of saying that the sinner's life was forfeited because of sin and, one way or another, life has to be offered in sacrifice to satisfy divine justice and for sin to be forgiven. The sin-offering was offered in order to **'purify the altar and make atonement'** for it (43:20). The Hebrew for 'atonement' (*kipper*) means 'to cover' or 'to wipe away'. Our sin needs to be 'covered' before we can approach God. Old Testament sacrifices were substitutes for the sinner's own life, and anticipated the coming of Jesus Christ, who was, and is, the sole source of cleansing and reconciliation for the sinner (1 John 1:7; Heb. 9:14; 1 Peter 1:18-19; Rev. 1:5; 7:14; 12:11). What is foreshadowed here are the words of Jesus at the Last Supper: 'This is my blood of the covenant, which is poured out for many for the forgiveness of sins' (Matt. 26:28).

3. Burning outside the sanctuary

The burnt offering was burnt outside the sanctuary (43:21; cf. Exod. 29:14; Lev. 16:17). The priests were allowed to partake of certain sacrifices (see Lev. 7); but there were certain sacrifices that they were not permitted to eat, such as the sin offerings and the annual sacrifices for sin offered on the Day of Atonement (Lev. 16). These were to be destroyed by fire *outside the camp*. The action of carrying the slaughtered carcass of the animal outside the ground was in order to signify that its place of holocaust was unholy ground. As a consequence, ceremonial cleansing was necessary before a man could return to the camp from outside (Lev. 16:26,28). All of this

was an anticipation of Christ's own death, for as the letter to the
Hebrews informs us, 'And so Jesus also suffered outside the city
gate to make the people holy through his own blood' (Heb. 13:12).
Jesus thereby completely identified with sinners, dying the death
they deserved. The very location of Calvary was one of defilement.

4. *The use of salt*

The ritual offerings designed to purify the altar were to be performed
with the addition of '**salt**' (43:24). Salt was an Old Testament
symbol of the covenant (Lev. 2:13). Greeks and Arabs are known to
have concluded covenants by eating salt together.[8] Salt was relatively indestructible in ancient times and therefore was a useful
means of suggesting that the covenant was eternal. The addition of
salt signified that God would not forsake his promise to forgive
whoever offered a sacrifice for the remission of sins.

5. *Peace offerings*

At the end of this ritual the worshipper was entitled to offer and
partake of a '**peace offering**'. Signifying as they did communion
with God (see note 7), peace offerings revealed the fact that, sin
having been covered, the sinner is now able to enjoy fellowship with
God. John exclaims with confidence: 'Our fellowship is with the
Father and with his Son, Jesus Christ' (1 John 1:3).

What Ezekiel is being shown here is a glimpse of the gospel:
forgiveness through the atoning blood of Jesus!

> He died that we might be forgiv'n
> He died to make us good,
> That we might go at last to heav'n,
> Saved by his precious blood.
>
> There was no other good enough
> To pay the price of sin;
> He only could unlock the gate
> Of heav'n, and let us in.

(Cecil Frances Alexander).

Summary

We have been given a glimpse of the temple and its furnishings. It is a glimpse of the coming of Christ, the Saviour, coming to atone for sin and to establish his kingdom.[9] In it we have seen the intricate detail of the plans reinforcing how meticulously God has planned the salvation of sinners. Nothing is left to 'chance', for he orders all things. In this work, which even the angels crave to glimpse (1 Peter 1:12), God spares no expense. He gives the finest and the best — his own Son! In the new age, of which Ezekiel has said much already (36:24-38; 37:1-14), renewed sinners will desire to worship the Lord who is in their midst and dwells in their hearts by faith. Ezekiel's apocalyptic vision is not so strange after all; it is a glimpse of the New Testament church coming before God through faith in his Son, Jesus Christ.

21.

A visionary tour of the future temple and its workings

Please read Ezekiel 44:1 - 46:24

'If you think of holiness as a circle embracing everything about God that is different from what we are,' writes J. I. Packer, 'the centre of the circle is God's moral and spiritual purity, which contrast painfully with our twisted sinfulness.'[1] Holiness is what these chapters teach: the holiness of God and its implications for the way we are to worship him.

Though chapter 44 begins with a continuation of the vision that occupied chapters 40-43 (44:1-3), the rest of this section deals with more practical matters relating to how worship is to be conducted in the restored visionary temple.

A glance back at chapters 8 and 9 of Ezekiel will remind us that the prophet has already seen the kind of improper use the Israelites had made of Solomon's temple. Access to the temple was to be strictly controlled — something that Israel had failed to implement. In the visionary temple of the New Jerusalem, things are to be different. Three sections of the community are singled out: the king (44:1-3), foreigners (44:4-9) and the priests (44:10-14).

The 'prince' (44:1-3)

As Ezekiel is taken back to the east gate in the outer wall of the court, the gate is firmly closed (44:1-2). This was the gate through which Ezekiel had witnessed the return of God's glory (43:1-4), and as a consequence no one would be allowed to pass this way.

The **'prince'** (i.e. king) may use some of the rooms in the gateway (see, 40:6-16) to eat his sacrificial meal, but he must enter these rooms via the portico at the western end of this gateway (44:3;

i.e. from the west — from inside — rather than through the gateway — from the east). This was, no doubt, a way of reflecting the privilege of the king's position, intimating, in part, the honour of God himself. Being allowed to eat in the eastern gateway, through which the glory of the Lord had passed, reflected the king's honour as God's representative ruler among his people. Nevertheless, the access given to the king is strictly limited. He may not abuse this privilege, as Uzziah did in his old age (2 Chron. 26: 16-20).

Of greater significance, however, is the shutting of the eastern gate. This, no doubt, was a way of symbolizing that the Lord, having once entered, was not about to leave the temple again. Having left once before because of Israel's sin, the Lord was now back — permanently. (As to the identity of the 'prince', see discussion on 45:13-25.)

Foreigners (44:4-9)

Moving forwards from the outer east gate, and round to the right, Ezekiel enters the inner court via the north inner gateway (44:4), coming face to face with the glory of God in the temple. Ezekiel falls on his face, something which Daniel was also to do (Dan. 8:17). It is an expression of unworthiness and defilement in God's presence.

Who may enter the temple and worship God? Only the covenant people of God. Foreigners, those who were **'uncircumcised in heart and flesh'** (44:7), were not permitted to enter. This was something which had been violated in Solomon's temple, when foreign guards had been placed in charge (44:8; cf. 2 Kings 11:4).These had permitted those who were spiritually unfit to enter the temple and thus defile it. Herod's temple, unlike Solomon's, provided a 'court' for Gentiles to meet. It more or less surrounded the temple area itself. Preventing access to the 'Court of Israel' was a four-and-a-half foot high stone wall acting as a kind of partition. On it was an inscription forbidding Gentiles to go any further on pain of death. According to Josephus, there were many such inscriptions written in Greek and Latin at equal distances from each other.[2] Two such notices were discovered (one in 1971 and the other in 1935) and read: 'No foreigner may enter within the barricade which surrounds the temple and enclosure. Anyone who is caught doing so will have himself to blame for his ensuing death.'[3]

The Levites (44:10-14)[4]

The duties of the Levites were threefold: keeping watch over access to the temple, thus acting as temple guards; slaughtering and cooking of sacrifices; and, thirdly, helping the worshippers with their worship (44:11). In contrast to the duties of the Zadokite priests (described in the next section, 44:15-27; cf. 43:19), these were relatively menial tasks. Forbidden to serve as priests, a privilege reserved, on penalty of death, for Aaron's sons (Num. 3:10; 10:8), the Levites were dedicated to an auxiliary role as ministers for the priests, especially in regard to the manual labour of caring for the tabernacle and later the temple of Solomon (Num. 3:5).

They had, however, been grossly irresponsible in the past, allowing idolatry (44:12) to mar the temple of God. This is something Ezekiel has been at pains to point out (6:3-6; 14:3-11; 16:18-21; 23:36-49; 36:17-18; 37:23). Judgement has now fallen on them and their tasks in Ezekiel's temple are greatly reduced in importance: **'They are not to come near to serve me as priests or come near any of my holy things or my most holy offerings; they must bear the shame of their detestable practices'** (44:13). Those who hold office in God's church are accountable to God. 'From everyone who has been given much, much will be demanded; and from one who has been entrusted with much, much more will be asked' (Luke 12:48).

Having mentioned three groups (the king, foreigners and the Levites) who had violated access to the temple in the past, Ezekiel is now shown the function of the Zadokites who are to serve as priests in the new temple.

The Zadokite priests (44:15-27)

As we have noticed, the priests were chosen from the line of Aaron's descent. However, a further narrowing of the priestly line took place at the time of David, when Zadok the priest successfully backed Solomon as David's successor (rather than Adonijah, 1 Kings 1). Only those Levites descended from Aaron through Zadok could serve as priests at the temple (1 Kings 4:2; 2 Chron. 31:10). According to

Ezekiel, it is the Zadokites alone who remained free from the charge of apostasy during the reign of the Israelite kings (44:15). They only are allowed to **'offer sacrifices of fat and blood'** (44:15). Following the sacrifice, the fat was burned (Lev. 3:14) and the blood poured out on the altar (cf. 43:20) as gifts to the Lord.

The priests' clothes

The priests were to wear **'linen clothes'** (44:17) not wool, while they ministered in the inner court, or inside the temple area. Likewise, they were to wear **'linen turbans'** (Ezekiel wore one, cf. 24:17) and **'linen undergarments'** (44:18). The reason lies in making sure that they did not **'perspire'**! (cf. Exod. 39:27-29; 16:4). Concern over bodily fluids was a source of uncleanness in Old Testament times, as it is today (cf. Lev. 12,13,18, etc.). No doubt this was to reinforce basic hygiene in relatively primitive times, but it was also to underline the fact that serving in the inner court meant proximity to God and therefore a necessity to be ceremonially pure. Consequently, these garments were to be kept in the chambers surrounding the inner court (44:18-19) and described in 42:1-9.

Sin is a state of uncleanness, as well as rebellion and guilt, and salvation involves at its heart the need to be washed and made clean. This was, in part, the lesson Nicodemus received from Jesus (John 3:5). The same lesson is reinforced by Paul when he writes to Titus and speaks of the 'washing of rebirth' (Titus 3:5). God had also spoken of this truth through Isaiah:

> '"Come now, let us reason together,"
>   says the Lord,
> "Though your sins are like scarlet,
>   they shall be as white as snow;
> though they are red as crimson,
>   they shall be like wool'
>
> (Isa. 1:18).

Other regulations concerning priests

Other regulations include a regular haircut (44:20): they were neither to shave their heads (a sign of mourning, 7:18), nor wear their hair long (a sign that they have taken a vow, Num. 6:5; Acts 21:23-25); the prohibition of drinking wine when on duty (44:21); marriage to virgins or widows of priests (44:22); and a prohibition against going near a corpse, unless it is that of a relative, in which case the priest will be rendered ceremonially unclean for seven days (44:25-27). These rituals, strange in themselves, taught the people the difference between what was clean and unclean, between what was **'holy'** and what was **'common'** (44:23). This had always been the function of the priest in Israel (Lev. 10:10). Similar lessons were taught by the differentiation of certain animals (Lev. 11) and illnesses (Lev. 12-15). Certain things were holy, set apart for special use and service. Behind it all lay the need to reinforce the truth of God's magisterial holiness. Worship, accordingly, must be strictly controlled by the requirement to place God at the head of all. There was to be no such thing as 'informal worship' in Israel.

The priests were given no inheritance in Israel — though a portion of the land immediately surrounding the temple is given to them (45:1-5; 48:9-12); God was to be their inheritance (44:28; cf. Num. 18:20,23-24; Deut. 10:9; Josh. 13:14,33; 18:7). They were to live off the various sacrifices in which they were allowed to share (44:29-31). This is a point the New Testament makes clear also, underlining the principle that those who live by the gospel are to be maintained by the gospel. Paul tells Timothy that elders 'who direct the affairs of the church' are 'worthy of double honour' — not 'double pay', as a few exegetes have said, but a twofold honour: the honour of respect and the honour of remuneration (1 Tim. 5:17; cf. 1 Cor. 9:7-14; 1 Thess. 2:9; 2 Cor. 11:8-9).

The allocation of the land (45:1-8)

Talk of land ownership can become a source of heated debate. 'Home ownership' became a political slogan during the political administration of the 'Thatcher years' in Britain (the 1980s). To the exiles along the banks of the River Kebar, whose land and homes had been taken away from them, talk of land ownership must have proved thrilling — more so, perhaps, than to us who read these chapters 2,500 years later!

Israel had been formed on the promise that everyone would be given his own portion of the land in which to live and work (Gen. 12:7). The exile had shown more clearly than anything the demise of this dream. No doubt they listened with great attentiveness as Ezekiel now described the division of the land in the New Jerusalem.

The best way to understand this portion is by consulting the map on page 294. A portion of the land is claimed by the Lord (all of it belongs to him!) which stretches from the Mediterranean on the west to the River Jordan on the east. This is divided into three sections, the middle third of which is further divided into a central section, to be inhabited by the priests and containing the temple plot as described in chapters 40-43 (45:1-4); a northerly section, to be inhabited by the Levites (45:5); and a southerly section which was to be occupied by the city of Jerusalem (45:6). The sections to the west and east are to be allocated to the **'prince'** (45:7). Since he possesses his own land, he will have no need to oppress the people with high taxation demands — a distressingly familiar picture of what had happened in the past (45:8; cf. 1 Kings 5:13; 12:4; 21:1-16). (As to the identity of the 'prince' see discussion on 45:13-25).

Justice: the mark of the new age (45:9-12)

Ezekiel now pleads for justice to be the hallmark of the new age. Even in the New Jerusalem as Ezekiel sees it, there is the possibility of sin: false measures and weights (45:9-12). This highlights the fact that Ezekiel's vision is not of heaven itself, but of the New Testament era. 'Honesty is the best policy,' runs the adage, and God's kingdom is to be characterized by honesty. Cheating may well bring short-term profit, but the God who sees all (Ps. 139:1-3) will not tolerate it. This is a theme that the prophets never grew tired of thundering (Amos 8:5; Micah 6:10-12).[5]

A mere glance at the layout of the land, as depicted in this vision, should prove sufficient to convince us that no literal fulfilment should be expected. The Jerusalem in this figure is of enormous proportions! 'In the kingdom of God, all will be in order, all will be just, and God will be at the centre,' comments Stuart.[6]

Offerings and holy days (45:13-25)

Land distribution, proper weights and measures — these have a place in the kingdom of God, but central to it is a concern for maintaining a pure system of worship, especially in the giving of offerings.[7]

The contributions are to be proportionate: a sixtieth in the case of **'wheat'** and **'barley'** (45:13); a hundredth in the case of **'oil'** (45:14); and one in two hundred in the case of **'sheep'** (45:15). The offerings in view include **'grain offerings, burnt offerings and fellowship offerings'**, each of which will be designed **'to make atonement for the people'** (45:15; cf. 45:17). These offerings are to be conducted by the **'prince'** (45:17). Sacrifices are to be made on the following occasions: New Year's Day (45:18-19), a week later (45:20), Passover (45:21-24) and the Feast of Tabernacles — **'the feast, which begins in the seventh month on the fifteenth day'** (45:25). This is the Feast of Ingathering (Exod. 23:16; 34:2), or Tabernacles (Deut. 16:16).

Two matters of interpretation force themselves on us at this point. They concern the offering of sacrifices in a future kingdom and the identity of the prince. (Both are somewhat technical and readers may wish to consult the references for further elucidation. The discussion in the text has been kept to a minimum.)

When are these offerings to be given?

Those who foresee a literal fulfilment of Ezekiel's visions at this point insist that the sacrifices offered in the restored temple in Jerusalem (though outside it in this vision) will be 'memorial' sacrifices, i.e. sacrifices in which there will be no shedding of blood.[8] This is to protect themselves against the charge that they do not believe that the work of Christ is complete, thus necessitating the end of all blood-letting sacrifices (cf. Heb. 10:18). This, however, will not do, for the exact same word for atonement is used here as it is throughout the Old Testament to imply a sacrifice of propitiatory significance (Lev. 6:30; 8:15; 16:6,11,24,30,32,33,34; Num. 5:8; 15:28; 29:5). If the sacrifices envisaged here are meant to be taken literally, they are *not* memorial sacrifices; and if they are not memorial sacrifices, the entire priestly work of Christ is called into question and our salvation is based on uncertain ground. For this reason alone, the vision unfolding in these chapters has to be taken as a symbolic depiction of the kingdom of God in the last days, leading up to the establishment of the new heaven and the earth.

Who is the 'prince'?

It is time to consider one of the most difficult issues in this entire section: the identity of the 'prince' (see 44:1-3; 45:1-8). The 'prince' of Ezekiel's vision is allowed access to the east gate of the temple courtyard (44:1-3), to receive tribute from the people (45:16), as well as exalting the worship of God in the temple in supervising the offerings (45:17). His identity is a 'puzzle to many'.[9] Some commentators readily see him as the Messianic king of the new age, as described in previous sections (e.g. 17:22-24; 34:23-31; 37:24), in other words, the 'prince' finds his fulfilment in the coming of Jesus Christ. Others are quite strongly insistent that this cannot be the case.[10] One of the problems in identifying him with Christ is the fact that he is said to offer a sin offering **'for himself and for all the people of the land'** (45:22).[11] Another problem is that the prince is said to have children (46:16).[12]

A Messianic interpretation seems, on the face of it, untenable. It seems that the 'prince' was meant to convey in the minds of Ezekiel's listeners the idea of a future leader who would lead them in worshipping God. Unlike past leaders who had led the people astray — one of the reasons why God had warned them not to crave after a king so as to be like the other nations (cf. Deut. 17:14-20; 1 Sam. 8:1-9) — the future 'leader' would be trustworthy and loyal. No one person is meant by this depiction of a future king. He is an ideal figure. To ask his identity is probably a mistake. None of the details of these chapters is to be pressed into hard realities in the future. Just as we do not expect any literal fulfilment of this massive temple complex, or the division of the land of Palestine in which the city of Jerusalem occupies the greater part, so also we should not expect the 'prince' to emerge as any one figure of definable identity. This is apocalyptic writing (See 'Focus on Ezekiel 40-48'). What we have in these chapters is an entire impressionistic tableau.

Readers who have followed the discussion above (and have read the references!) will appreciate how difficult some passages of Scripture can be to understand. Daniel confessed to being baffled by some of his own visions (Dan. 12:8). A confession of ignorance about the precise meaning of these passages is nothing to be ashamed of. Just because commentators are dogmatic about a certain interpretation is no guarantee that they are right. We need the illumination of the Holy Spirit to help us come to understand every word of Scripture. In passages like these, meekness is the best approach.

The role of the prince in worship (46:1-18)

Bearing in mind what we have already said about the apocalyptic nature of the 'prince' in these passages, certain matters are now elaborated upon. The east gate of the outer court was kept permanently closed (44:2). The prince, however, had access to the gateway from the inside (44:3). It is not this gateway, but the inner gateway which leads to the sanctuary that is now in view. Its doors, too, were to be kept closed, except on the Sabbath and new moons (46:1), but only the priests were allowed to enter this gateway into the inner courtyard (46:2-3).[13]

Various offerings are to be offered on these days (46:4-7), as well as on the festival occasions (46:11-15), the details deviating a little from the requirements mentioned in Moses' time. The burnt offering on the Sabbath calls for **'six male lambs and a ram'** (46:4); the Mosaic requirement calls for only two lambs (Num. 28:9). The daily offering, one lamb in the morning and one in the evening in Moses' legislation (Num. 28:3-8) is offered in the morning only (46:13). It may be that the increase in the number belonging to the future kingdom explains the increased requirement for the Sabbath.[14] In any case, we are not given a complete list of requirements here. In the festivals mentioned in 45:18 - 46:24, there is no mention of the Day of Atonement.

It may seem strange that 46:8-10 includes what are in effect traffic directions! The explanation is not difficult. The estimated numbers in Jerusalem at feast days in the time of Christ grew from 50,000 to 200,000. In this vision, the numbers are even greater. Anyone who has been in a crowd knows the need for good crowd control. One only has to think of what happened at such venues as Mecca in Saudi Arabia, or at some football stadiums, to see the sense of it.

The prince is permitted to make gifts of land to his sons, who are allowed to keep it as an inheritance (46:16-18). Gifts made to servants were leased, and to be returned **'in the year of freedom'** (46:17)— probably the year of jubilee, the fiftieth year (Lev. 25:10-13). In this way, all land stayed within the family and a system of justice and equity was maintained. In the new kingdom, justice and fairness will be its hallmarks.

Cooking of sacrificial meals (46:19-24)

Following a description of the sacrifices, Ezekiel now explains how and where they are to be offered, and in some cases, cooked. Bread was to be baked in ovens to be found at the western extremity of the north row of priests' chambers in the inner court (46:19-20). Worship, in the Old Testament, and in Ezekiel's visionary new kingdom, includes the fellowship of eating food with one another. After the Levites had cooked the offering, the worshippers gathered in family groups to eat. It is not haphazard that Jesus chose the Passover meal to institute one of the signs and seals of the new covenant administration: the Lord's Supper. Eating together shows, as almost nothing else does, our mutual love and respect for one another.

Summary

We have been given a glimpse of a future temple and its workings, together with its setting in the new Canaan. It is not meant to be more than a picture, an apocalyptic, or impressionistic picture given in terms which Ezekiel's companions would appreciate. Everything serves one end: the worship of God in an orderly, reverent fashion. Restrictions are placed on access to the inner court, where God dwells, restrictions which underline the fact the God is holy. Sacrifices abound, emphasizing man's inherent sinfulness and consequent inability to approach God. God's great work, something which he had depicted as a resuscitation of an army of corpses (37:1-14), includes the formation of a church in which access to God will be by means of the sacrifice of his own Son: 'But now he has appeared once for all at the end of the ages to do away with sin by

the sacrifice of himself.' 'Therefore, since we are receiving a
kingdom that cannot be shaken, let us be thankful, and so worship
God acceptably with reverence and awe, for our "God is a consuming fire"' (Heb. 9:26; 12:28-29).

22.
The promised land

Please read Ezekiel 47:1 - 48:35

In this final section of the book of Ezekiel we are given a glimpse of the promised land, including the city of Jerusalem. It must be understood immediately that what is portrayed here is something very different from the Israel (or Jerusalem) that we know today. Any attempt to convey a link between these chapters and the emergence of the State of Israel in 1948 is misguided.

The river of life (47:1-12)

The Bible begins with a description of a river which flowed through the Garden of Eden and broke up into four tributaries as it left (Gen. 2:10-14). This is a theme which runs right through the Bible. The psalmist speaks of a river 'whose streams make glad the city of God, the holy place where the Most High dwells' (Ps. 46:4). Several of the prophets picture something similar: Joel speaks of a 'fountain' which 'will flow out of the Lord's house' (Joel 3:18), and Zechariah of 'living water' which 'will flow out from Jerusalem, half to the eastern sea, and half to the western sea' (Zech. 14:8). And the Bible ends with a picture of the New Jerusalem, from which emerges a river flowing from God's throne (Rev. 22:1-2). This latter reference is, in fact, based directly on Ezekiel's vision in chapter 47 and the interpretation of the one, as we shall see, affects the other.

There is no way that any literal fulfilment of this river can even be imagined! The fact that at this point we are dealing with an impressionistic painting should be evident. A glance at a coffee table book depicting life in Egypt, for example, shows the effect of the River Nile on the surrounding countryside. Near the river bank, the land is rich and fertile ('life-giving'); further away, the land is desert! To those who lived in hot climates, as did the Israelites, there was no better way of depicting life than by a fresh, clean supply of water in a nearby river.

The river emerges from under the temple **'threshold'** (47:1), runs (apparently) underground to emerge under the eastern gate (47:2), through the city (eastwards, 47:3) and out into the countryside. After some 2,500 yards the river has become so wide and so deep that no man can cross it. This is some river! Eventually it empties into the Dead Sea (47:8). Along its banks are the signs of abundant life and prosperity (47:9-12). This is Eden restored (cf. 36:35). This is a picture of the kind of blessing God's people may expect in the new kingdom. Every provision for their need will be taken care of by the Lord himself.[1] God's kingdom is paradise.

There is a television commercial which goes something like this: a few men are sitting down at the end of a day's fishing on the porch of the house. Everything speaks of harmony and contentment. One opens a pack of six cans of lager, drinks one and says, 'It doesn't get better than this.' This is paradise! Sadly, for many, life gets no better than that. In fact it gets a great deal worse. For the believer, however, life gets much better. Knowing God and anticipating good things to come means that life *does* get better than this!

The key to understanding the river that flows from beneath the temple is found in John 7:37-39, where Jesus, on the final day of the Feast of Tabernacles, stands up and proclaims: "'If anyone is thirsty, let him come to me and drink. Whoever believes in me, as the Scripture has said, streams of living water will flow from within him." By this he meant the Spirit, whom those who believed in him were later to receive...' Every day of the Feast of Tabernacles, a priest took a golden flask holding about four and a half pints of water from the Pool of Siloam near Jerusalem, carried it through the Water Gate, went up the ramp to the altar, and poured it out.[2] It is thought that the pilgrims who watched this ceremony would have thought of Ezekiel 47.[3] In this understanding, Jesus quite deliberately identifies himself as the fulfilment of Ezekiel's prophecy.

Ezekiel's vision points to Christ as the true temple of God, who after his death, resurrection and ascension sent forth the Holy Spirit as his representative agent in the hearts of his people. Ezekiel 47 is a picture of Pentecost and the subsequent outpourings of the Spirit in revivals down through the ages. Given this interpretation, the restored temple which Ezekiel has described is 'a type of the Christian believer'.⁴ In the New Testament the individual believer has become the temple of God because the Holy Spirit dwells within him (1 Cor. 6:19; cf.3:16-17). Considered collectively, the church has also become God's temple (Eph. 2:21).

The land division (47:13-23)

The division of land in the middle section of Canaan has already been dealt with (45:1-8). Concern is now expressed for the outer limits of the land.

Reading through Joshua conveys the fact that Israel never did occupy all the land that God had allocated to her. A dangerous sign of Israel's waning enthusiasm for settlement comes in Joshua 13:13: 'But the Israelites did not drive out the people of Geshur and Maacah, so they continue to live among the Israelites to this day.' A similar danger showed up earlier when the Philistine cities of Gaza, Gath and Ashdod were listed as unconquered — a problem that was to cause Israel pain for centuries to come (Josh. 11:22; cf. Num. 33:55-56). Other examples include the failure to dispossess the Jebusites from Jerusalem (Josh. 15:63; cf. 16:10; 17:12-13).

In the history of Israel that followed, the land changed a great deal, depending upon who was judge or king at the time. By the time of Ezekiel, of course, Babylonian foreigners occupied all of it to the north and Edomite greed had excised a large part to the south. The northern territories occupied by Israel had long since gone when the Assyrians conquered the land. Ezekiel's promise of a land that, more or less, matched the original promise made to Israel in Numbers 34:1-12, must have sounded like music to their ears. Other references to the extent of God's promise to Israel include: 'from the river of Egypt to the great river, the Euphrates' (Gen. 15:18); 'from Dan to Beersheba' (Judg. 20:1); and 'from Lebo Hamath to the Wadi of Egypt' (1 Kings 8:65).

The boundaries described in Ezekiel 47 are as follows: to the west, the Mediterranean Sea (47:20); to the east, the Jordan River and the Dead Sea (47:18); to the north, from Tyre on the Phoenician coast on the western side, and on the eastern side, the southern tip of Syria—north of the Sea of Galilee (47:15); and to the south, from

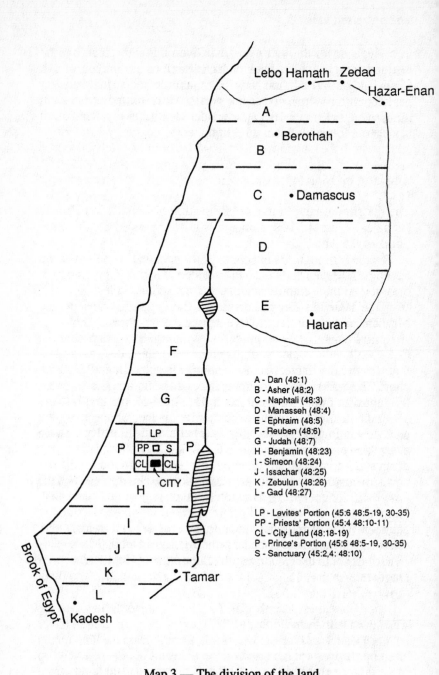

Map 3 — The division of the land

the Mediterranean to the Dead Sea along a route that is now unidentifiable (47:19). There is no land east of the Jordan (where Reuben, Gad and the half tribe of Mannaseh settled)! Ezekiel is depicting a land that is perfectly symmetrical. His point is not to convey real geography, but a far greater spiritual reality: that there is far more to the kingdom of God than we imagine. We are kings and priests in the kingdom of God (Rev. 1:6), but we often fail to live as children of the King! His royal treasure house is ours. The challenge is expressed in the hymn, 'Jesus, I my cross have taken':

Take, my soul, thy full salvation,
Rise o'er sin and fear and care;
Joy to find in every station
Something still to do or bear;
Think what Spirit dwells within thee,
What a Father's smile is thine,
What a Saviour died to win thee:
Child of heaven, shoudst thou repine?

(Henry Francis Lyte).

Of particular interest in this section is the inclusion of Gentiles (47:22-23). Since the 'uncircumcised in heart and flesh' were forbidden access to the inner courtyard (44:4-8), one might have expected Ezekiel's vision to contain no place for the Gentiles whatsoever. But this is not so. Ezekiel has already hinted at Gentile inclusion in the kingdom of God (14:7; 22:7). Now it is made explicit. Aliens who settled among the people of God (i.e. proselytes) were to be regarded as **'native-born Israelites'** (47:22; cf. Lev. 24:22; Num. 15:29). In a wonderful display of grace and pity, Jesus went to the land of Tyre to speak to a woman about her daughter (who was under the influence of an evil spirit) — a combination thought to be beneath the dignity of a rabbi (Mark 7:24-30). It was one of many expressions of the place of Gentiles in God's kingdom.

The seven northern tribes (48:1-7)

The allocation of the land in the time of Joshua seems to have been a fairly arbitrary affair — Judah and Ephraim having large areas,

while Benjamin, Dan and Issachar had only tiny tracts of land; and
Simeon's boundaries were so small that it was soon absorbed by
Judah. In the new kingdom, land allocation will be 'fair and square'[5]
The land allocation is best seen by consulting the map (p. 294). It
should be noted that the central portion (48:8-22; cf. 45:1-8),
consisting of Jerusalem and surrounding land belonging to the
prince, occupies some fifty square miles in this vision.

The city of God (48:30-35)

The city has twelve gates, three on each side, named according to the
twelve tribes of Israel, with 'Joseph' replacing his two sons,
Ephraim and Manasseh (48:32), and **'Levi'** taking the additional
place (48:31). Levi was given no land in which to dwell and is
therefore not mentioned in the land distribution of the preceding
sections (cf. Josh. 13:14). The point being made is that *everyone* in
Israel has access to the city of God.

And the name of this city? Not Jerusalem, or Zion, but *Yahweh-
Shammah* — 'THE LORD IS THERE' (48:35). This has been the
meaning of the entire vision: to point out to a despondent people in
exile that God is with them. The point of this vision has not been to
focus on the city of Jerusalem, or the temple in its gigantic proportions; still less to get sidetracked by discussions of its relevance to
modern Israel. Ezekiel wants his readers to be taken up with God and
his presence with his people. At the heart of the covenant was the
Lord dwelling among his people. 'I will be your God and you will
be my people,' had been the theme of ages. God commanded Israel
to construct a tabernacle that he might dwell among them (Exod.
25:8). It was to be the place where he would dwell among his people
(Exod. 29:42-44). Throughout Deuteronomy, God had spoken of a
place 'to put his Name ... for his dwelling' (Deut. 12:5; cf. 12:11,14;
14:23; 16:2,6,7,11). Ezekiel has already spoken in similar terms in
chapter 37: 'I will make a covenant of peace with them; it will be an
everlasting covenant. I will establish them and increase their numbers, and I will put my sanctuary among them for ever. My dwelling-
place will be with them; I will be their God, and they will be my
people. Then the nations will know that I the Lord make Israel holy,
when my sanctuary is among them for ever.'

This is the theme which emerges at the coming of Christ into the world, when God 'tabernacles' in human flesh by the presence of the incarnate Son (John 1:14; Ezekiel has foreseen this day, too, in his many prophecies of the coming of Christ). Paul takes up the same theme, saying that God's people become a 'temple in the Lord' (Eph. 2:1). The great multitude of the redeemed, which no man can number, serve the Lord day and night in his temple, having God's tabernacle spread over them (Rev. 7:15). And the Bible closes with this same theme: 'Then I saw a new heaven and a new earth, for the first heaven and the first earth had passed away, and there was no longer any sea. I saw the Holy City, the new Jerusalem, coming down out of heaven from God, prepared as a bride beautifully dressed for her husband. And I heard a loud voice from the throne saying, "Now the dwelling of God is with men, and he will live with them. They will be his people, and God himself will be with them and be their God"' (Rev. 21:1-3).

Summary

There were times in Israel's history when God withdrew his presence; Ezekiel saw the glory of God depart through the east gate of the temple in chapter 10. This was God's withdrawal from an apostate people.

Even though most believers can testify to knowing something about this in their own lives, when God's presence seems to be withdrawn (Ps. 22:1; 74:1; Isa. 40:27; 50:10), what they experience is something temporary and of a different order from what has happened to Israel in these chapters. God never forsakes any of his true children (Josh. 1:5; 1 Peter 1:5), but he does withdraw some of his blessings and help (Josh. 7:1-26).

What these final chapters have been about is ultimately heaven. The church which has been symbolically depicted by a temple will one day be the very glory of God. Its salvation from sin will be its eternal theme of gratitude. A day will dawn when God's people will know and experience an uninterrupted measure of God's presence and blessing.

In the depiction of the water of life flowing from the temple and into the Dead Sea, we have seen a picture of the coming of the Holy

Spirit on the Day of Pentecost. The gift of the Spirit, in which all in the church share, is described by Paul as the 'deposit, guaranteeing what is to come' (2 Cor. 1:22; 5:5), and as the 'first-fruits' of the full inheritance to be received at Christ's return (Rom. 8:23). The possession of the church is currently only partial. Only in heaven will the full reality of our possession and privilege become apparent.

Heaven is the ultimate fulfilment of Ezekiel's vision. These chapters, though difficult, must have greatly encouraged those in exile to persevere. Perhaps they spurred the likes of Daniel and his three friends to face the fires of persecution, knowing that God had a wonderful future planned for them. Reading Ezekiel should prove to be a similar source of encouragement for us, too.

References

Introduction
1. In Jewish rabbinical tradition, Ezekiel was a book reserved for study by mature students rather than beginners partly because of the delicate nature of chapters 16 and 23, with their references to prostitution and even nymphomania (16:28-29).
2. Lewis Carroll, *Alice's Adventures in Wonderland*, ch. 1.
3. J. M. Barrie, *Peter Pan*, Hodder & Stoughton,1928, p.111.
4. Thomas Watson, *A Body of Divinity*, Banner of Truth, 1958, p.25
5. D. Thomas, *God Delivers*, Evangelical Press, 1991.
6. E. Hengstenberg, *The Prophecies of the Prophet Ezekiel*, T. & T. Clark,1976, p.102. This quotation is cited again in the text.

Chapter 1 — Meeting God
1. C. H. Spurgeon, *Lectures to my Students*, Marshall, Morgan & Scott, 1970, p.349.
2. Cited by Sinclair Ferguson, *Daniel*, Word, 1988, p.147.
3. Jane Austen, *Northanger Abbey*, John Davie,1971, p.97
4. The story is recorded in 2 Kings 24:1-25:1, which ends with the statement: 'So Judah went into captivity, away from her land' (2 Kings 25:21).
5. Some commentators interpret the opening verse in a different way, suggesting that the 'thirtieth year' is a general title for the entire book and especially for the last nine chapters (40-48). Thus these latter chapters were delivered no later than thirty years after the captivity, i.e. 568 B.C. (See Douglas Stuart, *Ezekiel, The Communicator's Commentary*, Word, 1989, p.29). A more natural reading of the text would suggest that Ezekiel is giving us his own age.
6. During David's time the ages were altered to include those from twenty to fifty (1 Chron. 23:24-27), 'because there was no longer a need for mature Levites as porters' (*The Illustrated Bible Dictionary*, IVP, 1980, Part 3, 'Priests and Levites', p.1267). 'This regulation may be understood as referring to the age at which the Levites were to enter upon their duties after the people had taken possession of the land of Canaan, and it appears to have remained in force until the time of David who

substituted the age of twenty for that of twenty-five, because the necessity of carrying the tabernacle from place to place, which arose but seldom after the entrance into Canaan, finally ceased after the removal of the ark to Mount Zion. The time of service during the wanderings in the wilderness was from thirty to fifty (Num. 4:3,23,30), during which time the constant removal of the Tabernacle required the services of men in the full vigour of life' (C. J. Ellicot, *Leviticus — An Old Testament Commentary for English Readers,* Cassell & Co.,1897, p.506).

7. Iain Murray, *D. Martyn Lloyd-Jones: The Fight of Faith,* Banner of Truth, 1990, vol. 2, p.23.

8. Ezekiel 3:14 hints that Ezekiel may have had the liberty to walk some distance away from the main encampment of exiles as he received these visions. As to whether or not Ezekiel actually saw a dark cloud on the horizon which then led into a visionary experience, we do not know; nor is it that important.

9. See E. W. Hengstenberg, *The Prophecies of Ezekiel,* T & T Clark, 1869, p.7.

10. Such creatures may appear strange to us but they would not have done so to Ezekiel and his initial readers. Cherubim adorned the ark of the covenant (Exod. 25:18-22), the curtains and veil of the tabernacle (Exod. 26:31) and the walls of the temple (2 Chron. 3:7). The presence of God in his glory that was manifested at creation (Gen. 1:2) was replicated in the tabernacle (Exod. 25-40), which was itself a symbolic reproduction of the reality of the heavenly temple, where the God of glory is enthroned in the midst of the angelic divine council (Heb. 9:23-24). What Ezekiel saw was what countless priests had witnessed in the tabernacle and temple worship: a glimpse of heaven! (See Meredith Kline, *Images of the Spirit,* Baker, 1980, pp.39,40).

11. 'Wings' and 'clouds' are significant in Bible passages depicting God's *glory*. In the opening chapter of Genesis, we read that 'The Spirit of God was hovering over the waters' (Gen. 1:2). The verb 'to hover' is used again in Deuteronomy 32:11, to describe God leading Israel through the 'barren and howling waste' on the way to Canaan. The deliverance is likened to the action of an eagle hovering protectively over its young, spreading out its wings to support them. In Exodus 19:4 God similarly describes himself as bearing Israel on eagle's wings. It was in the pillar of cloud and fire that he went before them in the way and afforded them this overshadowing protection (see Kline, *Images of the Spirit,* p.14).

12. The 'living creatures' are also said to have had under their wings hands like those of a man (1:8) but these only seem to have significance later, in 10:7,8.

13. Light is often an attendant of God's glory in Scripture: 'God ... lives in unapproachable light' (1 Tim. 6:16); the radiance of a rainbow revealing the holy beauty of the Lord in his temple (Ezek. 1:28; Rev. 4:3; 10:1); the light of wisdom and truth, penetrating the darkness of sin (Ps. 139: 7-11), or 'the sun of righteousness' (Mal. 4:2).

14. John Calvin, *Commentaries on the First Twenty chapters of Ezekiel,* Baker, 1981, vol. XI, p. 97.

15. It is a pity that the NIV has omitted the repetition of the Hebrew word *qôl* ('voice', 'sound') in verses 24-28. Literally they read: 'When they [the cherubim]

went, I heard the *qôl* of their wings, like the *qôl* of many waters, like the *qôl* of the Almighty, the *qôl* of tumult like the *qôl* of an army... And there came a *qôl* from the firmament above their heads... Such was the appearance of the glory of the Lord. And when I saw it, I fell upon my face, and I heard the *qôl* of one speaking.'

16. See also such passages as 2 Sam. 5:24; Isa. 13:4-6; 30:30; Joel 2:11; 3:16; Zeph. 1:14. The Lord is pictured as the Divine Warrior coming to do battle with all the accompanying noise that such an onslaught brings (See Kline, *Images of the Spirit*, pp.100-102).

17. The Second Coming of Christ, far from being a 'secret' coming, is the noisiest event of all!

18. Patrick Fairbairn, *Ezekiel and the Book of his Prophecy*, T & T Clark, 1883, p.34.

19. John Calvin, *The Institutes of the Christian Religion*, 1:1:3

20. Lewis Carroll, *Complete Works*, chapter 7, *Alice Through the Looking Glass*, Nonesuch, 1939, p.196.

21. Wayne Grudem, *1 Peter, Tyndale New Testament Commentary*, IVP, 1988, p.66.

22. That which had proved to be a comfort to Hagar in her distress, when she exclaimed, 'I have now seen the One who sees me' (Gen. 16:13), is meant to be our source of comfort too.

Chapter 2 — Five commissions

1. Calvin, *Ezekiel*, p.107.

2. Walter Eichdrodt says it refers to 'the weakness of the creature to whom the Mighty Lord shows such condescension' (*Ezekiel*, Westminster Press, 1975, p.61). 'Here it stresses Ezekiel's inferiority to and dependence on God, who alone is sovereign' (Stuart, *Ezekiel*, p.39).

3. Gerard van Groningen, *Messianic Revelation in the Old Testament*, Baker, 1990, p. 740.

4. See comments on page 12.

5. J. I. Packer, *God's Words*, IVP, 1981, p.34.

6. Calvin, *Ezekiel*, vol. 1, p.109.

7. The Hebrew for 'hard' is *hazaq*, and 'Ezekiel' is *yehezqe'l*. (See, John B. Taylor, *Ezekiel: An Introduction and Commentary*, Tyndale Press, 1969, p. 66).

8. Calvin, *Ezekiel*, vol. 1, p. 137.

9. T. H. L. Parker, *John Calvin*, The Westminster Press, 1975, pp.151-2.

10. Calvin, *Ezekiel*, vol. 1, p. xxxviii.

11. Ezekiel constantly refers to 'Israel' even though he sometimes has the southern kingdom of Judah in mind. Once the northern kingdom had fallen it was customary for the prophets to think of Judah as Israel.

12. W. Stanford Reid, *Trumpeter of God: A biography of John Knox*, Baker, 1974, p.283.

13. *Hamlet*, Act 3, Scene 2.

14. Technically, it was to the people of Judah that Ezekiel ministered, Israel having

fallen into Assyrian hands a century earlier. By Ezekiel's time the 'house of Israel' and the 'house of Judah' are phrases often used interchangeably as a depiction of God's people (2:3; 3:4-7; 4:3; 8:1-12; 9:9; 11:15 etc.) .

15. *Tel Abib,* which was situated somewhere in southern Iraq, meant 'mound of the flood' (i.e. destruction), probably referring to the ruined condition of the site. It is not to be confused with the modern site of Tel Aviv on the Mediterranean coast of northern Israel.

16. Some have suggested that Ezekiel was merely identifying himself with God's righteous anger and indignation against Israel, and that he was not guilty of any sinful anger against divine providence.

17. Calvin, *Ezekiel,* vol. 1, p. 110.

18. The period of seven days may well be significant since it represented the prescribed period of mourning in Israel (Gen. 50:10; Num. 19:11; Job 2:13), appropriate enough considering the message he was asked to deliver. Seven days was also the period of time for a priest's consecration (Lev. 8:33). At thirty years of age, Ezekiel was being set apart as priest in a foreign land with a mission to perform for God.

19. *Shorter Catechism,* Answer 87

20. Fairbairn, *Ezekiel,* p. 43.

21. As above, p. 45.

Chapter 3 — The siege of Jerusalem

1. See article on 'Hophra' in K. Kitchen in *Illustrated Bible Dictionary,* vol. 2, pp.659-60.

2. The exact number of years from 931 B.C. to 539 B.C. is, of course, 392 years, which is rounded off to 390 years.

3. Actually this makes forty-seven years, but it may be that it is rounded down to forty so as to make the total 'days' of Ezekiel's enacted prophecy 430 'days' — Israel had spent 430 years in captivity in Egypt (Exod. 12:40). The allusion to the forty years spent wandering in the wilderness is also a likely reason for rounding off this number (See Stuart, *Ezekiel,* p.57). Others have argued that the number forty represents the long reign of wicked Manasseh before his repentance (2 Kings 21:11-15; 23:26-27; 24:3-4; 2 Chron. 33:12-13).

4. Examples of sin-bearing language are: Exod. 28:43; Lev. 5:17; 19:8; 22:9; 24:15; Num. 9:13; 14:34; 18:22.

5. Cited by Timothy George, *Theology of the Reformation,* Apollos, 1988 p.60.

6. Craigie, *Ezekiel,* pp.35-6.

7. Cf. 13:8; 21:3; 26:3; 28:22; 29:3,10; 30:22; 34:10; 35:3; 38:3; 39:1.

8. John Stott, *The Cross of Christ,* IVP, 1986, p.125.

9. The word 'spent' (Hebrew *kalah)* is a favourite word in Ezekiel. Other references are at 6:12; 7:8; 13:15; 20:8,21.

10. This is the first of sixteen such instances of God describing himself as 'the living God' in Ezekiel. The others are: 14:16,18,20; 16:48; 17:16,19; 18:3; 20:3,31,33; 33:11,27; 34:8; 35:6,11.

11. Calvin, *Ezekiel,* p.217.

Chapter 4 — The Day of the Lord

1. Asherah, sometimes (wrongly) translated 'grove' (AV), was a Canaanite fertility mother goddess represented by a wooden pole, thought to be of phallic significance. Baal was the supreme nature god of the Canaanites. Asherah was often worshipped along with Baal (Judg. 3:7; 2 Kings 23:6). During Elijah's time, Jezebel attempted to obliterate true religion, substituting Baalism as the official religion of Israel. 400 prophets of Asherah ate at Jezebel's table (1 Kings 18:19). Together, these religions encouraged ritual prostitution (Judg 2:17; Jer. 7:9; Amos 2:7) and child sacrifice (Jer. 19:5).

2. The reading 'Diblah' is disputed. It may refer to Beth Diblathaim, a city of Moab and mentioned in Jeremiah 48:22. Alternatively, a textual error known as orthography may be responsible, confusing two Hebrew characters which look very similar. Instead of reading Diblah, some copyists have read Riblah. Riblah is known to be a city which existed in the northern Syrian district of Hamath on the Orontes River and south of Kedesh. It was here that Pharaoh Necho put King Josiah in chains. It was also in Riblah that Nebuchadnezzar had his headquarters and that Zedekiah, Judah's last king, was executed (2 Kings 25:6).

It must be noted, however, that no evidence for such an error exists. It may be that a place called Diblah did indeed exist and may one day come to light.

3. Readers should note that in some versions chapter 7 is laid out in the form of poetry (e.g. NKJV). The NIV, which is used in this commentary, does not.

4. Cited by John Blanchard, *More Gathered Gold,* Evangelical Press, 1986, p.179.

5. Taking a rod to imply an instrument of punishment, other commentators have suggested that it is the pride of Nebuchadnezzar, as God's instrument of judgement, that is in view. See, Ralph H. Alexander, *The Expositor's Bible Commentary,* edited by Frank E. Gabalein, Zondervan, 1986, vol. 6, p.777.

6. Sinclair Ferguson, *A Heart for God,* Banner of Truth, 1987, p.123.

7. Cited by Richard J. Foster, *Money, Sex and Power,* Hodder & Stoughton, 1985, p. 19.

8. As above, p.26

9. Calvin, *Ezekiel,* p. 237.

10. Hymn: 'O Love that wilt not let me go', published in 1882.

Chapter 5 — Revelations of the temple

1. Because of this lengthy gap of fourteen months, chapters 8-19 are sometimes referred to as the second cycle of predictions regarding Jerusalem, covering the first twenty-four chapters of Ezekiel. The outline of the book then becomes: first cycle (1-7), second cycle (8-19), third cycle (20-23) and fourth cycle (24) (e.g. Hengstenberg, *Prophecies of Ezekiel,* p.68). The next dated reference in Ezekiel (20:1) is eleven months away, suggesting that the contents of chapters 8-19 were all delivered within that time-scale.

2. Why some prophets received more visions than others is not clear. Geerhardus Vos suggests that 'Some of the prophets may have been of a more imaginative type of mind than others' (Geerhardus Vos, *Biblical Theology,* Eerdmans, 1973, p.240).

3. We must always remember,' O. T. Allis comments, 'that we are dealing with

visions, with dreams, which may or may not correspond exactly to the realities of earthly life and experience. In this respect the visions of the Old Testament may be compared with the parables of the New' (O. T. Allis, *The Old Testament: Its Claims and its Critics,* Presbyterian and Reformed, 1972, p.47).

4. Kline, *Images of the Spirit,* p.62.

5. Taylor, *Ezekiel,* p.96.

6. Calvin, *Institutes,* 2.8.18

7. Craigie, *Ezekiel,* p.58.

8. John Owen, *Works,* Banner of Truth, 1974, vol. 6, p. 47.

9. The translation of 8:17 is difficult. Commentators sometimes point out that the word 'branch' normally means 'twig' and that putting a twig to one's nose was part of the ritual practice of sun worship (Alexander, *Expositor's Bible Commentary,* p. 785).

10. Calvin, *Ezekiel,* vol. 1, p. 298.

11. John Stott is of the opinion that the statement, 'God's patience runs out,' is *not* appropriate to God. Speaking of the prophets of the exile and their use of the language of provocation, he says, 'They did not mean that Yahweh was irritated or exasperated, or that Israel's behaviour had been so "provocative" that his patience had run out. No, the language of provocation expresses the inevitable reaction of God's perfect nature to evil. It indicates that there is within God a holy intolerance of idolatry, immorality and injustice' (*Cross of Christ,* p.124). But this is, I think, a mistaken interpretation of the word 'patience'. God's 'patience' is his slowness to anger. It is not limitless. The fact that it runs out does not necessarily imply a loss of control.

12. Jerry Bridges, *Transforming Grace: Living Confidently in God's Unfailing Love,* NavPress, 1992, p.29.

13. It is true that the last letter of the Hebrew alphabet is shaped like an 'X' in the oldest Hebrew script, but, as the reader can see by turning to the reference to *'Taw'* given as a superscription to Psalm 119:169-176, in later Hebrew script the letter bears no visual relation to a cross.

14. H. L. Ellison, *Ezekiel: the Man and his Message,* Eerdmans, 1956, p. 44.

Chapter 6 — The chariot of God

1. *Matthew Henry's Commentary,* Marshall, Morgan & Scott, 1953, vol. 5, p.97.

2. Craigie, *Ezekiel,* p.71

3. *Westminster Confession of Faith,* 25:v

4. This is a different Jaazaniah from the one in 8:11, their respective fathers being Azzur and Shaphan.

5. C. H. Spurgeon, *The Metropolitan Tabernacle Pulpit,* Pilgrim Publications, 1979, vol. 59, p.510

6. J. C. Ryle, *Holiness,* James Clark, 1956, p.1.

7. Hengstenberg, *The Prophecies of Ezekiel,* p.102.

8. See Fairbairn, *Ezekiel,* pp.113-15.

9. B. B. Warfield, *Biblical and Theological Studies,* Presbyterian & Reformed, 1968, pp.357-8.

10. John Murray, *Collected Writings,* Banner of Truth, 1977, vol. 2, p.171.

11. As above, p.173.

12. Jonathan Edwards, 'The Distinguishing Marks of the Spirit of God', *Works,* Banner of Truth, 1974, vol.2, p.266.

Chapter 7 — False prophets and prophetesses

1. Spurgeon, *Metropolitan Tabernacle Pulpit,* vol. 20, p.169.

2. Calvin, *Ezekiel,* vol.1, p.405.

3. John Murray, *Principles of Conduct,* Tyndale Press, 1971, p.232.

4. Other eighth-century prophets warned of Judah's (and Jerusalem's) downfall, only to fall on deaf ears (see Hosea 5:10-14; Micah 1:8-9; Isa. 22:1-14).

5. D. Martyn Lloyd-Jones, *Expository Sermons on 2 Peter,* Banner of Truth, 1983, p.168.

6. Stuart, *Ezekiel,* p.120.

7. The facts are these: Miriam, Moses' sister, was a prophetess; she, however, was punished with leprosy for an act of rebellion against Moses (Num. 12). Afterwards there is no record of any suspicion against her. Though no woman ever became an author of any Bible book, her song of victory over the Egyptians is recorded in Scripture (Exod. 15), along with inspired songs by Deborah, Hannah and Mary.

Deborah was both a prophetess *and* a judge (Judg. 4:4). In King Josiah's time (when Ezekiel would have been a boy) it was Huldah the prophetess who spoke God's word to Josiah and other important men, even though Jeremiah was available at the time (2 Kings 22:13). Joel confirmed the propriety of prophetesses (Joel 2:28-29) and the New Testament gives testimony to the fact that they existed (Anna, Luke 2:36-38; Philip's four daughters, Acts 21:9). According to Calvin, God permitted the use of prophetesses 'to shame the men', but this does not seem to explain Huldah's role when Jeremiah was evidently available (2 Kings 22).

Women were permitted to pray and prophesy in the New Testament church: 'And every woman who prays or prophesies with her head uncovered dishonours her head...' (1 Cor. 11:5). Various interpretations are available for this verse: the praying and prophesying of women did not occur in the church (Hodge); it is mentioned that it did take place in the church, but it is not condoned (Plummer); it is allowed and condoned in the church (Hurley, Knight). Objections to prophetesses usually arise from the fact that Paul denies a woman the right to teach and exercise authority over a man (1 Cor. 14:34; 1 Tim. 2:12). But prophecy was an act in which the person was essentially passive and does not necessarily imply headship over a man (Knight, Foh). 'Preaching is a form of teaching, and as such was forbidden to women in 1 Timothy 2:11-15. Prophecy is different in that God puts the very words into the mouth of the prophet (2 Pet. 1:21-22)' (Foh, p.104). See Charles Hodge, *I & II Corinthians,* Banner of Truth, 1974; James B. Hurley, *Man and Woman in Biblical Perspective,* Zondervan, 1981; George Knight III, *The New Testament Teaching on the Role Relationship of Men and Women,* Baker, 1977; Susan Foh, *Women and the Word of God: A Response to Biblical Feminism,* Presbyterian & Reformed, 1979.

8. Calvin, *Institutes*, 3:2:11
9. Calvin, *Ezekiel*, vol.2, pp.17-18.
10. Craigie, *Ezekiel*, p. 97.
11. Calvin, *Institutes*, 1:18:2.
12. Calvin, *Ezekiel*, vol. 2, p.58.
13. As above.
14. As above, p.59
15. Calvin, *Institutes*, 1:18:2
16. As above, 3:24:13
17. As above.
18. As above
19. The Hebrew spelling is, in any case, 'Danel'.

Chapter 8 — Grapes, a wayward woman and two eagles

1. God's people in covenant relationship with Christ are the 'true' vine (John 15:1), where the adjective is *alethinos*, not *alethes*: not meaning true as opposed to false, but genuine as opposed to spurious; the reality as opposed to the shadow.
2. C. H. Spurgeon, Sermon on Ezekiel 16:62-63 entitled 'The Heart Full and the Mouth Closed', *Metropolitan Tabernacle Pulpit*, p.217.
3. *Works of Goodwin*, 2:lxii, cited by Joel R. Beeke, *Assurance of Faith: Calvin, English Puritanism, and the Dutch Second Reformation*, Peter Lang, 1991, pp.325-6.
4. J. I. Packer, *Knowing God*, Hodder & Stoughton, 1973, pp.153-4.
5. As above.
6. R. V. G. Tasker, *The Epistle of James*, Tyndale New Testament Commentary, Tyndale, 1956, p.106, cited by Packer, *Knowing God*, p.154.
7. Owen, *Works*, vol.6. p.249.
8. *Westminster Confession*, 25:v
9. Calvin, *Ezekiel*, vol. 1, p. 159.
10. Calvin, *Ezekiel*, vol.2, p. 176.
11. *Westminster Confession*, 25:v
12. Palmer Robertson, *The Christ of the Covenants*, Presbyterian and Reformed, 1980, p.284, n.15. Robertson adds that the predominant usage of the Hebrew word used here is '"making null and void". The term is used of a vow that is "made null and void" by subsequent action. A wife may commit herself by vow; but the husband may proceed to void the wife's vow (cf. Num. 30:8-15). The husband does not "break" the vow, since only the wife could perform that action. Instead, he "nullifies" the oath his wife has made.'
13. Cited by Sinclair Ferguson, *Children of the Living God*, Banner of Truth, 1989, p.113.
14. Nebuchadnezzar was compared by Jeremiah to a lion (Jer. 4:7; 49:19; 50:44), and an eagle 'spreading its wings' (Jer. 48:40). Daniel combines both images, likening Nebuchadnezzar to a lion with eagle's wings (Dan. 7:4).
15. Calvin, *Ezekiel*, vol. 2, p.207.

16. Owen, *Works,* vol. 8, p.322.
17. Calvin, *Ezekiel,* vol. 2, p.219.

Focus on the nature of the covenant
1. Calvin, *Institutes,* 2:2:8
2. Calvin makes the following comment on Ezekiel 16:61: 'A contrast must be understood between the people's covenant and God's', writes Calvin. 'He is mindful of his own agreement, and yet it had been dissipated, broken, and abolished. He shows that it was fixed on his own side, as they say, but vain on the people's side' (*Ezekiel,* p.176. cf. similar comments in his *Institutes,* 4:15:22; 4:16:9,26).
3. Calvin, *Harmony of the Gospels,* I:36-37 (Comment on Luke 1:49).
4. Calvin, *Institutes,* 3:21:7
5. Calvin, *Ezekiel,* p.121. Calvin makes similar comments on Ezekiel 11:16-17 and 18:25.
6. Compare his comments on Romans 9:6: 'God's condescension in making a covenant of life with a single nation is indeed a remarkable illustration of undeserved mercy, but this hidden grace is more evident in the second election, which is restricted to a part of the nation only.' The words of Andrew Woolsey are helpful here: 'It is not only proper to speak of a general and secret election, it is also appropriate to speak of a general and a secret application of the covenant' (A. A. Woolsey, *Unity and Continuity in Covenantal Thought: A Study in the Reformed Tradition to the Westminster Assembly,* Ph.D. Thesis, Glasgow, 1988, 2.28). I am grateful to Dr Woolsey for many of these quotations from Calvin.

Chapter 9 — 'I am, Yours sincerely...'
1. For the Bible's account of Israel's exile into Assyria, see 2 Kings 17:7-23; and for that of Judah into Babylon, see 2 Kings 22:16-17.
2. Calvin, *Ezekiel,* vol. 2, p.238.
3. B. B. Warfield, *Biblical Doctrines,* Banner of Truth, 1988, pp.24-5.
4. Murray, *Collected Writings,* vol. 4, p.131.
5. Calvin, *Commentary on the First and Second Epistles of Peter,* Baker, 1981, vol. 22, pp. 419-20.
6. Donald Macleod, *Behold Your God,* Christian Focus Publications, 1990, p.5.
7. J. C. Ryle, *Old Paths,* William Hunt and Co., 1884, p.468.
8. Calvin, *Ezekiel,* vol.2, p.247. For a further treatment of this subject, see R. L. Dabney, 'God's Indiscriminate Proposals of Mercy, as related to his Power, Wisdom and Sincerity', in *Discussions: Evangelical and Theological,* Banner of Truth, 1967, vol. 1, pp.282-313.
9. Others have insisted that verses 5-9 refer to Jehoiachin, who also ruled for three months in 598 B.C. before being taken into exile in Babylon (2 Kings 24:8-16). He had been the king when Ezekiel and his companions had been taken prisoner. It was also Jehoiachin that they considered to be the last legitimate king of Judah. Jehoiachin was an impressive king (19:7), but foreigners (Babylonians) captured

him (19:8) and brought him into exile, in Babylon, so that 'His roar was heard no longer' (19:9) (see Douglas Stuart, *Ezekiel*, p.168).
10. From the hymn, 'There is a green hill far away,' by Cecil Frances Alexander.

Chapter 10 — Dumb idols
1. Calvin, *Ezekiel*, vol.2, p.285. Hengstenberg adds: 'Those who wish to have another answer must repent beforehand' (*Prophecies of Ezekiel*, p.168).
2. Calvin, *Ezekiel*, vol. 2, p.291.
3. Stuart, *Ezekiel*, p.182.
4. *New Dictionary of Theology*, IVP, 1988, p.105.
5. A. Blackwood, Jr, *Ezekiel: Prophecy of Hope*, Baker, 1965, p.133. Cited by Yoshiaki Hattori, 'Divine Dilemma in Ezekiel's View of the Exodus' in *The Law and the Prophets: Old Testament Studies in Honour of Oswald T. Allis*, Presbyterian and Reformed, 1974, p.420.
6. From C. S. Lewis' introduction to *St Athanasius on the Incarnation*, Mowbray, 1953, p.9. Cited by John Stott, *The Contemporary Christian*, IVP, 1992, p.26.
7. See Focus on Chapters 40-48.
8. Fairbairn, *Ezekiel*, p.230. For a fuller discussion of the principles of interpretation involved, see discussion on Ezekiel 34 and especially chapter 40.
9. Calvin, *Ezekiel*, vol. 2, p.345.
10. Editorial note at the close of Calvin's expository lectures on Ezekiel, vol. 2, p. 346.
11. Parker, *John Calvin*, p.151.

Chapter 11 - The sword of the Lord and no intercessor
1. Readers of the English text should note that the Hebrew is very difficult and some of the translation is tentative.
2. Edmund P. Clowney, *The Unfolding Mystery: Discovering Christ in the Old Testament*, NavPress, 1988, p.131.
3. Julia Ward Howe (1819-1910), written in December 1861.
4. Cited by Douglas F. Kelly, *If God Already Knows, Why Pray?*, Wolemuth & Hyatt, 1989, pp.184-5.
5. Among those who take this view are the following: Fairbairn, *Ezekiel*, p.244; Hengstenberg, *Christology of the Old Testament*, Macdonald, vol. 2, p.761; Taylor, *Ezekiel*, p.165.
6. The Hebrew has 'prophets', while the Septuagint (the Greek translation of the Old Testament) has 'kings'. The NIV has translated the word 'princes'.
7. See Kelly, *If God Already Knows, Why Pray?*, p.187.

Chapter 12 — Oholah and Oholibah: a tale of two cities
1. Stuart, *Ezekiel*, p.223.
2. See comment by Derek Kidner, *Love to the Loveless: The story and message of Hosea*, IVP, 1981, p.72, n.3

3. Frederick Beuchner, *Godric,* Chatto and Windus Ltd, 1981, p.153, cited by Foster, *Money, Sex and Power,* p.104.

4. *Westminster Confession of Faith,* 25:v.

5. G. R. Beasley-Murray, *The New Bible Commentary Revised,* edited by D. Guthrie, J. A. Motyer, A. M. Stibbs and D. J. Wiseman (IVP, 1970), p.676.

6. Fairbairn, *Ezekiel,* p.257.

7. Calvin speaks of 'illegitimate children' within the covenant in his comments on Genesis 17:7. Referring in his comments to Romans 9:8, he speaks of 'illegitimate children' who received the promise of the covenant, but were not children of the promise. They were children only in the general, outward sense, but not in the spiritual and inward sense (*Genesis,* pp.447-9). Commenting further on Ezekiel 16:21, Calvin says, 'There was a twofold election of God, since speaking generally he chose the whole family of Abraham. For circumcision was common to all, being the symbol and seal of adoption ... this was one kind of adoption or election. But the other was *secret,* because God took to himself out of that multitude those whom he wished; and these are the sons of promise' (*Ezekiel,* vol. 2, pp.121-2).

Chapter 13 — 'Something's burning!'

1. Calvin, *Ezekiel,* vol.2, p.250.

2. Cited by Richard Alderson, *No Holiness, No Heaven,* Banner of Truth, 1986, p.93.

3. Stuart, *Ezekiel,* p. 243.

4. Craigie, *Ezekiel,* p.185.

5. J. I. Packer, *A Passion for Holiness,* Crossway, 1992, p.249.

6. Craigie, *Ezekiel,* p.185.

7. Stuart, *Ezekiel,* p. 243.

Chapter 14 — How the mighty are fallen!

1. Cited by Roy Clements, *When God's Patience Runs Out: The truth of Amos for today,* IVP, 1988, p.13.

2. Ammon's relationship with Israel was tense: it was they who hired the false prophet Balaam against Israel (Deut. 23:3-6), who oppressed Israel in the days of Jephthah (Judg. 3:13; 10:6-11:33) and Saul (1 Sam. 11), and likewise Judah in the days of King Jehoshaphat (2 Chron. 20). Amos likened Ammon's expansionist policies to that of terrorists (Amos 1:13-14).

3. One bright spot appears in the life of Naomi. Her widowed daughter-in-law, Ruth the Moabitess, professed faith and married Boaz who became the great-grandmother of King David (Ruth 4:17). Her appearance in the genealogy of Jesus in Matthew 1:5 marks her out as a trophy of God's grace to one of Israel's enemies.

4. It is not hard to understand that following the rivalry between Isaac's twin sons, the relationship between Israel and the Edomites was a tense one. Amos, speaking at an earlier time than that of Ezekiel, had referred to the brutality of the Edomites (Amos 1:11-12; see also Num. 20:18-21; 1 Sam. 14:47, where they are referred to

as the 'enemies' of God's people; 1 Kings 11:14-22; 2 Kings 8:20; 14:7; 2 Chron. 28:17). However, it is the book of Obadiah that is wholly devoted to the fate of the Edomites.

5. The Idumeans (as the Edomites were known) were, in fact, compelled by John Hyrcanus to adopt Judaism by compulsory circumcision!

6. The Philistines had been Israel's first major enemy. Having originally come from Crete (cf. Gen. 10:14), they settled in the coastal plains, south-west of Canaan, roughly during the period covered by the Exodus. In occupying Canaan, the Israelites had taken deliberate steps to avoid 'the road through the Philistine country' (Exod. 13:17). In the time of the judges, relationships between Israel and the Philistines wavered. Samson married a Philistine wife, but his eventual capture and ridicule at their hands revealed their mutual hostility. In Saul's time, it was the Philistines who captured the ark of the covenant (1 Sam. 4). They had by now occupied not just the coastal plains between Egypt and Gaza, but the Negeb and much of the hill country.

In particular, the Philistines were noted for their skills in iron and the making of weapons and chariots (1 Sam. 13:19-22). Saul's victory at the famous battle of Michmash came only by means of divine intervention: a storm that caused the chariots to get bogged down (1 Sam. 14). David's victory over Goliath also revealed the hand of God (1 Sam. 17-18). Philistine power was seriously curtailed by another of David's victories (2 Sam. 5:25), but following his death their power once more increased. Isaiah mentions the threat they posed during the reign of Ahaz (Isa. 9:12) and warns of God's judgement (Isa. 14:28-32).

7. Apart from Genesis 3:15, the word is used on only four other occasions: Num. 35:21,22; Ezek. 25:15; 35:5.

8. Though no month occurs in this date-reference, verse 2 implies that Jerusalem has fallen. This would mean that it must be the eleventh or twelfth month — a few weeks after Jerusalem's collapse. Ezekiel 33:21 implies that it was not until the 'twelfth year ... in the tenth month,' i.e. a full eighteen months following the prophecy given in chapter 26, that news finally reached the exiles of the fall of Jerusalem. However, this refers to the official confirmation delivered by some refugee who had taken this length of time to reach the Kebar River, off the Tigris River, avoiding Babylonian troops along the way. It seems incredible but that the exiles would have been taunted by news of Jerusalem's fall by their captors from the very beginning.

9. 'Phoenicia' is a word coined by the Greeks and is not found in the Old Testament. The NIV includes the word in Isaiah 23:11, but the Hebrew is 'Canaan'. The inhabitants of Phoenicia called themselves 'Canaanites' in Old Testament times. Phoenicia is roughly the same as modern Lebanon.

10. Cf. 1 Kings 5:18; Ps. 83:7.

11. By the middle of the eighth century B.C. Tyre's strength had waned. In Isaiah's time, Assyria threatened but never conquered Tyre, but Luli, King of Tyre, was forced to flee to Cyprus in 701 B.C. (the year that Sennacherib besieged Hezekiah's Jerusalem). Where Sennacherib failed, his son Esarhaddon succeeded. Throughout

the century that followed, Tyre (like Judah) looked to Egypt for help against Assyrian aggression, until at last Assyria's decline set in. Tyre regained her independence for a short period until the rise of the Babylonians. A thirteen-year siege under Nebuchadnezzar brought Phoenicia to an end in 572 B.C. An attempt to regain some power during the days of Alexander the Great resulted in the total destruction of both Tyre and Sidon in 332 B.C. It is to this decline of Tyre's fortunes that Ezekiel 26:3-5 refers. The cities never recovered from it. Hellenistic culture took over, the language of the Phoenicians was lost and by New Testament times the inhabitants of the region were known as Syro-Phoenicians, reflecting their Hellenistic identity. It was a fulfilment of Ezekiel's warning: **'You will never be rebuilt'** (26:14), and especially: **'You will be sought, but you will never again be found'** (26:21). Outside Phoenicia some managed to maintain their identity and culture. One of Phoenicia's most famous sons is Hannibal, of Alps and elephants fame.

12. Stuart, *Ezekiel*, p.254.

13. It is possible that the prophets knew of specific breaches of treaty obligations towards Israel. Jehu's violent overthrow of Omri's dynasty in Samaria, with the assassination of the queen mother Jezebel, must have caused considerable ill-feeling against Israel in Phoenicia.

14. Taylor, *Ezekiel*, p.192.

15. I am indebted to J. I. Packer for this phrase. See, 'Infallible Scripture and the Role of Hermeneutics' in *Scripture and Truth*, edited by D. A. Carson and John D. Woodbridge, IVP,1983, p.350.

16. Cf. 26:20, though a different Hebrew word for 'pit' is used there.

17. Cf. Packer, *God's Words*, p.87.

18. Calvin, *Ezekiel*, vol. 1, p.368, commenting on Ezekiel 11:17.

Chapter 15 — Egypt

1. Following the defeat of Egypt by the Assyrian king, Esarhaddon, in 671B.C. (foretold by Isaiah in Isaiah 19:4), the nation was to remain under Assyrian domination for only a brief period. In 663 B.C. the so-called Saite dynasty (663-525 B.C.) was to be one of Egypt's last ruling families with any claim to power, its early rulers endeavouring to recover some of its past glories. Just before the time of Ezekiel (604-594 B.C.) Pharaoh Necho, in alliance with the Assyrians, conquered Josiah at Megiddo (609 B.C.) and installed Jehoiakim on the throne in Jerusalem as an Egyptian vassal. Egypt's hopes were dashed, however, by the rise of Babylonian power under Nebuchadnezzar, suffering two major defeats in 605 B.C. Necho's successors, Psalmist II and Hophra, continued their anti-Babylonian policies, putting a great deal of pressure on Judah's last king, Zedekiah, to rebel against Nebuchadnezzar. When Zedekiah finally yielded to Egyptian pressure, Egypt sent an army to help him which succeeded for a time in thwarting the Babylonian aggression. But Egypt's help was in the end to prove worthless, and Judah was to fall to Babylonian domination. Egypt did, though, provide a haven of refuge for many Judeans, including, of course, Jeremiah.

From then on Egypt declined dramatically. In 525 B.C. the Persian king Cambyses conquered the country. For the next four centuries, Egypt was held under the grip of the Persian, Alexander the Great, and finally the Romans.

2. The time reference is a year earlier than the one mentioned at 26:1. At the commencement of the Tyre prophecy, Jerusalem had already fallen to the Babylonians. Here it has not.

3. Water-beasts figured largely in the Babylonian mythology of creation. Bible-writers were not averse to using mythological figures to underline their message. In mentioning such figures as Sebek, the Egyptian crocodile-god, Ezekiel is saying, 'It is the Lord alone who can destroy the chaos-powers you believe in. He alone is the God of creation' (Meredith Kline, *The Structure of Biblical Authority*, Eerdmans, 1971, pp.79f.).

4. See Thomas, *God Delivers*, ch.10.

5. The cedar was one of the grandest of all the trees and grew in abundance in the northern regions of Lebanon. It was a common symbol of greatness and is used by the psalmist to depict the true stature of a Christian adorned with holiness: 'The righteous will flourish like a palm tree; they will grow like a cedar of Lebanon' (Ps. 92:12).

6. So-called 'Conditionalists' argue that the words 'Hades' and 'Sheol' always refer simply to the grave.

7. *The Works of Jonathan Edwards*, Banner of Truth, vol.2, p.10.

8. Cited by Eryl Davies in *The Wrath of God*, Evangelical Press of Wales, 1984, p. 67.

9. Fairbairn, *Ezekiel*, p. 353.

Chapter 16 — Watchmen and shepherds

1. It has been argued that verse 11 should be translated in the following way: 'I have no pleasure in the death of the wicked but *when* the wicked turns from his way and lives.' In this case, it is claimed that the verse merely suggests that God is pleased *when* the wicked turns, rather than the notion that God longs for their turning, whether they do in fact turn or not. John Murray argues that 'It is not in any way denied that this kind of delight is embraced in the expression. But to limit the concept to this notion is without warrant and is not borne out by the usage' (*Collected Writings*, vol. 4, p.124). Furthermore, Murray argues that in any case the verse suggests quite categorically that God does not delight in the death of wicked. 'This does not mean simply that God does not delight in the death of the wicked *when* he dies. The denial is much more embracive.'

2. The command to turn, argues John Murray, is given 'to all men without any discrimination or exception. It expresses the will of God to repentance. He wills that all should repent. Nothing less than that is expressed in the universal command. To state the matter more fully, he wills that all should repent and live or be saved' (*Ibid.*, p.125). This will is not the will of God's decree — a will that decrees the eternal death of some wicked, a will that God is pleased to decree — rather, this is God's

w*ill of benevolence.* It is a will which is, of course, in many instances, unfulfilled. God knows what it is to live with extreme disappointment.

3. In chapter 16:1-14, God has been represented in terms of another figure altogether than that of a shepherd, that of a husband and a father to his people.

4. Ezekiel uses the verb 'to scatter' twenty-six times to indicate the coming of the exile (5:2,10,12; 6:5,8; 10:2; 11:16,17; 12:14,15; etc.).

5. For a similar analysis of the shepherd's task, see Jeremiah 3:14-17; 23:1-8.

6. Taylor, *Ezekiel,* p.223.

7. 'The new covenant, promised by Israel's prophets, does not appear as a distinctive covenantal unit unrelated to God's previous administrations. Instead, the new covenant as promised to Israel represents the consummate fulfilment of the earlier covenants' (Robertson, *Christ of the Covenants,* p.41).

8. Douglas MacMillan, *The Lord our Shepherd,* Evangelical Movement of Wales, 1983, p.13.

9. The 'covenant of peace' is not therefore identical to the 'new covenant' as Jeremiah proclaimed it (Jer. 31:31-34). See Van Groningen, *Messianic Revelation in the Old Testament,* p.776; A. A. Hoekema, *The Bible and the Future,* Paternoster Press, 1978, p.285.

Focus on the land of promise
1. New Scofield Bible, p.888. It does not, however, concede this principle to the entire section.

Chapter 17 — Mountains
1. Preaching the same sermon the following week at Kilmarnock, however, produced no converts at all — proving that God is sovereign in the sending of revival (See John Gillies, *Historical Collections of the Accounts of Revival,* Banner of Truth, 1981, pp.198-9.

2. This is a much harsher fate than that of either Egypt (29:13-16) or Ammon (25:1-7).

3. Thomas Watson, *The Doctrine of Repentance,* Banner of Truth, 1987, pp.83-4.

4. Joni Eareckson Tada, *Secret Strength,* Scripture Press, 1989, p.69.

5. See, Van Gronigen, *Messianic Revelation in the Old Testament,* p.777.

6. All secretions of bodily fluid were considered to be unclean and surrounded with rigorous purification laws, partly, no doubt, as a means of enforcing elementary rules of cleanliness, thus minimizing the risk of the spread of disease (Lev. 15).

7. Murray, *Collected Writings,* vol. 2, 'Regeneration', p.169.

8. *Ibid.,* p.170

9. B. B. Warfield, *Biblical and Theological Studies,* 'On the Biblical Notion of "Renewal"', Presbyterian and Reformed, 1968, p.351.

10. Commenting on this passage, John Murray says, 'This passage we may properly regard as the Old Testament parallel of John 3:5 and there is neither reason nor warrant for placing any other interpretation upon "born of water" than that of

Ezekiel 36:25' (*Redemption Accomplished and Applied*, Banner of Truth,1961, p.100).

11. The difference between the Old and New Testament ministry of the Holy Spirit is not one of *kind*, but of *degree*. As J. I. Packer put it, 'The Holy Spirit's ministry was enlarged at Pentecost, without being in any way diminished from what it was before. Prior to Pentecost ... the Spirit sustained creation and natural life, renewed hearts, gave spiritual understanding, and bestowed gifts for service both in leadership and in other ways, and all this he still does. The difference since Pentecost is that all his present ministry to Christian believers relates not to Christ who was to come, as was the case when he ministered to Old Testament saints (see, for hints of this, John 8:56-59; 1 Cor.10:4; Heb.11:26; 1 Pet.1:10); nor does it relate any more to Christ present on earth, as it did when Simeon and Anna recognized him (Luke 2:25-38), and during his three years of public ministry; it relates now to Christ who has come and has died and risen and now reigns in glory. It is primarily in these terms that the newness of God's era, so far as the Spirit is concerned, ought to be defined, just as it is primarily in terms of fellowship with this Christ that the newness of life which Christians have enjoyed since Pentecost ought to be explained' (*Keep in Step with the Spirit,* IVP, 1984, p.90).

12. 'Two errors, therefore,' adds W. G. T. Shedd, 'are to be avoided: First, that all men are saved; secondly, that only a few men are saved' (*Dogmatic Theology,* Klock & Klock,1979, vol. II, p. 712).

13. Jonathan Edwards, *Works,* ed. W. Goold, Banner of Truth, 1967, 4:518.

14. 'The scriptural principle is, not that favours are by our importunity wrung from the reluctance of the Divine Being, but that they antedate the prayer in the determinations of his sovereign and gracious will; and the true spirit of prayer, which he also imparts, is the sign and pledge of the gift to be conveyed. Prayer, then, as already stated, is not the cause which procures through its own efficiency, but merely the antecedent condition upon which a predetermined benefit is suspended' (B. M. Palmer, *Theology of Prayer,* Sprinkle Publications, 1980, p.140).

15. Cited by Douglas Kelly, *If God Already Knows* ..., pp. 82-3).

Chapter 18 — The valley of dry bones

1. Packer, *Keep in Step with the Spirit,* p.57.

2. As above, p.257.

3. Stuart, *Ezekiel,* p.347.

4. Readers are referred to 'Focus on the Land of Promise', as well as comments made on Ezekiel 40-48.

5. Ephraim and Manasseh were Joseph's two sons born to him before the years of famine. Jacob blessed Ephraim with his right hand and Manasseh with his left (Gen. 48:13-14), signifying that Ephraim would become the greater (Gen. 48:19). Even during the exile, Ephraim retained a privileged position: 'I am Israel's father, and Ephraim is my firstborn son' (Jer. 31:9).

6. Robertson, *Christ of the Covenants,* pp. 277-8.

7. As above, p. 42.

8. See, 'Focus on the land of promise'.
9. John Calvin, *Commentaries on the Prophet Jeremiah and the Lamentations,* Baker, 1950, 4:220.

Chapter 19 — Gog

1. This, in part, is due to the fact that 'prince of' can also be 'Rosh' (the Hebrew for 'prince') which in English, of course, sounds a little like the beginning of 'Russia'. It is a pity that neither Ezekiel nor the vast majority of Russians speak English!
2. Stuart, *Ezekiel,* p. 355.
3. Persia was to the east of Israel, across the Tigris River; Cush (Ethiopia) was south of Egypt in North Africa; Put (Libya) was far to the west of North Africa; Gomer (along with Meshech and Tubal, Gomer was a son of Japheth, Gen. 10:2-3) was further north than Gog in what is today Armenia; and Beth Togarmah is where Armenia is situated today.
4. I say, 'if not exclusively,' because some interpreters refer this entire prophecy to the days of persecution against God's people instigated by Antiochus Epiphanes of Syria in the second century B.C. I am unable to agree with this interpretation. Willem A. Van Gemeren cites J. G. Aalders to this effect: 'Ezekiel's prophecy has already received its incipient and direct fulfilment in the historical events associated with the Seleucid aggression against Israel, in the name of Antiochus Epiphanes and his successors, but it will be completely and finally fulfilled in the eschatological opposition of a world power, opposed to God and to the Christian church' (*Interpreting the Prophetic Word,* Zondervan, 1990, p. 335). This appears to be about right.
5. Cited by Ferguson, *Daniel,* p.215.
6. Thomas à Kempis, *The Imitation of Christ,* 1.19.
7. It is just here that we need to evaluate a little some of the main theories relating to the expectation of a future battle against the church. Certain views of prophecy, e..g. classical postmillennialism, find difficulty with seeing any great battle of Satan against the church at the end of history, assigning such prophecies as Gog and Magog exclusively to historical battles that have already occurred. Instead, this view believes that the present age will gradually merge into the millennial, or 'golden' age, as more and more of the world's population are converted to Christianity. As far as Gog and Magog are concerned, they are seen as having been fulfilled in the onslaught of Antiochus Epiphanes against the Jews in the second century B.C.

Other views of prophecy do expect a period of tribulation at the end of the age, including historic premillennialism. This view posits that when Christ comes again, believers who have died will be raised, to meet those who are still alive. Both will be transformed and glorified, and having been caught up to meet Christ in the air, will descend and accompany Christ to earth. Following the slaying of Antichrist, and the conversion of the Jews to Christ, the millennial reign of Christ will be established, near the end of which Satan will be loosed in order to deceive the nations. He will gather the rebellious nations together for the Battle of Gog and

Magog. Satan will, however, be consumed by fire from heaven and then be cast into the lake of fire.

Dispensationalism, too, expects a period of tribulation, teaching that Christ's return will be in two stages, the first a rapture which can occur at any moment, in which risen believers and transformed believers are taken with Christ into heaven for seven years to celebrate the marriage feast of the Lamb. During this seven-year period (a fulfilment of Daniel's seventieth week prophecy, Dan. 9:24-27) several things will take place, including the great tribulation of Daniel 9:27, the reign of Antichrist, the return of 144,000 Israelites to Jesus as Messiah and the Battle of Armageddon, in which the armies of the beast and the false prophet gather together to attack the people of God. This is the fulfilment of Ezekiel's prophecy of Gog and Magog. The difference between dispensationalism and premillennialism is that the former expects the church to be raptured before the tribulation takes place, while the latter does not.

The view taken in this commentary has been in line with amillennial interpretations. Amillenialists believe that the millennium spoken of in Revelation 20:1-3 covers the entire period of history from the first to the second advents of Christ. Expecting that Christ will return after this millennial reign is over, amillenialists do expect the Second Coming to be heralded by certain precursors, including the worldwide preaching of the gospel (Matt. 24:14), the conversion of Israel (though variously understood as meaning 'all the true Israel including both Jews and Gentiles', or 'all elect Jews in a dramatic conversion of Jews at the end of the age' on the basis of Romans 9-11), and the revelation of the man of sin, together with its accompanying tribulation.

8. See J. A. Thompson, *Deuteronomy, Tyndale Old Testament Commentary*, IVP, 1974, p.276.

9. Cf. Ferguson's comment: 'Scripture promises us that the last days (that is, the period between Pentecost and the return of Christ, Acts 2:16-17) will be punctuated by times of special stress and danger (2 Tim. 3:1). This will reach a climax at "the time of the end"...' (*Daniel*, p.242).

10. For this interpretation see, A. A. Hoekema, *The Bible and the Future*, p.150. Others, however, are of the opinion that Matthew 24:1-28 refers entirely to the destruction of Jerusalem in A.D. 70. See John Murray, 'The Interadventual Period and the Advent: Matthew 24 and 25', *Collected Writings*, vol. 2, p. 389.

11. J. C. Ryle, *Practical Religion*, James Clarke, 1959, p. 130.

Focus on Ezekiel 40-48

1. J. I. Packer, *Keep In Step with the Spirit*, p.88.

2. Ralph A. Alexander complains that such an interpretation means that in this case 'Different aspects of the passage mean whatever the interpreter desires'(*Ezekiel*, p.943). This need not be the case, since the details of the visions are not to be pressed, in the same way as parables are not.

3. *An Introduction to the Old Testament*, Eerdmans, 1949, p.248.

References

317

Chapter 20 — The Lord's return to Jerusalem
1. Stuart, *Ezekiel*, p. 372.
2. Ezekiel's temple is larger than Solomon's, but about half the size of Herod's temple in Christ's time, which measured some thirty acres.
3. The *burnt offering* was the commonest of all the Old Testament sacrifices and was used for what we may call 'everyday' sins (Lev.1:1-17). *Guilt offerings* were designed to atone for two particular sins: a trespass against holy things or a trespass against God's holy name by uttering false oaths in a court (Lev. 5:14-26). *Sin offerings* (Lev. 4:1-5:13) were offered less frequently, and were designed to cope with 'a subsidiary problem created by human sin pollution and defilement' (G. J. Wenham, *The International Commentary on the Old Testament: The Book of Leviticus*, Hodder & Stoughton , 1979, p.95. The sin not only had to be atoned for (thus, a burnt offering was to be offered), its after-effects had also to be considered (and hence the sin offering). Ezekiel 42:13 also mentions **'grain offerings'**; these always accompanied the daily burnt offering (Num. 28). Unlike the burnt offering, it was n*ot* an animal offering! By means of grain offerings, the worshipper renewed his covenant obligations to live before God in holiness.
4. Priests were allowed to eat certain sacrifices (Lev. 2:3; 5:13; 6:16,26,29; 7:6,10).
5. It was the practice of Parliamentary interference in the affairs of the church in Scotland that caused 474 ministers to withdraw and establish the Free Church of Scotland. One of the issues at stake in this dramatic moment in Scottish church history was the right of individual congregations to call their own minister and not be forced to accept one imposed upon them by an external, and independent, aristocracy.
6. Cf. 44:15. Zadok traced his lineage to Aaron through Aaron's son Eleazar (1 Chron. 6:50-53). In David's time he served along with Abiathar (2 Sam. 8:17). In the divisions that developed, Zadok supported Solomon (Abiathar supported Adonijah) and was rewarded with service in Solomon's temple (1 Kings 1).
7. 'Fellowship offerings' are generally taken to mean the same thing as peace offerings (see note 3 above on 40:39). Peace offerings were more like communal meals; only the fat parts were burnt on the altar, while the flesh was consumed by the worshipper and the priests. They signified communion with God.
8. G. J. Wenham, *New International Commentary on the Old Testament: The Book of Leviticus*, Hodder & Stoughton, 1979, p.71.
9. See 'Focus on Ezekiel 40-48'.

Chapter 21 — A visionary tour of the future temple and its workings
1. J. I. Packer, *Laid-Back Religion? A Penetrating Look at Christianity Today*, IVP, 1987, p.35.
2. Josephus, *Antiquities*, XV.11.5. The Jews accused Paul of violating this very principle, and thus tried to kill him, because he had supposedly taken Trophimus with him into the temple area (Acts 21:27-32).
3. Cited by F. F. Bruce, *Commentary on the Book of the Acts*, Eerdmans, 1954, p.434.

4. There is much controversy with regard to the exact identity of both Old Testament 'priests' and 'Levites'. The priesthood was reserved for the sons of Aaron. The Levites served in an auxiliary capacity as servants to the priests. The Levite clan had three families: the Kohathites, the Gershonites and the Merarites (Num. 3-4). One of the most important functions of the Levites was to act as substitutes for each tribe's first-born (Num. 3:40-41). Although Deuteronomy frequently uses the expression 'the Levitical priests' (e.g.17:9; 18:1; 24:8; 27:9), giving rise to the idea that no distinction is to be made between 'priest' and 'Levite', this is a mistake. The NIV translation 'the priests, who are Levites' (44:15) is meant to convey the fact that not all Levites were priests. Different sections are assigned to each (Deut. 18:3-5,6-8). Since Aaron was himself descended from Kohath, this has given rise to the view that all the Kohathites served as priests. (See *The Zondervan Pictorial Encyclopaedia of the Bible*, ed. Merrill Tenney, Zondervan, 1977, Vol. 4, 'Priests and Levites', pp. 852-67). This, probably, is also mistaken, for when Eleazar, the priest in Joshua's time, reminds Joshua of Moses' command concerning Levitical cities (Josh. 21:1-3), the Kohathites are divided into two groups: those who have descended from Aaron (i.e. the priests) and the rest (Josh. 21:4-5).

5. 'Since ancient balances had a margin of error of up to 6%,' writes D. J. Wiseman, '... and no two Hebrew weights yet found of the same inscribed denomination have proved to be of exactly identical weight, the importance of this exhortation can be seen' (*New Bible Dictionary*, article on 'Weights and Measures', cited by Taylor, *Ezekiel*, p. 274, n.1).

6. Stuart, *Ezekiel*, p. 401.

7. This section deals with only a few of the regulations for offerings and feasts. Ezekiel 45:13-25 should be seen as an example of what is expected at every other feast.

8. 'The reference to sacrifices is not to be taken literally, in view of the putting away of such offerings, but is rather to be regarded as a presentation of the worship of redeemed Israel, in her own land and in a millennial temple, using the terms with which the Jews were familiar in Ezekiel's day.' This is the note provided on page 888 of the New Scofield Bible. This is an astonishing, and terminal admission, for if the thesis of literal interpretation fails here, why should we expect it to be upheld anywhere else?

Ralph H. Alexander, in a lengthy and involved discussion, argues similarly that the sacrifices envisaged for the millennial age are of a 'memorial' nature: 'The sacrifices in the millennial sacrificial system of Ezekiel appear to be only memorials of Christ's finished work and pictorial reminders that mankind by nature is sinful and in need of redemption from sin' (*Ezekiel*, p. 951). Alexander argues, further, that all the sacrifices made in the time of Moses were also 'memorials', using such passages as Hebrews 9:23-28; 10:1-11 to support the view. Since the sacrifices made in the Old Testament could not take away sin (only Christ's sacrifice could do that) there is no problem in the reintroduction of such sacrifices at some point in a future millennium. To add support to his argument he comments:

'The Lord's Table is itself a memorial of Christ's death.' The point needs to be made, however, that neither the Lord's Table nor baptism involves the shedding of blood (as did the Passover and circumcision).

Furthermore, it is quite wrong to think that the sacrifices made in the time of Moses were mere memorials. They were expiatory and efficacious. Nor can appeal be made to the book of Hebrews. 'To make use of the "beggarly elements"', comments O. T. Allis, 'before the reality had come, and to do this when directly commanded to do so, was one thing. To return to them after the reality has come and expressly commanded not do so, would be quite another thing... The thought is abhorrent that after He comes, the memory of His atoning work will be kept alive in the hearts of believers by a return to the animal sacrifices of the Mosaic law, the performance of which was so emphatically condemned in passages which speak with unmistakable plainness on this very subject. Here is unquestionably the Achilles' heel of the Dispensational system of interpretation' (*Prophecy and the Church,* Presbyterian and Reformed, 1945, p.248).

9. Alexander, *Ezekiel,* p. 974.

10. Those who do not interpret the 'prince' as Messianic include Van Groningen, *Messianic Revelation in the Old Testament,* pp. 783-4, and the commentaries by Taylor, Alexander and Craigie. Craigie, in fact, makes the astonishing claim that Ezekiel's 'prince' was a prophecy of a restored monarchy after the exile, 'and in that particular', he comments, 'Ezekiel was wrong'! (Taylor, *Ezekiel,* p. 303).

Among those who do interpret 'the prince' in a Messianic way is Stuart, who refers to him as 'the messianic king of the new age foreseen in the vision' (*Ezekiel,* p. 400), though Stuart adds later, 'The "prince" is not exactly the same as the Messiah,' (p.406}. Others who adopt a similar interpretation are Willem A. Van Gemeren, *Interpreting the Prophetic Word,* Zondervan, 1990, p.336; and E. W. Hengstenberg, who says, 'The prince finds his closing appearance in the Messiah, according to 34:24, 37:25; but in the centuries which lay between him and the prophet, the prince appeared in various forms as well as in the kingly' (*The Prophecies of Ezekiel,* p. 434).

11. Ralph A. Alexander, who translates 'prince' as 'leader', comments: 'If the "leader" were Jesus Christ, then he, the Messiah, would need cleansing from sin. Such was not possible (cf. Heb. 4:15)' (*Ezekiel,* p. 974).

12. Hengstenberg, who was in favour of seeing the prince as Messiah in 44:3 (p.434 of his commentary), is less sure in his comments on 45:22: 'That the prince must offer the bullock as a sin-offering, not merely for the people, but also for himself, shows quite clearly that we should understand by him neither exclusively nor immediately the Messiah' (p. 459). A few pages later, commenting on 46:16, he is quite sure that the prince is *not Christ!* 'The prince here cannot be Christ,' he says (p.465).

13. This limitation of access to the prince into the inner courtyard via the east gate underlines the difficulty of interpreting him as the Messiah.

14. Stuart, *Ezekiel,* p. 406.

Chapter 22 — The promised land

1. 'The river with its water of life symbolizes the inexhaustible grace of God', writes P. E. Hughes, commenting on Revelation 22:1 (*The Book of Revelation*, IVP, 1990, p.232). 'They speak of the gloriously satisfying and God-given life of the church of God in glory', comments Richard Brooks on the same passage (*The Lamb is All the Glory*, Evangelical Press, 1986, p.192). 'The river suggests God's provision,' writes John Goldingay in a comment on Psalm 46 (*Songs from a Strange Land: Psalms 42-51*, IVP, 1978, p.105).

2. See *Mishnah Succah*, 4:9,10.

3. See D. A. Carson, *The Gospel According to John*, IVP, 1991, p.322.

4. Packer, *Keep In Step with the Spirit*, p.88.

5. cf. Stuart, *Ezekiel*, pp.418-9.